The Making of International Trade Policy

NGOs, Agenda-Setting and the WTO

Hannah Murphy

University of Tasmania, Australia

Edward Elgar
Cheltenham, UK • Northampton, MA, USA

Published by
Edward Elgar Publishing Limited
The Lypiatts
15 Lansdown Road
Cheltenham
Glos GL50 2JA
UK

Edward Elgar Publishing, Inc.
William Pratt House
9 Dewey Court
Northampton
Massachusetts 01060
USA

A catalogue record for this book
is available from the British Library

Library of Congress Control Number: 2010927660

MIX
Paper from
responsible sources
FSC
www.fsc.org   FSC® C018575

ISBN 978 1 84980 018 1

Typeset by Cambrian Typesetters, Camberley, Surrey
Printed and bound by MPG Books Group, UK

Contents

Tables

Foreword

The discipline of international relations is in disarray, now that sovereign national states are no longer its exclusive actors. But what can non-state, non-governmental actors accomplish – or prevent from happening? In this pioneering work, Hannah Murphy explores both the potentialities and limits of NGO intervention in the substantive arena of international trade policy. Her empirical findings are paradoxical: the WTO does not formally include such organizations in its negotiations, yet its agenda and member-state alliances are informally influenced by them. Her theoretical conclusions are unorthodox: the influence of these NGOs is neither confined to their 'radical' capacity for the mobilization of protest, nor to their 'constructivist' impact upon the norms of national representatives, nor to their 'realist' conformity to prevailing conceptions of national interest. Rather, she finds the answer in the obscure corridors of something called 'governance' where public and private actors interact, try to convince each other, exploit momentary crises, provide alternative wordings, form transnational factions, and sometimes contribute to forming a consensual rather than a hegemonic solution.

Philippe C. Schmitter
Professor Emeritus
European University Institute

Acknowledgements

This book is the outcome of my PhD research that began in February 2005. I am indebted to the School of Government at the University of Tasmania and especially to my dedicated supervisors Professor Aynsley Kellow and Dr Matthew Sussex. I cannot thank them enough for their help and support. I also wish to acknowledge Professor Philippe Schmitter for generously taking the time to talk over important aspects of the research – I very much benefited from his advice. Last but not least, I am grateful to the NGO representatives and WTO representative who generously participated in interviews. I dedicate this book to my mother and father, and to Luke, who has been an unwavering source of support.

Abbreviations

ACP	African, Caribbean and Pacific Group
APEC	Asia-Pacific Economic Cooperation
ASEAN	Association of South East Asian Nations
BIT	bilateral investment treaty
CAFOD	Catholic Agency for Overseas Development
CIEL	Center for International Environmental Law
COSATU	Congress of South African Trade Unions
CPTech	Consumer Project on Technology
CUT	Central Única dos Trabalhadores
CUTS	Consumer Unity and Trust Society
DSB	dispute settlement body
ECOSOC	Economic and Social Council
ETUC	European Trade Union Confederation
EU	European Union
FDI	foreign direct investment
FOEI	Friends of the Earth International
FTA	free trade agreement
FTAA	Free Trade Agreement of the Americas
G-20	Group of 20 (interest grouping at WTO)
G-77	Group of 77 (interest grouping at WTO)
G-90	Group of 90 (interest grouping at WTO)
GATS	General Agreement on Trade in Services
GATT	General Agreement on Tariffs and Trade
GSP	Generalized System of Preferences
HAI	Health Action International
Health GAP	Health Global Access Project
IATP	Institute for Agriculture and Trade Policy
ICC	International Chamber of Commerce
ICFTU	International Confederation of Free Trade Unions
ICSID	International Centre for Settlement of Investment Disputes
ICTSD	International Centre for Trade and Sustainable Development
IGTN	International Gender and Trade Network
IISD	International Institute for Sustainable Development
ILO	International Labour Organization
IMF	International Monetary Fund

IP	intellectual property
ITO	International Trade Organization
ITSs	international trade secretariats
LDCs	least developed countries
MAI	multilateral agreement on investment
MFN	most-favoured nation
MIGA	Multilateral Investment Guarantee Agency
MNCs	multinational corporations
MSF	Médecins Sans Frontières
NAFTA	North American Free Trade Agreement
NGO	non-governmental organization
OECD	Organisation for Economic Co-operation and Development
OME	Office of Monitoring and Enforcement
PhRMA	Pharmaceutical Research and Manufacturers of America
PI	portfolio investment
PSI	Public Services International
QUNO	Quakers United Nations Office
SEATINI	Southern and Eastern African Trade Information and Negotiations Institute
TAC	Treatment Action Campaign
TAG	Treatment Action Group
TILS	Task Force on Trade, Investment and Labour Standards
TNCA	Thai NGO Coalition on AIDS
TRIMs	Trade-Related Investment Measures
TRIPS	Trade-Related Intellectual Property Rights
TSMO	Transnational Social Movement Organization
TUAC	Trade Union Advisory Committee
TUC	Trades Union Congress
TWN	Third World Network
UNCHR	United Nations Commission for Human Rights
UNCTAD	United Nations Conference on Trade and Development
UNGASS	United Nations General Assembly Special Session
USTR	United States Trade Representative
WDM	World Development Movement
WGTI	Working Group on Trade and Investment
WHA	World Health Assembly
WHO	World Health Organization
WIPO	World Intellectual Property Organization
WSF	World Social Forum
WTO	World Trade Organization
WWF	World Wide Fund for Nature

1. Introduction: NGOs and the WTO

In recent decades the negotiation of international rules to manage trade liberalization has become increasingly controversial. Whereas free market proponents claim that trade liberalization can deliver a range of benefits such as job creation, increased efficiency and technology transfer to the least developed countries (LDCs), critics maintain that it destroys national industries, displaces workers, negatively impacts the natural environment and threatens national identity. For these reasons the World Trade Organization (WTO), since its establishment in 1995, has become a major target for non-governmental organizations (NGOs) representing a diverse range of interests. Contrary to popular perception, the NGOs that target the WTO do not simply stage street demonstrations outside WTO ministerial conferences – typified by the 1999 'Battle of Seattle' protests outside the WTO's third ministerial conference – but undertake a variety of lobbying activities in their efforts to impact the negotiating positions of WTO member states.

Beginning in the mid-1970s, political scientists, international relations scholars and NGO practitioners have contributed to the burgeoning literature on the activities of NGOs in global governance, particularly in regard to the policy domains of human rights, development and the environment. But far less systematic research has been conducted into NGO activities in international economic policy arenas where conditions for influencing policy outcomes are generally considered to be less propitious for NGOs seeking to represent social or environmental interests. Given the formal constraints on NGO decision-making input at the WTO and the considerable economic and political costs and benefits of trade liberalization for states, the WTO arena serves as a good test case for assessing the contributions of NGOs to international policymaking.

By focusing on the activities of NGOs in relation to the international trade policymaking process, this book seeks to add to the emerging scholarship on agency in international relations, in particular, the parameters of NGO agency in global governance. Specifically I examine the campaign tactics employed by NGOs in contesting international trade issues and their dynamic relationships with WTO member states and intergovernmental organizations in order to discover more about their roles in international trade governance. The overarching question that this study tackles is: what impact, if any, do NGOs have on international trade governance at the WTO?

To help address this question, the case study chapters of the book employ NGO campaign materials, WTO documents, interview data and existing scholarly literature to investigate three prominent NGO campaigns directed at the WTO. These NGO campaigns pertain to the issues of labour standards, intellectual property (IP) rights and foreign investment rules. Each case study traces the campaign tactics used by NGOs and the ways in which NGO campaign activity impacted trade negotiations at the WTO. The cases were selected on the basis that they provide insight into the nature of relationships between NGOs, intergovernmental organizations and a variety of WTO member states. The policy issues raised in regard to each campaign led to interesting and differing 'alliances' between NGOs, WTO member states, as well as intergovernmental organizations in related policy domains. Each campaign also sees NGOs advocating different scales of policy change at the WTO and this sheds light on the varied roles and impacts of NGOs in the international trade regime. A core task of the book is to elucidate some of the key constraints and opportunities that NGOs must navigate in order to exert influence in international policymaking.

THE WTO AND NGOs

Established in 1995 with its headquarters in Geneva, Switzerland, the WTO is a legal institution that provides an arena for member states to negotiate the rules governing the multilateral trading system, work towards trade liberalization and settle trade disputes. It also periodically reviews the trade policies of member states to assess their openness to trade. As of November 2009 the WTO had 153 member states, while another 30 (mostly developing countries) were awaiting accession. For 2009 the organization had a budget of approximately $US 188 million and a secretariat staff of 629, which provides technical support, analyses world trade and manages the WTO's relations with the public and media. The small size of the budget and secretariat staff (in comparison with other intergovernmental organizations) reflects the role of the WTO as a negotiating forum and governance mechanism rather than a funding source for nations suffering balance of payment problems or other economic crises. This is the role of the WTO's sister organizations, the World Bank and International Monetary Fund (IMF).

According to Robert Keohane and Joseph Nye (2001a), the recent politicization of global economic institutions, particularly the WTO, is largely due to their achievements. In addition to the 1947 General Agreement on Tariffs and Trade (GATT) dealing with trade in goods, the WTO administers a broad range of accords, which include (among many others) IP rights, trade in services, agriculture, textiles, civil aircraft, food safety, electronic commerce and government procurement. Once negotiated, these agreements and articles are mandatory for all WTO members through the imposition of legal obligations. Although the ongoing attempts to finalize the 2001 Doha Round of trade negotiations have been thwarted by the significant variations in the distribution of costs and benefits of the round for member states, in terms of its judicial and regulatory powers, the WTO nonetheless remains one of the most effectual intergovernmental organizations currently in existence (see Gilpin 2001: 382).

The broad range of issues dealt with at the WTO spanning food safety, textiles, agriculture, trade in services and IP reflects the growing trend towards global governance whereby domestic policy issues are increasingly transferred to the international level of decision-making, thus consolidating interdependencies among nation-states. This phenomenon has meant that NGOs and other types of non-state actors no longer work solely within domestic contexts to influence policymaking. Since the 1970s most major intergovernmental organizations have consequently experienced a growth in direct exchanges with NGOs, although there is little consensus about how these relationships should be conducted and for what purpose. In regard to the WTO, member states have repeatedly concurred that the distinctive trade treaty basis of the organization precludes the involvement of NGOs in the decision-making process. Instead the WTO directs those seeking to influence international trade negotiations to their national representatives.

Despite the limits on formal NGO participation at the WTO, the expansion of global trade law through the WTO and the recent explosion in the number of NGOs operating internationally (see Katz 2008; Union of International Associations 2008–9) has seen a vast number of grassroots, national and international NGOs developing an interest in the activities and decision-making processes of the WTO. Professional international NGOs, such as Catholic Agency for Overseas Development (CAFOD), World Wide Fund for Nature (WWF) and the International Centre for Trade and Sustainable Development (ICTSD), concede the necessity of global trade rules but seek to shape WTO decision-making. Their campaigns often highlight the negative impacts of WTO rules on the environment, public health, labour standards, national culture and identity, and the provision of public services.

In addition to social, environmental and other alleged side-effects of WTO rules and agreements, the organization has also come under fire from both scholars and NGOs deeply concerned with a perceived lack of democratic accountability in WTO decision-making procedures. These criticisms, particularly in the wake of the 1999 Seattle Ministerial Conference, have revolved around the transparency of decision-making processes and the absence of meaningful NGO consultation and/or participation mechanisms. For example, Rorden Wilkinson (2002) claims that powerful member states dominate WTO decision-making, business actors have disproportionate access and influence at the organization, and day-to-day working practices are closed to public scrutiny. It is further argued that WTO member states are constrained by the neoliberal framework underpinning the international trade regime, committing national governments to the liberalization and deregulation of their national economies. Indeed, Jackie Smith contends that at the WTO, economic policy decisions are simply considered technical, rather than inherently political, decisions (2002: 209).

While the sources of civil dissatisfaction with trade liberalization and the WTO have received a satisfactory level of scholarly attention, much remains to be understood about the tactics employed by NGOs in targeting the WTO and the resultant roles they play in the functioning of the international trade regime. The broad range of NGOs that seek to influence international trade policy at the WTO not only wage public campaigns on policy and procedural issues but also engage with various WTO member states on a regular basis, sharing information and in some cases obtaining positions on official governmental delegations to the WTO. Similarly, limits on formal NGO participation at the WTO have not prevented an increasing number of NGOs from attending WTO biennial ministerial conferences as observers.

Despite the growing number of NGOs, their increasingly active engagement with international trade issues and evolving relationships with nation-states, much of the academic literature in this area has focused on the untapped potential of NGOs to improve the WTO's legitimacy. This theoretical debate is at odds with the empirical reality of the growing number of NGOs seeking to influence decision-making at the WTO. While there is some discussion in the WTO-NGO literature regarding the success of single NGO campaigns leading to NGOs playing important roles in affecting the negotiation of particular WTO agreements, there is little examination of the mechanisms or patterns of NGO influence at the WTO, the reasons why some NGO campaigns succeed and others fail to achieve their goals, or the roles they play in international trade governance more generally. This book aims to address this mismatch between the existing WTO-NGO literature and the real world activities of NGOs to assess their contribution to the international trade policy process.

NGOs AND TRANSNATIONAL ACTIVISM

The focus on the democratizing potential of NGOs for the WTO parallels developments in the literature on NGOs and transnational activism more generally. Despite their presence in the global polity for over a century, it has only been in recent decades that international relations scholars have begun to consider the important roles that actors other than nation-states play in international politics. The literature on NGOs and transnational activism is an emerging inter-disciplinary field that represents an attempt to bridge at least two sets of scholarship: first, the literature on transnationalism, regimes, and norms in international relations; and second, the discourse on the globalization of social movements and the diffusion of norms in sociology (see Tarrow 2001 and Risse 2002 for thorough and insightful reviews of developments in these areas). Of most relevance to this study are the contributions concerning international NGOs (Weiss and Gordenker 1996; Willetts 1996; Keck and Sikkink 1998; Bob 2005; DeMars 2005); the organizational patterns of different types of non-state actors beyond the state (Smith, Chatfield and Pagnucco 1997; Stiles 2000; Smith and Johnston 2002; Bandy and Smith 2005; della Porta and Tarrow 2005); and NGO activity in relation to particular issues and institutions (Sikkink 1993; Wapner 1995; Ayres 1998; Fox and Brown 1998; Price 1998; O'Brien et al. 2000; Nelson 2002; Joachim 2007).

Across the transnational NGO advocacy literature, the majority of contributions, many emanating from the 'normative turn' in international relations scholarship (see Tarrow 2001), have focused on successful NGO campaigns, often in the areas of human rights and the environment. Such accounts detail the role of NGOs in creating and disseminating ideas that are said to overwhelm the instrumental goals and interests of other actors, including nation-states and business organizations. For example, Keck and Sikkink's (1998) landmark text, *Activists Beyond Borders*, explains that successful NGO action against a government's human rights violations involves weak, resource-poor domestic NGOs linking up with more powerful international NGOs, other governments and international institutions, who then place external pressure on the recalcitrant government to reform. Similarly Paul Wapner (1995) illustrates how NGO campaigns that publicize the environmentally unfriendly practices of large corporations can result in these corporations capitulating to NGO demands and altering their production techniques. In ceasing their offending activities, seemingly more powerful actors are said to have had their interests, or even their sovereignty in the case of nation-states, 'reconstructed' by the moral pressure of NGOs (see also Sikkink 1993; Klotz 1995; Price 1998; Risse, Ropp and Sikkink 1999; Khagram, Riker and Sikkink 2002; Joachim 2007).

The normative cast of research in this area has resulted in scholars attempting to demonstrate that NGOs are important actors in international politics with the potential to rival nation-states. But in emphasizing the power of moral values *vis-à-vis* the interests of nation-states, much of the NGO scholarship does not pay sufficient attention to specifying the conditions that *constrain* NGO activity. These may include the structure of the international system; the material and political interests of nation-states; the profit-maximizing behaviour of business;

alternative or competing moral values; and the rules, practices and decision-making processes of international institutions. By claiming that norms and ideas disseminated by NGOs can reconstruct interests, insufficient attention is paid to the ways in which the normative goals of NGOs and the strategic, material and political interests of nation-states (and other actors) may be complementary. This suggests that a different characterization of the role of NGOs in international politics might be more accurate. Instead of being simply categorized as agents of moral pressure, the effects of NGO activity in international politics may additionally involve enhancing the clout of particular states in international negotiations and increasing the likelihood that certain policy decisions will be taken over others. It is in this direction that this study proceeds to investigate the role of NGOs in the international trade policy process at the WTO.

The emphasis on the issue areas of human rights and the environment in the norms-based literature on NGOs in international politics has also diverted attention away from NGO advocacy in economic policy areas, especially international trade, where NGO success has been more nuanced and thus less visible (see O'Brien et al. 2000). The prevailing constructivist model of NGO advocacy, whereby states and other actors reconstruct their interests to accommodate the ideas and values created and disseminated by NGOs, does not easily apply to NGO activism at the WTO. This is because international trade is a policy arena dominated by states and business actors seeking to realize their economic and political interests. NGOs have not been granted participation status at the WTO and trade negotiations are technical and complex. Yet despite this, the number of NGOs that actively campaign on WTO issues is steadily increasing. This study attempts to address this puzzle and, in doing so, boost understanding of NGO advocacy in international economic policy arenas.

RATIONALE AND APPROACH

In this book I seek to understand more about the activities of NGOs in relation to international trade governance to highlight the varied roles of NGOs in international politics. Specifically I do so by examining (1) the strategies and tactics employed by NGOs in attempting to influence decision-making at the WTO; and (2) the ways in which NGOs contribute to the international trade policy process.

Of the many different types of NGOs, I focus on public interest, non-profit advocacy organizations, such as Oxfam International and Third World Network (TWN), which have broadly reformist platforms in relation to the WTO. In contesting the international trade regime, NGOs join together to wage international campaigns, using a number of different strategies to influence WTO policies and decision-making processes. I do not examine professional associations that represent business interests such as the International Chamber of Commerce (ICC) (for typologies of non-governmental actors in the WTO context see Bellmann and Gerster 1996: 35 and Scholte et al. 1999: 112–16). Unlike the normative literature on NGOs in international politics that heralds their democratizing potential, I do not necessarily seek to cast NGOs as inherently noble actors. Additionally I do not explicitly debate the accountability or representativeness of NGOs – I contend that they play roles in the international policy arena regardless of whether they possess these desirable attributes.

In adopting a governance-centred approach based upon notions of complex interdependence (Keohane and Nye 1977; 2003) and global public policy networks, I focus on the international trade policy process and the interactions of political actors in this process. This approach enables sufficient scope to examine not only the normative values and ideas disseminated by NGOs and the role of states' interests (and how the two intersect), but also the institutional characteristics of the WTO. Given that NGOs are formally excluded from directly participating in WTO decision-making, I investigate how NGOs support, through normative argument, the interests of particular WTO member states with whom they share common objectives in relation to given issues at the WTO. Additionally I examine the institutional characteristics of the WTO in terms of its rules, norms, practices and decision-making procedures that shape interactions among governments and NGOs, affecting their capacity to realize their objectives.

I employ a comparative case study method to investigate the role of NGOs in the governance of international trade by way of three international NGO campaigns on trade-related issues. The selected NGO campaigns are: (1) the campaign for the incorporation of core labour standards into WTO rules; (2) the access to medicines campaign challenging the application of the WTO's Trade-Related Intellectual Property Rights (TRIPS) Agreement to pharmaceutical products required in developing member states; and (3) the campaign against the development of a comprehensive foreign investment agreement at the WTO. Each set of NGO campaigners attempted to mobilize international consensus for their campaign positions to convince nation-states with compatible objectives to pursue an issue at the WTO and simultaneously pressure states with opposing positions. I draw upon the insights of Alexander L. George (1979) in designing the case study framework.

Each of the three campaign issues broadly split WTO members along North/South lines. The goals of NGOs in relation to TRIPS and investment closely resonated with those of developing member governments, while the goals of the labour standards campaigners aligned with the objectives of the

US and several European nations. The NGO campaigns also differ in the type of action or policy change demanded of WTO members. The access to medicines campaigners attempted to modify an existing WTO agreement, the investment campaign attempted to remove an issue from the WTO agenda, while the labour campaign sought to enact a new WTO accord. Whatever their goals for the WTO arena, all three worked alongside various WTO member states in an attempt to get their issues addressed inside the organization. The case study chapters of the book examine in detail how NGO campaigners attempt to build support for their goals and engage WTO members on their issues.

The selection of the above NGO campaigns to evaluate the contribution of NGOs to the policy process at the WTO provides an opportunity to see how issues raised by NGOs are dealt with by WTO members in different ways once on the WTO agenda. While both the issues of access to medicines and investment were addressed in a manner broadly supporting the goals of NGOs and developing countries, the labour standards issue, backed by more powerful WTO members, did not result in any substantive policy change at the organization. This study shows that the resolution of issues is heavily conditioned by WTO decision-making procedures. Specifically, the organization's 'single undertaking' and consensus decision-making procedures, and the one-state, one-vote system heavily condition whether actors in the policy process (be they states or NGOs) can achieve their goals (see Chapter 2 for a detailed discussion of these processes). That influential WTO member states did not achieve their objectives on any of the three campaign issues further highlights the significance of WTO decision-making procedures.

DATA SOURCES

The case study chapters of NGO campaigns draw upon two types of data: NGO and WTO web-based documentation and media reports; and existing literature that provides information and analysis of the NGO campaigns and WTO proceedings. The major types of NGO material used are campaign documentation including mission statements, campaign statements and declarations; NGO research reports; and accounts of workshops and other NGO-sponsored meetings. From the WTO website, the major resources used were those pertaining to the ministerial conferences including ministerial conference declarations, statements of WTO members, explanations of WTO agreements and news items.

As a tool of preliminary investigation, semi-structured interviews were conducted with representatives of five NGOs: Global Trade Watch Australia and Oxfam Community Aid Abroad Australia, in December 2005; and Oxfam

International (Geneva Advocacy Office), MSF, and the ICFTU, in September 2006. A representative of the WTO's external relations division was interviewed in September 2006. These interviews comprised broad discussion of:

(1) the relations between NGOs, WTO member states, the WTO and other non-state actors;
(2) the WTO's mechanisms for engagement with NGOs;
(3) the relationships between selected WTO member states and NGOs;
(4) the strategies used by NGOs in their medicines, investment and labour standards campaigns; and
(5) the impact of the above campaigns.

Finally, I attended and participated in the September 2006 WTO Public Forum. The annual WTO Public Forum is a two-day event held at the WTO headquarters in Geneva open to civil society, academics, WTO members and the business community, as well as the general public, to discuss the challenges for the multilateral trading system. Importantly the WTO invites NGOs to submit topic proposals for sessions at the forum. I attended sessions closely linked to the NGO campaign issues examined in this study, including 'Can trade deliver decent work in the XXIst century?' organized by the ICFTU; 'G-20 civil society views on the WTO' organized by the Friedrich-Ebert Foundation (FES) and Consumer Unity and Trust Society International (CUTS); and 'Stocktaking of WTO negotiations: concerns of developing countries' organized by the South Asian Association for Regional Cooperation Chamber of Commerce (SCCI). Attendance and participation in these sessions was valuable for hearing alternative views and discussing issues relevant to the selected NGO campaigns with stakeholders.

ORGANIZATION OF THE BOOK

After providing some background information about WTO operations and the growing role of NGOs in international politics, the following chapter reviews and critically analyses the WTO-NGO and transnational activism literature. In regard to the WTO-NGO literature, I explain that normative understandings of NGOs as democratizing agents come at the expense of analysis into the mechanisms and impact of NGO advocacy directed at the WTO and the role of relations between NGOs and member states. The second part of the chapter turns to the literature on NGOs and transnational activism in general. It assesses the relevance of the constructivist, social movement, and what I call 'governance-centred' perspectives for understanding NGO influence at the WTO. The governance-centred perspective incorporates global public policy and neoliberal institutionalist views about the role of NGOs and other non-state actors in international politics and takes account of normative values, interests and institutional practices. In contrast, the constructivist and social movement approaches, while offering important insights into how NGOs attempt to build and disseminate norms at the international level, suffer from a number of limitations that restrict their applicability to NGOs in the WTO context. The constructivist perspective does not account for the important role of interests and power structures within world politics, while social movement scholars are primarily concerned with the factors that may sustain and strengthen social movements on a global scale. Instead a governance-centred approach that situates NGO activity within the broader international trade policy process is the best lens for investigating NGO advocacy in relation to the WTO.

Having outlined the terrain of the transnational NGO literature in Chapter 2, Chapter 3 begins with the key research questions guiding this study. The remainder of the chapter is dedicated to setting up the methodological framework for assessing NGO influence at the WTO. Drawing upon the comparative case study method, which provides guidance for establishing appropriate terminology, case study selection and theory building, the chapter discusses conceptualizations of civil society, NGOs and NGO collective action. The chapter ends by introducing the three case studies of NGO campaigns and justifies their particular merits for responding to the research questions.

Chapters 4, 5 and 6 comprise the empirical component of the book. Each contains a case study of an NGO campaign directed against the WTO. Chapter 4 details the campaign to incorporate core labour standards into WTO rules. Chapter 5 outlines the access to medicines campaign directed at clarifying the safeguard provisions within the WTO's IP agreement. Chapter 6 presents the campaign against the development of a WTO foreign investment agreement. Each chapter provides the background to the campaign issue, describes the key actors involved, outlines the chronology of the campaign and the tactics and strategies employed by NGOs. The manner in which each of the campaign issues raised by NGO campaigners is ultimately dealt with inside the WTO arena is discussed. Comparing and contrasting the insights of the case studies, Chapter 7 outlines the key roles played by NGOs in the governance of international trade. It explains that despite their very limited formal status at the WTO, NGOs play interesting and varied roles in the international trade regime at the agenda-setting stage. Chapter 8 summarizes the findings of the book and proposes avenues for future research to ascertain the significance of NGO activity at other stages of the international trade policymaking process.

2. NGOs, states and the WTO: towards a governance-centred perspective

INTRODUCTION

There is not a great deal written about NGOs in regard to the governance of international trade. This is surprising given the proliferation of studies on NGOs within the international relations literature, combined with ongoing debates surrounding international trade liberalization. Most of the contributions on this topic (from both scholars and NGO practitioners) limit their focus to the formal relations between NGOs and the WTO. The key thread within such discussions is prescriptive, revolving around the deficiencies of existing arrangements for NGOs at the organization and the supposed benefits of bolstering their status to allow NGOs to participate in WTO decision-making alongside nation-states. Proponents of increasing the level of formal NGO input at the WTO, such as Steve Charnovitz (2000; 2002; 2004), Daniel C. Esty (1998; 2002), and Payne and Samhat (2004), have primarily understood NGOs as democratizing agents that possess the capacity to rectify the WTO's 'democratic deficits'. This viewpoint reflects that found in the norms-based literature in international relations more generally: as Kathryn Sikkink claims for instance, 'NGOs and networks are informal, asymmetrical, and ad hoc antidotes to domestic and international representational imperfections' (2002: 316). This study instead adopts a broader view of the role of NGOs in the international trade regime that focuses on their activities external to the decision-making arena of the WTO and their relations with member states. This is because even a brief investigation of NGO activity related to the WTO reveals that limits on their formal participation have not deterred NGOs from waging international campaigns on a plethora of international trade issues.

While the debate over formalizing NGO participation to reduce the WTO's legitimacy problems is an important one, it remains a theoretical discussion that has deflected attention from the current roles of NGOs in the international trade regime. Though some existing studies deal with certain aspects of NGO activity in relation to the WTO, such as the use of the internet to facilitate NGO campaigns (Smith and Smythe 2003), national-level consultation procedures put in place by WTO member states (Capling and Nossal 2003; Capling 2005) and NGO contributions in the form of *amicus curiae* briefs to

WTO dispute settlement proceedings (Charnovitz 2000; Howse 2003), there are no comprehensive studies detailing how NGO campaigns contribute to the international trade regime. This represents a gap in the WTO-NGO literature, especially given the increasing numbers of NGOs dedicated to international trade issues, the rise in NGO campaigns that have targeted the WTO, evidence that NGOs are working closely with WTO member states in relation to partic- ular trade issues, as well as accounts claiming that NGOs played a role in the renegotiation of particular WTO accords such as the TRIPS Agreement (see Abbott 2002; 't Hoen 2002; Shadlen 2004). Consequently the goal of this book is to understand more about the current role of NGOs in international trade poli- tics rather than simply reiterate their legitimizing potential for the WTO system.

This chapter begins with a brief description of the WTO and its decision- making procedures, before providing an overview of the WTO-NGO litera- ture. This overview comprises an outline of the WTO's mechanisms for engagement with NGOs and civil society, the inadequacies of which have been a catalyst for generating this body of literature. The arguments and proposals put forward by those advocating greater formal involvement of NGOs at the WTO are examined. I then contend that this preliminary investigation of recent NGO activity in relation to international trade issues reveals that the normative debate that dominates the WTO-NGO literature does not align with the current practice of international trade politics and governance. Only a small number of contributions in this area, such as those of Dunoff (1998), Scholte et al. (1999), Abbott (2002), Tuerk (2003) and Shadlen (2004), provide some insight or starting point for considering how NGO activity impacts the governance of international trade.

The paucity of the WTO-NGO literature means that a wider examination of the general literature on NGOs in international politics is necessary for under- standing how NGOs affect the international trade regime. This is undertaken in the second part of the chapter. I examine the governance-centred (compris- ing complex interdependence and global public policy perspectives), construc- tivist, and global social movement approaches to understanding NGO activity in international politics. I find that a governance-centred perspective that views non-state actor behaviour in the context of institutional structures and practices, and takes into account both normative values and instrumental objectives, provides the best platform for investigating the contribution of NGOs to international trade governance.

THE WTO

The WTO is primarily a legal institution that provides a permanent forum for discussing the rules, norms and principles for governing international trade

Table 2.1   WTO ministerial conference meetings

Year/date	Location	Outcomes
1996 (9–13 December)	Singapore	Review of first two years of WTO activity and implementation of Uruguay Round commitments. Introduced the Singapore issues
1998 (18–20 May)	Geneva (Switzerland)	Celebration of 50 years of the GATT
1999 (30 November to 3 December)	Seattle (US)	Collapse – failure to launch 'Millennium Round'
2001 (9–13 December)	Doha (Qatar)	Launch of Doha 'Development' Round
2003 (10–14 September)	Cancún (Mexico)	Collapse over agriculture and the Singapore issues
2005 (13–18 December)	Hong Kong (China)	Modest progress. No progress on agricultural market access
2009 (30 November to 2 December)	Geneva	An attempt to prepare member states to bring the Doha Round to conclusion in 2010

liberalization, monitoring the trade policy of member states and adjudicating their trade disputes. The chief governing body of the WTO, the Ministerial Council, consists of each member's trade minister or equivalent representative. The Ministerial Council meets every two years, although because of the current difficulties in completing the Doha Round, there was a four year gap between the formal ministerial conference involving all members held in December 2005 (Table 2.1) and the most recent ministerial conference held in December 2009. The WTO's General Council manages the day-to-day work of the organization and comprises the diplomatic representatives of member states. Additionally there are a large number of specialized, issue-specific committees, working groups and working parties that deal with individual WTO agreements and other trade-related areas such as the environment, development, membership applications and regional trade agreements. Each of these bodies reports to the General Council.

The WTO's General Council also meets as the organization's Dispute Settlement Body (DSB), considered one of the most effective enforcement mechanisms of any intergovernmental organization. As Keohane and Nye explain, the DSB acts as a 'circuit breaker' in dealing with trade disputes among WTO member states by awarding the 'winner' of a dispute the right to take action equal to the damages inflicted by the state deemed to have violated WTO rules (2001a: 228). For a DSB ruling to be rejected, there must be unanimity among the states involved. But since the 'winner' of the dispute would never reject a decision in its favour, this effectively makes DSB rulings automatically binding. Additionally, if a member refuses to accept the ruling, the DSB may levy a fine. This aspect of WTO governance renders the organization relatively effective in upholding international trade rules. In terms of its judicial and regulatory powers, the WTO is therefore unique among international organizations. As Robert Gilpin states, '[i]t approaches the neoliberal ideal of an effective supranational institution' (2001: 382).

In contrast to the operation of the DSB, trade negotiations at the WTO are cumbersome, tedious and slow, with trade rounds taking several years to complete. For example, the Uruguay Round, which resulted in the establishment of the WTO, took seven and a half years to negotiate. The current Doha Round, launched in 2001, shows little sign of satisfactory completion in the near future despite the WTO's Director-General Pascal Lamy urging members at the November/December 2009 ministerial conference to conclude the round in 2010. The difficulty with trade negotiations is linked not only to the political ramifications for member states of decreasing protection for particular industries and sectors, but the decision-making procedures that underpin the trade liberalization regime itself.

Officially, WTO decision-making is based upon the three principles of consensus, one member/one vote, and the 'single undertaking'. In regard to consensus, Article IX of the Marrakesh Agreement that established the WTO states that: '[t]he WTO shall continue the practice of decision-making by consensus followed under the GATT. Except as otherwise provided, where a decision cannot be arrived at by consensus, the matter at issue shall be decided by voting' (WTO 1994). Members are formally considered equals and as such, there is no allocation of voting shares: '[a]t meetings of the Ministerial Conference and the General Council, each Member of the WTO shall have one vote' (WTO 1994). The WTO's decision-making procedures are therefore very different to those of other international economic institutions such as the World Bank and IMF, where voting power is determined by a member state's weight in the global economy. For example, the United States (US) holds over 16 per cent of the vote in both the IMF and the International Bank for Reconstruction and Development (IBRD), while most LDCs possess less than one percent each (World Bank 2007a; IMF 2007). Additionally trade negotiations at the WTO can only be finalized with the agreement of all members on every aspect of every issue (the 'single undertaking' approach). In other words, nothing is agreed until everything is agreed (see Sampson 2001;

Steinberg 2002). WTO member states therefore are formally considered equals and as a consequence the most powerful nations do not always control the organization's agenda.

In practice, the WTO's formal decision-making procedures have given rise to the formation of a large number of bargaining coalitions with overlapping memberships (see Table 2.2). These have developed in order to bypass some of the impracticalities of a large number of participants in the negotiations. Various combinations of the US, European Union (EU), Japan, India, Brazil, Canada and Australia comprise the most powerful of these coalitions. For example, the 'Quad' consists of the US, EU, Japan and Canada. Since large developing countries have become more prominent in the negotiations, the Quad has evolved into slightly larger groupings involving Brazil, India and Australia that have been variously known as the 'new Quad', the 'Four/Five Interested Parties' (FIPS), the 'Quint' and the 'Group of 6' (G-6). In effect, trade negotiations in any area are not feasible unless these parties agree to them. Since 2004, up to six of these members have worked together in an attempt to break deadlocks, particularly over agriculture. This was the case with the FIPS following the collapse of the 2003 Cancún Ministerial Conference. It should also be noted that the EU – known officially in WTO business as the 'European Communities' – has a single external trade policy. As such, the EU is a WTO member in its own right, but so too are each of its 27 member states.

In addition to the above groupings, there are several coalitions of developing country member states (for an excellent description and discussion of their evolving nature and successes at the WTO see Narlikar 2003). These include the African Group, the LDC Group, and the African, Caribbean and Pacific Group (known as the ACP countries). At the Cancún Ministerial Conference, these three groupings came together to form the Group of 90 (G-90). Another coalition, the G-20, also comprises developing nations and its goal is to obtain a better deal in relation to agriculture. Reflecting its changing composition, the G-20 has also been known as the G-21, the G-23 and the G-20+. Coalitions such as these have been particularly helpful for the very poorest of developing countries that typically lack the resources to form a studied position on all of the areas under negotiation. Another coalition, the Cairns Group, led by Australia but comprising both developed and developing countries, also seeks to decrease barriers to agricultural trade in the US and EU.

As was the case during the GATT years, WTO members have also attempted to overcome the difficulties of a large membership by undertaking negotiations in smaller meeting groups of between 20 and 40 delegations. Known as the 'green room' consultative process (a phrase taken from the informal name of the GATT director-general's conference room), their purpose is to 'beat the consensus into shape'. There are no formal rules

Table 2.2   Selection of key bargaining coalitions at the WTO

Name of group	Number of members	Members	Objective
Four/Five Interested Parties (FIPS) also known as the 'new Quad', the 'Quint' and the 'G-6'	4, 5 or 6 of the members depending on issue at stake	Australia, Brazil, EU, India, Japan, US	To break deadlocks in the negotiations, particularly over agriculture
Group of 20 (G-20) sometimes known as the G-21, G-22 or the G-20+	22 members since 21 November 2006	Argentina, Bolivia, Brazil, Chile, China, Cuba, Egypt, Guatemala, India, Indonesia, Mexico, Nigeria, Pakistan, Paraguay, Peru, Philippines, South Africa, Tanzania, Thailand, Uruguay, Venezuela, Zimbabwe	To promote interests of agriculture-exporting developing countries
African, Caribbean and Pacific Group (ACP Group)	56 WTO members out of a regional total of 79	Angola, Antigua and Barbuda, Barbados, Belize, Benin, Botswana, Burkina Faso, Burundi, Cameroon, Central African Republic, Chad, Congo, Cote d'Ivoire, Cuba, Democratic Republic of the Congo, Djibouti, Dominica, Dominican Republic, Fiji, Gabon, The Gambia, Ghana, Grenada, Guinea, Guinea-Bissau, Guyana, Haiti, Jamaica, Kenya, Lesotho, Madagascar, Malawi, Mali, Mauritania, Mauritius, Mozambique, Namibia, Niger, Nigeria, Papua New Guinea, Rwanda, St Kitts and Nevis, St Lucia, St Vincent and the Grenadines, Senegal, Sierra Leone, Solomon Islands, South Africa, Suriname, Swaziland, Tanzania, Togo, Trinidad and Tobago, Uganda, Zambia, Zimbabwe	To promote sustainable development, poverty reduction, agriculture and other development issues for developing countries

Group	Membership	Description
African Group	All African members of the WTO, currently 41 countries	Angola, Benin, Botswana, Burkina Faso, Burundi, Cameroon, Central African Republic, Chad, Congo, Côte d'Ivoire, Democratic Republic of the Congo, Djibouti, Egypt, Gabon, The Gambia, Ghana, Guinea, Guinea Bissau, Kenya, Lesotho, Madagascar, Malawi, Mali, Mauritania, Mauritius, Morocco, Mozambique, Namibia, Niger, Nigeria, Rwanda, Senegal, Sierra Leone, South Africa, Swaziland, Tanzania, Togo, Tunisia, Uganda, Zambia, Zimbabwe	To represent the interests of African WTO members
Least Developed Countries (LDCs)	32 WTO members	Angola, Bangladesh, Benin, Burkina Faso, Burundi, Cambodia, Central African Republic, Chad, Democratic Republic of the Congo, Djibouti, Gambia, Guinea, Guinea Bissau, Haiti, Lesotho, Madagascar, Malawi, Maldives, Mali, Mauritania, Mozambique, Myanmar, Nepal, Niger, Rwanda, Senegal, Sierra Leone, Solomon Islands, Tanzania, Togo, Uganda, Zambia	To represent the interests of the least developed WTO members
Group of 90 (G-90)	64 WTO members of the African, ACP and LDC groups	Angola, Antigua and Barbuda, Bangladesh, Barbados, Belize, Benin, Botswana, Burkina Faso, Burundi, Cambodia, Cameroon, Central African Republic, Chad, Congo, Côte d'Ivoire, Cuba, Democratic Republic of the Congo, Djibouti, Dominica, Dominican Republic, Egypt, Fiji, Gabon, The Gambia, Ghana, Grenada, Guinea (Conakry), Guinea Bissau, Guyana, Haiti, Jamaica, Kenya, Lesotho, Madagascar, Malawi, Maldives, Mali, Mauritania, Mauritius, Morocco, Mozambique, Myanmar, Namibia, Nepal, Niger, Nigeria, Papua New Guinea, Rwanda, Saint Kitts and Nevis, St Lucia, St Vincent and the Grenadines, Senegal, Sierra Leone, Solomon Islands, South Africa, Suriname, Swaziland, Tanzania, Togo, Trinidad and Tobago, Tunisia, Uganda, Zambia, Zimbabwe	Promote issues of importance to landlocked and island economies, less developed countries, and commodity-dependent nations; removal of preferential domestic subsidies by the EU and the US to allow G-90 products greater access to foreign markets

Table 2.2 continued

Name of group	Number of members	Members	Objective
Like-Minded Group	20 members	Algeria, Bangladesh, Belarus, Bhutan, China, Cuba, Egypt, India, Indonesia, Iran, Malaysia, Myanmar, Nepal, Pakistan, the Philippines, Sri Lanka, Sudan, Syria, Vietnam, Zimbabwe	To promote the interests of developing countries, oppose the Singapore issues and labour standards
Cairns Group	18 members	Argentina, Australia, Bolivia, Brazil, Canada, Chile, Colombia, Costa Rica, Guatemala, Indonesia, Malaysia, New Zealand, Paraguay, Peru, Philippines, South Africa, Thailand, Uruguay	Agricultural trade liberalization

Source: WTOa and WTOb.

concerning the agenda, member constitution, or frequency of such meetings (Narlikar 2003: 37). They can take place at ministerial conferences as well as in between conferences in order to progress negotiations. As such, several commentators have likened the process to that of a private club (Ricupero 1998; Keohane and Nye 2001a; Howse 2003). Those left out, especially small developing countries, have often criticized green room meetings. Since the 1999 Seattle Ministerial Conference, however, the representation of developing countries in green room meetings has improved.

THE WTO AND NGOs

The WTO's limited formal relations with NGOs have been a source of controversy since its inception in 1995. 'WTO exceptionalism', a term coined by Steve Charnovitz (2000: 187), sees the organization departing from what some commentators consider a norm in global governance whereby NGOs are granted some form of consultative status at international organizations, particularly those related to the United Nations (UN). The UN Economic and Social Council (ECOSOC), for example, grants consultative status to an NGO if it has a democratically adopted constitution, representative structure and accountability mechanisms. Through ECOSOC's Committee on Non-Governmental Organizations, NGOs may request that the secretary-general place items on the provisional agenda of the council, submit written statements to ECOSOC meetings and make oral presentations.

Although Article V of the Marrakesh Agreement that established the WTO states that '[t]he General Council may make appropriate arrangements for consultation and cooperation with non-governmental organizations concerned with matters related to those of the WTO' (WTO 1994), it did not specify how this should occur. Given this lack of guidance, it was not until mid-1996 that the WTO's General Council adopted the 'Guidelines for Arrangements on Relations with Non-Governmental Organizations', which clarified the relationship between the WTO, member states and NGOs (WTO 1996a). While this decision recognized the need to improve the transparency of the WTO to NGOs and citizens, it stipulated that given the unique nature of trade negotiations, NGOs should *not* be directly involved in the work of the WTO and that it is incumbent upon member states to consider the public interest in trade policymaking. Specifically, the decision directed WTO member states to provide citizens with sufficient information about WTO activities, to essentially act as conduits for citizens and non-state groups to the WTO. The decision also instructed that contact between NGOs and chairpersons of WTO councils and committees 'shall be in their personal capacity unless that particular council or committee decides otherwise' (WTO 1996a).

The General Council's decision regarding NGOs also specified a public relations role for the WTO secretariat. It instructed the WTO secretariat to make de-restricted WTO documents (reports of dispute panels, trade policy review reports and summaries of proceedings of the WTO's various committees) more promptly available on the WTO website in all three official WTO languages (English, French and Spanish). It was also agreed that the WTO secretariat would host public symposia on WTO-related issues, develop arrangements to receive and disseminate information that NGOs wish to make available to interested member states, and respond to NGO requests for general information and briefings on WTO activities.

Further, it was decided that for WTO ministerial conferences, the WTO secretariat would establish an accreditation process for NGOs to attend, as long as their activities were 'concerned with those of the WTO' (WTO 1996a). Even so, there was concern from some states prior to the inaugural Singapore conference that NGOs would have the right to participate in the conference, which resulted in the secretariat replacing the word 'observe' with 'attend' in all official documents relating to the conference (Payne and Samhat 2004: 112). At WTO ministerial conferences, accredited NGOs are housed in an 'NGO centre', with communication facilities and office equipment, often separate from the main conference site. NGO representatives are able to view only the plenary sessions via video conference or in an NGO gallery, as was the case for the 1998 Geneva conference when the NGO facilities were in the same location. This enabled NGOs to have informal interaction with governmental delegates and distribute materials. For all conferences, a representative of the WTO secretariat briefs NGOs on the progress of negotiations.

Two years after the General Council issued the first set of guidelines regarding contact with NGOs, on 17 July 1998, WTO director-general Renato Ruggiero announced an enhanced set of initiatives, albeit within the framework of the 1996 guidelines. The new initiatives included a programme of regular briefings for NGOs on the work of WTO committees and working groups; the provision of a list of documents, position papers and newsletters submitted by NGOs to be made available to member states on demand; and a section of the WTO website devoted to NGO issues. In announcing the new initiatives, Ruggiero stated that the onus was still on WTO member states, rather than the WTO, to establish relations with NGOs. Similarly, while the secretariat was granted some flexibility with respect to consulting with NGOs, other issues were not resolved. These included opening dispute settlement hearings and other WTO meetings to NGOs and the general public, which remains dependent upon the approval (by consensus) of member states.

Following the fierce public opposition to the WTO and trade liberalization expressed outside the 1999 Seattle Ministerial Conference, the WTO established an annual WTO public forum, aimed at the interested public, NGOs, academics, WTO members and the business community. The WTO secretariat invites NGOs and other types of organizations to submit topic proposals for sessions in line with their particular interests, which the NGOs then host. Since its inception in 2000, the WTO website has contended that 'the WTO Public Forum has become one of the most important platforms for dialogue amongst the stakeholders of the multilateral trading system. It is now a significant feature of the international calendar' (WTO 2007).

The trend towards greater openness and transparency at the WTO continued at the 2001 Doha Ministerial Conference. The Doha Declaration contained the following pledge: '[w]hile emphasizing the intergovernmental character of the organization, we are committed to making the WTO's operations more transparent, including through more effective and prompt dissemination of information, and to improve dialogue with the public' (WTO 2001a). In line with this statement, on 14 May 2002, WTO members agreed to further relax the rules for de-restricting official WTO documents (WTO 2002). Although in 2001, some 65 per cent of the more than 21,000 WTO documents were publicly available, the de-restriction procedures had been continually criticized by NGOs and other commentators for being too slow. In response, the May 2002 decision reduced the time period for de-restriction from the previous nine months to an average of six to 12 weeks. Henceforth, it was decided that the majority of WTO documents would be freely available from the outset.

In sum, the WTO's mechanisms for engagement with civil society consist of five core elements. These are:

(1) NGO attendance at the biennial ministerial conferences (as spectators not participants);
(2) WTO-organized issue-specific NGO dialogues and briefing sessions;
(3) the annual WTO public forum (since 2000);
(4) informal day-to-day contact between the WTO secretariat and NGOs; and
(5) WTO website space for NGOs, including NGO position papers, community e-forums and video debates (WTOc).

Since taking office in 2005, WTO director-general Pascal Lamy has frequently used the organization's website to reach out to NGOs, for example, making himself available for 'chat events' (WTOd). For the Hong Kong Ministerial Conference, he even uploaded his 'conference diary' outlining his view of the meeting's progress (WTO 2005a). In line with the emphasis on web-based communication with NGOs and the general public, the WTO secretariat upgraded the WTO website in 2006, based upon input from the public via online surveys.

Since its establishment in 1995, the WTO has certainly made advances in its transparency, with the level of information accessible to the public having steadily increased. NGOs and other non-state actors have been kept at arms-length, largely due to the distinctive nature of trade negotiations in terms of legal complexity and bargaining processes, not to mention the consensus decision-making procedures that require all members to agree to an increase in the formal access for NGOs to the WTO. This exclusion of NGOs from the WTO's decision-making procedures has attracted a great deal of attention from NGOs and academic commentators alike.

THE WTO-NGO LITERATURE: NGOs AS DEMOCRATIZING AGENTS?

The limits on formal NGO input at the WTO – combined with the expansion of trade liberalization, secretive decision-making processes and concerns that some member states fail to balance economic interests with social justice and environmental issues – has fostered a small but dedicated literature debating the merits of allowing NGOs greater participation rights. The majority of contributors contend that boosting the participation of NGOs at the WTO holds the potential to rectify some of the organization's 'democratic deficits' (see Bellman and Gerster 1996; Marceau and Pedersen 1999; Trebilcock and Howse 1999: 509–10; Scholte et al. 1999; Wallach and Sforza 1999; Charnovitz 2000, 2002 and 2004; Atik 2001; Loy 2001; Petersmann 2001; Esty 2002; Wilkinson 2002a, 2002b and 2005; Howse 2003; Tuerk 2003; van der Ven 2003; Lacarte 2004; Nanz and Steffek 2004; Payne and Samhat 2004; Wallach, Woodall and Nader 2004; Willetts 2004).

The argument that increasing NGO input at the WTO will improve WTO decision-making has generated a response from those concerned that the presence of NGOs would compromise international trade negotiations (see Robertson 2000a, 2000b; Barfield 2001; Kellow 2001). Others warn that the participation of NGOs would only help improve the reputation of the WTO without achieving any substantive accountability benefits (Buchanan 2003; Ford 2003). This debate intensified following the collapse of the Seattle Ministerial Conference in 1999. Below, I explore the key criticisms levelled against the WTO's decision-making procedures and mechanisms for contact with NGOs. This is followed by an overview of some of the specific arguments for and against the formalization of NGO participation at the WTO.

Critics of the WTO's provisions for contact with NGOs point to the inequities within the current arrangements. For example, Scholte et al. (1999) and Wilkinson (2005) argue that the WTO's NGO accreditation process for attendance at ministerial conferences provides privileged access for business associations over public interest NGOs and grassroots organizations from the developing world (see also Buchanan 2003). This is because trade liberalization is seen to benefit business interests (in a general sense) and business actors are more readily accepted by both member states and the WTO secretariat as having a legitimate interest in the work of the organization. It has been suggested that multinational corporations (MNCs) and other business groups seeking to expand their exports and investments abroad provide a powerful constituency for the WTO. These firms and their industry associations have influential voices in policy councils in domestic politics and strong interests in continued liberalization (Keohane and Nye 2001a). Moreover, Charnovitz (2000) claims that in effect, nation-states engage in WTO dispute settlement processes on behalf of business interests. State-controlled access to dispute resolution procedures at the WTO is said to pose a significant constraint to the inclusion of issues not easily reconciled with national economic interests such as social justice and environmental issues (Mason 2004).

According to several scholars, business influence on the international trade regime pre-dates the WTO. For example, Ostry explains that American MNCs played key roles in establishing the global trading system as it exists today as corporations were the only actors other than states allowed to influence the Uruguay Round negotiations and the transformation of the GATT into the WTO (2000; McMichael 2000: 466). Sell and May contend that pharmaceutical MNCs were instrumental in having international IP rules placed on the negotiating table during the Uruguay Round, leading to the eventual constitution of the TRIPS Agreement (2005; Sell and Prakash 2004). Critics of TRIPS have observed that IP rights are a form of protection for business actors, illustrative of the WTO's treatment of business as a 'special' interest group (Wai 2003). Further, Tuerk (2003) claims that corporations based in developed countries play a major role in determining countries' market access requests for trade in services liberalization under the WTO's General Agreement on Trade in Services (GATS).

In addition to the privileged role of business groups at the WTO, the organization's focus on internet-based communication as the major tool for contact with NGOs is seen as problematic. Wilkinson (2005) argues that it benefits resource-rich international NGOs, but neglects small grassroots organizations, especially in developing nations, which may have only limited access to the internet. The WTO's use of its website is thus said to underscore the organization's focus on responding to 'noisy' NGOs based in developed countries (especially following the Seattle conference) rather than engage with a broad cross-section of NGOs. It has therefore been alleged that relations between the WTO and civil society have reinforced global structural inequalities in world politics (Wilkinson 2002b). Scholars have also criticized the absence of permanent NGO accreditation for ministerial conferences and other symposia as well as the lack of a dedicated civil society liaison committee (Charnovitz 2002; Scholte et al. 1999). Most critics have thus dismissed the WTO's overtures to civil society as a public relations exercise designed to limit criticism of the organization in the wake of the failure of the Seattle conference in 1999.

The WTO's preference for members to deal with NGOs at the national level has also been criticized. The WTO's accountability to citizens, through their respective national governments, is said to be too indirect, preventing adequate public scrutiny of the organization's decision-making processes and policies (Wilkinson 2005). Charnovitz (2004) argues that this indirect accountability is a particular problem for citizens of undemocratic nations, who make up a large proportion of WTO members. Compounding this democratic deficit is the claim that nations are constrained to join the WTO and must commit themselves to alter their laws and regulations to align with the international trade regime (Scholte et al. 1999). Although international governance is dependent on national ratification, Nanz and Steffek (2004: 317) state that 'non-elected experts negotiate the WTO's everyday norms and standards', while the powerful dispute settlement process is deemed to provide the institution with some relative autonomy from, and power over, the governments that subscribe to it.

Some commentators have also been highly critical of the procedures and rulings of the WTO's DSB. During the 1990s, the GATT/WTO attracted the ire of environmentalists with some controversial DSB decisions that ruled against the application of discriminatory tools against imported goods on the basis of their production techniques. In 1991, the GATT ruled against a US ban on imported tuna harvested by methods that killed dolphins, and in 1998, the DSB ruled against a US law that protected sea turtles and therefore prohibited the importation of prawns harvested using methods harmful to these creatures. These controversial rulings have led to claims from more radical environmental groups that trade liberalization and environmental protection are incompatible and that the WTO should be abolished. More moderate environmental NGOs and some scholars have called for the DSB process to be opened up to allow NGOs to provide evidence and outline their interpretations of WTO rules (Trebilcock and Howse 1999: 409–510; Howse 2003). This has begun to take place with the DSB now accepting both solicited and unsolicited submissions by NGOs, though formal legal standing remains confined to states.

The WTO's decision-making procedures have been widely criticized over their democratic legitimacy and the level of secrecy. In particular the green room consultative process, as noted above, has been labelled undemocratic and to the disadvantage of resource-constrained developing countries. Given these constraints, many developing countries cannot afford to staff their Geneva offices or obtain staff with the appropriate level of expertise. Staff that are in place must often represent their nation not just at the WTO but also at a number of other international organizations in Geneva.

The WTO has attempted to respond to these issues in a number of ways. Various WTO committees and meetings have offered resources and proposed strategies to enhance LDC participation and improve transparency of trade negotiations, while wealthy WTO member states periodically donate funds for capacity and technical assistance (see WTO 2003e; Payne and Samat 2004: 107–9). Procedural improvements such as timely circulation of reports and advance notice of informal consultations were new elements agreed upon at Doha in 2001 with the aim of improving LDC participation. Several NGOs and scholars charge that these responses have either been poorly implemented or do not go far enough (Scholte et al. 1999; Charnovitz 2004; Nanz and Steffek 2004).

Given the range of criticisms directed at the WTO's decision-making procedures and its provisions for contact with NGOs, a major element of the WTO-civil society literature concerns the potential benefits of boosting NGO participation in the organization. Several NGO proponents suggest that NGOs are ideally placed to rectify the WTO's accountability and legitimacy issues. They argue that NGOs may improve the quality of policy outcomes to reflect social and environmental realities, as well as reformulate priorities to better address popular needs rather than elite special interests (see Goodman 2002: xvii).

Nanz and Steffek, for example, state that external transparency at international organizations is necessary for informed political debate. They advocate the development of a 'global public sphere' in which civil society plays a key role (2004: 328). The formalization of NGOs at the WTO is said to generate alternative perspectives on issues thereby forcing the organization to explain, clarify and reconsider its policy positions (Scholte et al. 1999). In this respect, Esty views the role of NGOs as 'intellectual competitors' (1998: 9). Charnovitz concurs, stating that the participation of NGOs may improve WTO decision-making by injecting new energy, ideas and values and that '[i]deas are weighted not by how many people hold them but their scientific or philosophical merit' (2004: 681). Charnovitz additionally advocates a participatory role not only for NGOs but also other intergovernmental organizations and national parliamentarians (2004).

For Tuerk (2003) and van de Ven (2003) the most promising aspect of NGO participation at the WTO is its capacity to improve the status of developing countries at the organization by providing technical expertise and information services to address problems related to non-transparent decision-making processes (see also Scholte et al. 1999; Payne and Samat 2004). They claim that the involvement of NGOs in trade policy discussions at the WTO may improve policy outcomes given that NGOs can provide important data and analysis that would be useful for policy formulation, implementation and review.

In contrast only a small number of scholars question the benefits of increasing NGO participation at the WTO, arguing that 'opening up' the WTO to NGOs would compromise, rather than enhance, the decision-making process (Robertson 2000a, 2000b; Barfield 2001; Kellow 2001; Wolf 2001). In essence these scholars contend that NGOs and their academic 'cheerleaders' greatly overstate the power of the WTO by portraying it as a monolithic body, rather than constituted by its member states. Instead the accountability and representativeness of NGOs is questioned. Robertson asserts that 'most NGOs are run centrally by small powerful elites and are unaccountable to their societies' and that 'their political stances are often disguised by well-meaning objectives' (2000a: 4). In relation to NGOs in global governance generally, William DeMars (2005: 22) questions the desirability of the power and influence of NGOs *vis-à-vis* other types of citizens' organizations such as labour unions, governments or nationalist movements, many of which have more transparent and structured lines of accountability and representation.

Another concern, expressed by Aynsley Kellow (2001), is that permitting NGOs to participate in WTO policy processes would allow some NGOs not one but two opportunities to influence international trade policy: via their own nation-states in the first instance, and directly at the WTO. In relation to NGOs based in the EU, direct participation at the WTO would allow NGOs not two but three opportunities for input. Given that EU member states and the European Commission are WTO members in their own right, European NGOs already lobby at the national and regional levels on WTO issues. Permitting NGOs to contribute directly at the WTO would potentially give European-based NGOs an even greater advantage over NGOs from the global South. Kellow also makes the point that NGOs would need to accept greater responsibilities in terms of accountability if they are to gain greater rights in international policy processes, contending that there should be 'no representation without taxation' (2001: 77). Thus on the basis of the uniqueness of the trade negotiation process, equity concerns, and questions surrounding NGO accountability and representativeness, these critics maintain that NGOs should be kept out of the WTO decision-making process.

A different set of scholars reject the incorporation of NGOs at the WTO for other reasons based on their opposition to neoliberal institutions in general and the supposed embedded power structures within NGO networks. From a critical, Gramsci-inspired perspective, writers like McMichael (2000), Wilkinson (2002a, 2002b, 2005) and Goodman (2002) question the capacity of neoliberal institutions to ever deliver equitable policy outcomes, pointing to the dominance of elite interests in international economic policymaking. Specifically the WTO is viewed as a flawed institution dominated by business interests and powerful states seeking to advance capitalist hegemony. McMichael contends for instance that the establishment of the WTO should be seen in context, as part of 'the corporate attempt to secure global market rule, framed by a pervasive discourse of neoliberalism' (2000: 466). These critics focus upon the hegemonic and paradigmatic power of dominant states and economic liberalism and as a consequence they are cautious about advocating an enhanced role for NGOs within such a framework, fearing that NGOs would be co-opted. In any event, this perspective already views most international NGO networks as reflective of global structural inequalities. Critical theorists instead advocate a different strategy for greater global economic equality: the fusion of local autonomy with universal norms, to be simultaneously pursued transnationally through the development of a global civil society and locally through the defence of grassroots autonomy (see Goodman 2002: xxi; Buchanan 2003; Ford 2003).

In summary, the key debate within the WTO-NGO literature centres on the democratizing potential of NGOs for the WTO system. NGO proponents argue that opening up the WTO to NGOs would boost the WTO's legitimacy and alleviate its democratic deficits. Opponents question the representativeness and accountability of NGOs themselves and highlight the need to preserve the unique nature of the international trade negotiation process. Critical theorists highlight the power structures embedded in the WTO and question the capacity of NGOs to rise above such structures.

While the democratizing potential of NGOs for the WTO is an important theoretical discussion, it is the contention of this book that it has sidelined systematic empirical inquiry into the *current* impact of NGO campaigns on the WTO, how NGO activity contributes to the international trade negotiation process and whether it supports or challenges this regime. It is in this direction that this study attempts to advance the WTO-NGO literature. Below I briefly survey some of the activities currently and routinely undertaken by NGOs in relation to the WTO.

NGOs IN INTERNATIONAL TRADE POLITICS: A GROWING TREND

In spite of the limitations on their formal participation at the WTO, a vast number of different types of NGOs, ranging from business associations and MNCs to environmental, human rights, religious and development organizations, are actively engaged with international trade and WTO issues. Evidence about the extent of NGO activity in this area is apparent in the number and range of international NGO campaigns directed at the WTO, many against specific WTO agreements. These include an ongoing campaign against GATS, as well as campaigns that have targeted aspects of the WTO's agriculture agreement, including Oxfam International's high-profile 'Make Trade Fair' and 'Rigged Rules and Double Standards' campaigns, and the 'Bite Back: WTO Hands Off Our Food' campaign (about genetically modified foods). Meanwhile NGO activity under the umbrella of 'fair trade' also seeks to highlight inequities in WTO rules by representing a symbolic ethical counterpoint to the current operation of the international trade regime.

Several NGO campaigns have aimed to stall negotiations at WTO ministerial conferences. The campaign known as 'WTO – Shrink or Sink! The Turn Around Agenda' aimed to prevent the launch of the Millennium Round of trade negotiations at Seattle in 1999, while 'No deal is better than a bad deal' was the campaign slogan of the NGOs attempting to halt progress at both the 2003 Cancún and 2005 Hong Kong ministerial conferences. In contrast other NGO campaigns have effectively advocated the strengthening of the WTO framework by proposing new WTO agreements linking trade rules to labour and environmental standards.

The increasing number of NGOs that have attended WTO ministerial conferences provides further evidence that NGOs are active on international trade issues. Table 2.3 below reveals that the WTO's formal participation mechanisms have not posed a deterrent to NGOs attending the biennial WTO ministerial conference, though these figures include NGOs representing business and well as public interests. The table shows that while only 108 NGOs attended in 1996, this figure rose to 765 for the 2005 Hong Kong Ministerial Conference.

Yet another avenue pursued by NGOs (and actively encouraged by some states) is to lobby for a place on official national delegations to WTO ministerial

Table 2.3   Number of NGOs in attendance at WTO ministerial conferences

Year	WTO ministerial conference location	Number of NGOs in attendance
1996	Singapore, Republic of Singapore	108
1998	Geneva, Switzerland	130
1999	Seattle, United States	476
2001	Doha, Qatar	949
2003	Cancún, Mexico	954
2005	Hong Kong, China	765

Notes: The figure for the Cancún conference refers to the number of NGOs *accredited* prior to the event and may vary from the number that actually attended.

Source: adapted from Katz 2008: 325.

conferences. For example Ddamilura and Halima (2003) describe how the governments of Kenya and Uganda established multi-stakeholder advisory committees on trade policy and the WTO that led to NGOs becoming part of national delegations to WTO ministerial conferences. At the Singapore Ministerial Conference, NGOs were accredited to the official government delegations of the US, Canada, New Zealand, Denmark, Norway, Egypt, Tunisia, Burkina Faso and South Africa, giving them important access to government briefings and government officials (O'Brien et al. 2000: 89). At the 1999 Seattle Ministerial Conference, NGO representatives were present on the government delegations of the US, Norway, the United Kingdom (UK), Denmark, the Netherlands, the EU, Kenya and Sweden, to mention but a few (Trades Union Congress 2000: 117; Anner 2001; Coulby and Ndrangu 2001: 4; Ahnlid 2002: 11; Payne and Samat 2004: 113). Even though their access was dependent upon states, the admission of NGOs via national delegations has offered selected NGOs an alternative route for gaining access to the WTO decision-making arena.

This preliminary evidence of increasing NGO engagement with international trade issues and the WTO also sits alongside the expansion in the number of international NGOs in recent years (see Boli and Thomas 1997, 1999; Katz 2008; Union of International Associations 2008–9). Table 2.4 below highlights the existence of a large number of NGOs operating internationally and offers a breakdown of their different types according to Union of International Association categories (see Union of International Associations 2009). The table shows that as of 2007–8, the total number of NGOs engaged internationally was 21,443. 'Internally oriented national organizations' accounted for

Table 2.4   Number of NGOs operating internationally

Union of International Association organization type	2007–8	% of total
A. Federations of international organizations	35	0.16
B. Universal membership organizations	468	2.18
C. Intercontinental membership organizations	1,051	4.90
D. Regionally oriented membership organizations	5,963	27.80
E. Organizations emanating from places, persons, bodies	2,689	12.54
F. Organizations of special form	4,342	20.25
G. Internationally oriented national organizations	6,895	32.16
Total	21,443	100

Sources: adapted from Katz 2008: 318 and Union of International Associations 2009.

32.16 per cent of this total followed by 'regionally oriented membership organizations' at 27.80 per cent.

To explain the rise of NGOs at the international level, many commentators point to rapid leaps in communication technology and affordable international travel (Alger 1997; Cohen and Rai 2000). The growing number and range of NGOs operating beyond a single nation-state is also a product of the increasing number of policy issues that are dealt with multilaterally by intergovernmental organizations (Reinicke 1998; Tarrow 2001). In relation to the WTO, a key factor in understanding the increasing numbers of NGOs engaged with trade issues is the evolution of international trade governance. The transformation of the GATT secretariat into the WTO (a new and permanent institution with an expanded mandate and effective regulatory and judicial processes), the progress in multilateral trade liberalization, and the growth of bilateral and regional free trade agreements (FTAs) has served as a magnet for NGOs concerned with a wide range of international trade-related issues.

Ultimately Jeffrey L. Dunoff was correct when, only three years after the creation of the WTO, he recognized that the preoccupation in much of the WTO-NGO literature with the formal constraints to NGO participation at the organization did not represent current practice because it overlooked the ways in which NGOs *already* contributed to the international trade regime (1998: 434). As outlined above, increases in the number of NGOs contesting international trade policy through campaigning, NGO attendance at WTO ministerials and evolving relations between NGOs and WTO member states suggest that NGO activity external to the WTO may be of growing significance. In order to provide a more solid theoretical basis for understanding the relationship between NGO activity and international trade governance than that offered by the existing WTO-NGO literature, the remainder of this chapter investigates the broader literature on NGOs in international politics.

CASTING A WIDER NET: PERSPECTIVES ON NGOs IN INTERNATIONAL POLITICS

Beginning in the late 1980s, the literature on NGOs in international politics has proliferated in line with interest in the roles and impacts of norms, values and identity in the international relations discipline. The beginnings of the literature on non-state actors in international relations can be traced back to the early 1970s. In 1971 Keohane and Nye edited a special issue of the journal *International Organization* entitled 'Transnational relations and world politics' that spearheaded an important debate about the emerging significance of non-state actors in international politics. In this issue they challenged the dominant realist paradigm in international relations in which all actors other than nation-states are regarded as peripheral. In attempting to initiate a new liberal, pluralist framework for understanding world politics, Keohane and Nye (1972: 1977), along with Samuel Huntington (1973) and James Rosenau (1980), claimed that in addition to nation-states, non-state actors operating in the global sphere, such as labour unions, MNCs, religious organizations (such as the Catholic Church) and revolutionary movements, should be considered significant if they participate in political relationships autonomously from governments.

Though neorealists such as Kenneth Waltz (1979) attempted to dismiss the relevance of non-state actors *vis-à-vis* nation-states, the debate spearheaded by Keohane and Nye nonetheless marked the beginning of an ongoing discussion about the impact of non-state actors in international politics. It spawned the literature on international regimes (Krasner 1982; Young 1982), epistemic communities (Haas 1990, 1992), and examinations of the role of non-governmental activist groups, or pressure groups, in international politics (Willetts 1982, 1996; Risse-Kappen 1995). This, in turn, led to the new research agenda on NGOs as 'sovereignty-free actors' working for the public interest or 'common good' and signified the emergence of social construc-tivism as a major new perspective in the international relations discipline (Wendt 1987; Kratochwil 1989; Rosenau 1990). Among the major catalysts for the interest in NGOs and civil society as normative agents in international politics was the supposed role of new ideas in bringing an end to the Cold War (Thomas 2001) and the associated growth of non-governmental civil society groups in Eastern Europe (Mendelson and Glenn 2002). The fundamental question that continues to guide the NGO research agenda was articulated by Peter Willetts back in 1982: how do 'small, overworked and under-funded NGOs with little formal authority manage to oversee changes in the practices of nation-states and international organizations?' (1982: 24). Most research has centred on the activities of NGOs and other non-state actors on human rights violations (Sikkink 1993; Klotz 1995; Keck and Sikkink 1998; Price 1998; Joachim 2007), environmental policy (Haas 1990, 1992; Wapner 1995; Princen and Finger 1994; Newell 2000; Humphreys 2004), and social/economic justice (Smith, Chatfield and Pagnucco 1997; Smith and Johnston 2002; Goodman 2002; della Porta and Tarrow 2005).

A number of theoretical approaches have been adopted in an attempt to understand the varied roles and impacts of NGOs in international politics. Chief among these are governance-centred perspectives, constructivist perspectives, and global social movement perspectives. Though they share common concerns across key issue areas, each perspective focuses on different aspects of NGO activity. Governance approaches encompass global public policy and neoliberal institutional perspectives and highlight the relationships between NGOs, other non-state actors, states and intergovernmental organizations.

NGOs are viewed as contributors to the operation of international regimes, especially as the transfer of policy issues from national to international arenas increases. Alternatively, constructivists focus predominantly on the role of NGOs as agents of moral values that work to disseminate norms and ideas with the power to 'reconstruct' state interests and thus impact international agreements. Global social movement scholars, informed by both social constructivism and institutionalism, examine how global social movements are constituted and maintained, and attempt to map the processes surrounding norm development, dissemination and diffusion.

It should be noted that neo-Gramscian scholars and other critical theorists have made important contributions to the literature on NGOs in international politics. However, they adopt quite a different approach to the above perspectives, warning about the potential of NGOs to become co-opted into global power structures. As such, critical theorists often differentiate between professional NGOs and supposedly more authentic grassroots organizations focusing on, for example, the anti-globalization protests and other attempts to 'resist' neoliberalism (McMichael 2000; Goodman 2002; Wood 2004; Starr 2005). Given that they are primarily concerned with the counter-hegemonic potential of transnational civil society activism, most Gramsci-inspired contributions do not reveal much about how NGO activity contributes to the operation of international institutions, especially those that underpin the neoliberal economic order. As such I focus upon the governance, constructivist, and social movement perspectives of NGOs in international politics, the major insights of which are detailed below. I then explain why a governance-centred approach is the most suitable framework for understanding the roles played by NGOs in relation to the international trade regime.

THE GOVERNANCE PERSPECTIVE: NGOs IN INTERNATIONAL POLICY PROCESSES

Governance approaches to understanding NGOs in international politics view NGO activity in the context of international policymaking (see Fox and Brown 1998; Kellow 2000; O'Brien et al. 2000; Ronit 2007). NGOs are treated as contributors to the international policy process rather than simply 'norm entrepreneurs' or international manifestations of domestic social movements. Governance-centred approaches provide a role for both norms and interests in understanding how NGOs impact decision-making at international institutions like the WTO. The interests of nation-states, in the form of the economic gains to trade as well as a host of domestic political factors, are paramount in determining the negotiating positions of member states at the WTO. By emphasizing structural and interest-based factors alongside norms, identity and institutional practices, governance approaches allow for an understanding of how NGOs work strategically in their attempts to impact international decision-making.

The governance approach, with its foundations in the neoliberal institutional perspective in international relations, views the very presence of international organizations as fostering incentives and opportunities for NGO advocacy. As Keohane and Nye contend in *Power and Interdependence* (1977), increasing international interdependence is contributing to the growth of trans-governmental coalition-building and political bargaining, which provides space for the growth of non-state actors beyond the nation-state. According to this view, intergovernmental institutions are said to *facilitate* interstate communication, consensus and coalition building, from which there is a 'spillover effect', leading to 'the proliferation of international activities by apparently domestic agencies' (Keohane and Nye 2001b: 241). In this respect, Tarrow (2001: 15) likens intergovernmental institutions to 'coral reefs' to which non-state actors such as NGOs are drawn (see also Kellow 2000: 6). Indeed the significant amount of work conducted by the UN on human rights, the environment and development has helped foster the growth of NGOs and activists in these areas (see Willetts 1996). This was also demonstrated in the discussion above on the establishment of the WTO and the rise of NGOs engaged with international trade issues (see Table 2.3).

One particularly visible example of the way in which intergovernmental institutions foster NGO activity is the growth of NGO 'counter-summits'. International meetings of NGOs, such as the World Social Forum (WSF), are often staged to coincide with the meetings of intergovernmental institutions. The first WSF meeting in 2001 was timed to coincide with the annual World Business Forum in Davos, Switzerland. Since then the WSF has evolved into a venue for exploring alternatives to neoliberal globalization (Smith 2004: 415; Pianta and Silva 2003). Other counter-summits have shadowed meetings of the World Bank, IMF and various UN conferences. With high-profile meetings of international organizations providing the platform, counter-summits are said to build links between NGOs, strengthen their mobilization capacities, build knowledge of the policy issues, formulate alternative solutions, and attract the attention of the media (Pianta 2001).

Intergovernmental institutions also benefit from international NGO activity. NGOs can serve to boost their legitimacy, enhance acceptance of policy decisions and improve policy implementation (see Jacobson 2000). As Reinicke states, effective global governance requires that governments 'enlist the active cooperation of nonstate actors' (1998: 219). To harness these capabilities, international institutions establish engagement or consultation mechanisms for NGOs (such as those at the WTO discussed above) to maximize the benefits of NGO participation whilst minimizing the costs. As stated on the

World Bank's website, '[b]y tapping the knowledge of specialized CSOs [civil society organizations] and giving voice to the poor by consulting with CSOs whose membership comprises poor people, the Bank can have a richer and more complete basis on which to base its decisions' (World Bank 2007b). Similarly, the aim of the IMF in consulting with NGOs has been not only to boost the institution's legitimacy but also improve policymaking and implementation (Thirkell-White 2005: 251).

NGOs, due to their organizational flexibility, also carry out work that intergovernmental institutions are ill equipped to perform (Risse 2002: 260). For example, NGOs monitor states' compliance with internationally agreed rules, which is especially important in regard to environmental standards and human rights. NGOs provide alternative sources of information that states and international organizations may not otherwise easily obtain. In the area of forest protection, NGOs have reported on states' compliance with the tropical timbers regime, thereby creating disincentives for states to 'cheat' on internationally agreed rules for preserving tropical forests. Intergovernmental institutions often contract out various functions to the NGO and business sectors. The World Bank, for instance, lends between $US 15 and $US 20 billion per year to developing countries to carry out various infrastructure projects, which effectively amounts to investment and business opportunities totalling approximately 40,000 contracts each year for NGOs and business firms (World Bank 2007c). In this sense, NGO activity serves to facilitate the ongoing operation of various international regimes.

In essence, institutional arrangements, decision-making processes and informal practices of international institutions condition interactions among governments and NGOs and thus structure the way in which NGOs attempt to realize their goals. The increasing authority of international institutions has provided 'a fulcrum for the formation of alliances of different state and nonstate actors' (della Porta and Tarrow 2005: 236), and these interactions are evolving as global policy problems become increasingly complex (Reinicke 1998, 1999–2000; O'Brien et al. 2000; Boehmer-Christiansen and Kellow 2002; Ronit 2007). Reinicke argues that 'global public policy networks' comprising loose alliances among international organizations, governments, the business sector and civil society are emerging in order to manage knowledge, correct market and intergovernmental failures and broaden participation in international governance (1999–2000). But less is known about how the growing role of NGOs in governance networks is affecting their strategies for realizing their goals (but see Edwards and Hulme 1996; Hulme and Edwards 1997; Bob 2005; DeMars 2005).

Only a limited number of studies have adopted a governance-centred approach to analyse the activities of non-state actors in contesting international economic policymaking. Fox and Brown's 1998 volume traces the contention among NGOs, the World Bank and its member governments over NGO attempts to incorporate environmental values into the organization's decision-making. Through a number of case studies, they examine the impact of transnational NGO campaigns directed at the major donor governments that fund World Bank projects in developing nations, as well as the degree to which NGO action has impacted the World Bank itself. Fox and Brown (1998) demonstrate that World Bank decision-making rules and procedures and inter-actions between World Bank 'insider reformists' and NGOs were integral factors in facilitating organizational change and an improved recognition of environmental issues. In particular, the power imbalance in favour of donor nations at the World Bank proved a political opportunity for NGO campaign-ers. The success of the NGO campaign against the World Bank's Arun III dam project in Nepal during the 1990s was dependent upon NGOs from develop-ing countries working with local NGOs to gain the support of the World Bank's US executive director. Continued NGO pressure on the World Bank, the dissemination of proposals for smaller-scale alternatives, the publication of studies detailing the negative impacts of the dam, and NGO lobbying of other powerful executive directors led the German and Japanese governments to question the merits of the project (Fox and Brown 1998: 486–7). In 1995 the ongoing controversy and the political sensitivities generated by the NGO campaign led the incoming World Bank president to overrule the organiza-tion's management to dismiss the dam project.

Fox and Brown's Arun III dam case study illustrates that governments (both local and national), private sector interests, and the institutional characteristics of the World Bank all played a part in conditioning the impact of NGO advo-cacy. Fox and Brown's interactive model, which explains how NGOs achieved influence at the institution, acknowledges that NGOs not only campaign inde-pendently to gain support for their goals, but foster productive links with nation-states to impact the decision-making process at the World Bank. Fox and Brown find that the degree to which states can reform the World Bank depends upon their level of support from outsiders including civil society and the governments of other nations.

Although Peter Willetts argues that the power advantage of NGOs lies in their ability to mobilize legitimacy, which is dependent on their reputation for fighting for 'good causes' (1982: 24), NGOs also need government support, or at least assent, to exert influence in international politics. William DeMars (2005) posits that NGOs should be seen as international institutions that are constituted not only by their principled normative mandates and 'simplistic universal causal theories', but also their partners. According to DeMars, these partners are of two types: political partners may include governments and international organizations, while societal partners may include religious groups, MNCs, entrepreneurs or ethnic groups. The significance of NGO partners is said to lie in the 'latent agendas' which they attach to NGOs (DeMars 2005: 45). Essentially DeMars explains that the instrumental objectives of other actors can pose significant constraints and/or create opportunities for NGOs, and that the more partners NGOs can garner though the perception of shared objectives, the more likely NGOs are able to affect international policy processes. The examination of NGO partners is an important factor in assessing the impact of NGO activity, particularly where NGOs do not possess formal participation status at the international institutions they target.

In a significant and often cited comparative study, O'Brien et al. (2000) investigated the emerging relations between global social movements (operationalized as NGOs) on the World Bank, WTO, and IMF. By lobbying for institutional reform and attempting to shift public opinion on global economic issues, the authors claim that NGOs are challenging these institutions to alter their agendas to better address the social impacts of their policies. In response to NGO campaigning, O'Brien et al. examined how the institutions have modified and assessed their motivations for engagement with NGOs as well as the significance of the emerging relationships (2000: 17–22). They found that the key factors determining each institution's response include institutional factors such as the *raison d'être* of the organization, the institutional structure and culture, the role of the executive head, and instrumental factors such as the vulnerability of the institution to NGO pressure in successfully implementing its policy agenda. Though it does underplay the role of relationships between NGOs and states, O'Brien et al.'s study is an important contribution to the literature on NGOs and intergovernmental institutions in that it identifies some of the key institutional factors that condition the influence of NGOs in international economic policy arenas.

In summary, the governance-centred perspective offers a pluralist view of international politics. It permits an understanding of how cooperative and antagonistic relations between NGOs, intergovernmental institutions, governments, and other non-state actors shape the capacity of NGOs to affect international policy processes. As the selected accounts outlined above demonstrate, NGO campaigning involves the formation of alliances or partnerships with formal sources of authority (nation-states) and navigation of an organization's institutional structures. By taking into account the institutional characteristics and practices of intergovernmental institutions while retaining realist insights about the role of power and interests, the governance perspective, as articulated here, provides a sound basis for analysing the roles and impacts of NGOs in international trade governance.

I now provide a brief overview of two other prominent approaches to understanding NGOs in international politics – the constructivist and global social movement approaches.

THE CONSTRUCTIVIST PERSPECTIVE: NGOs AS 'NORM ENTREPRENEURS'

In their efforts to demonstrate that NGOs, not just nation-states, are important actors in world politics, scholars such as Sikkink (1993), Klotz (1995), Price (1998), Khagram, Riker and Sikkink (2002), and Joachim (2007) have emphasized the significance of norms, ideas, and identity over state power and interests. In doing so, they have understood NGOs as 'norm entrepreneurs', who contribute to the creation of new identities that can override national identities, reconstruct national interests and affect international decision-making (Haas 1990, 1992; Sikkink 1993; Gordenker and Weiss 1995; Klotz 1995; Wapner 1995; Keck and Sikkink 1998; Price 1998; Risse et al. 1999; Florini 2000; Khagram et al. 2002; Joachim 2003, 2007). Some go further, arguing that these new identities will eventually constitute a new form of international organization – a global civil society – to rival states. In this vision, citizenship is no longer territorially confined, but based upon a shared sense of morality or ethics (Falk 1995; Wapner 1995; Lipschutz 1996; Florini 2000; Anheier, Glasius and Kaldor 2001). These normative accounts elevate the status of NGOs in international politics at the expense of nation-states and, depending upon the issue at stake, they often highlight the combative rather than productive or complementary relationships between the two.

Focusing on the potency of principled-issue norms harnessed by NGOs *vis-à-vis* state power and interests, constructivist writers have produced a substantial body of scholarship. A prominent strand is dedicated to understanding how NGOs work together in transnational advocacy networks in order to challenge human rights violations perpetrated by various nation-states. For example, Sikkink (1993) illustrated how NGOs mobilized international allies to generate political, economic and diplomatic pressure on the governments of Argentina and Mexico, to put an end to their human rights abuses in the 1970s. Similarly Audie Klotz (1995) examined the anti-apartheid NGOs that worked to project the civil rights movement in the US onto South Africa, ultimately contributing to the downfall of the apartheid regime. Richard Price, in 1997, detailed the role of NGOs in the international campaign to ban landmines. Exploring their role in issue generation, moral persuasion, network development and 'norm grafting', Price argued that NGOs persuaded states that the military utility of landmines is overshadowed by their humanitarian costs (1997: 614). Though Price claimed that his article broke the mould by examining NGO activity in the area of international security, he too focused on how NGOs promoted the human rights rationale for banning landmines.

In the environmental issue area, Paul Wapner has highlighted that NGOs or 'world civic activists' disseminate normative values that not only influence states and international organizations, but also affect the behaviour of larger

collectivities throughout the world (1995: 320). Using NGO campaigns targeting the environmentally damaging practices of MNCs as examples, Wapner
contended that when certain values and ideas gain resonance, standards of
conduct can shift and activists can persuade people and corporations to change
their practices (1995: 312–13). In doing so, NGOs employ consumer activism
tactics, such as boycotts and sensationalist media stunts, to alert consumers to
undesirable MNC behaviour. Such activities are said to 'transcend the civil
sphere' from which they originate, resulting in widespread changes in social
and MNC behaviour, eventually becoming officially cemented by changes in
government policy (1995: 325). The key point that Wapner put forward is that
NGOs can provide 'governance without government', an enduring theme
within the literature on NGOs and other non-state actors (1995: 329; Rosenau
and Czempiel 1992; Cutler, Haufler and Porter 1999; O'Brien et al. 2000).

In their seminal book, *Activists Beyond Borders* (1998), Keck and Sikkink
employed case studies from both the human rights and environmental areas to
develop their 'boomerang' model, which describes the mechanisms through
which NGO networks may affect the behaviour of nation-states. Specifically,
the model explained how local or grassroots NGOs bypass their own undemocratic governments by alerting international allies of a national griev-
ance, who in turn mobilize international consensus to generate global
condemnation of a government, thereby pressuring the government to reform
its practices (Keck and Sikkink 1998: 12). The focus on human rights continued in Risse et al.'s 1999 volume in which they argued that NGO and social
movement activity was central in reducing the human rights violations of a
number of developing nation-states in Eastern Europe, Africa, Southeast Asia
and South America. These groups did so 'by creating new issues and placing
them on international and national agendas, providing crucial information to
actors, and most importantly by creating and publicizing new norms and
discourses' (Sikkink 1999: 306). Risse et al. extended the boomerang model
through their five-stage 'spiral' model explaining human rights change as a
result of transnational NGO action. Comprising several 'boomerang throws',
this model operationalized the process of norm dissemination and specified
how international human rights norms affect domestic political and social
structures (Risse et al. 1999: 17–35).

In addition to targeting individual nation-states and MNCs, constructivists
have also investigated the ways in which NGOs draw upon their moral authority to target international actors on a range of issues. Khagram et al.'s 2002
edited volume, for example, contained contributions from both scholars and
NGO practitioners that compare and contrast NGO advocacy across the security, environmental, developmental and economic policy issue areas.
Specifically, contributors deal with international women's rights, NGOs and
the World Bank, human rights violations in Chile, campaigns to reduce Third

World debt, the impact of NGOs in Indonesia, and the international labour movement. Focusing on how NGOs 'reconstitute' the sovereignty of particular nation-states and the authority of international institutions, Khagram et al. explained that the role of NGOs in creating and disseminating new norms is delineated by 'opportunity structures' that, in addition to intergovernmental organizations, are said to include international norms already established by NGOs. In this manner, these scholars remain overly optimistic about the strength of NGO agency in international politics.

Though the constructivist approach is helpful for understanding how NGOs work to disseminate norms in world politics, it suffers from a number of short-comings that limit its utility for examining the role of NGOs at the WTO. First and foremost, constructivist scholars downplay the role of power and interests, which are fundamental to politics at the WTO where states essentially attempt to balance the economic 'gains to trade' with domestic political imperatives. In claiming that the moral persuasion tactics of NGOs brought an end to South Africa's apartheid regime, for example, Klotz (1995) did not adequately take into account global power shifts such as the impact of the end of the Cold War in altering US interests in South Africa's apartheid regime. Nor did she explore the possible negative electoral consequences for US congressional representatives in *not* supporting regime change in South Africa. Instead it is implied that the racial equality norm was significant enough to overcome any alternative interest-based motivations for the apartheid regime. Furthermore the 'globalization' of the racial equality norm is better viewed as an extension of a US domestic norm than a global coalescence and is thus reflective of US power.

Likewise Wapner implied that MNCs engaging in environmentally-harmful production practices simply came to accept the moral rationale of NGO campaigners (1995: 327). A more plausible explanation is that the MNCs under attack from NGOs changed their production practices for instrumental reasons (reputation protection and profit margins) rather than a sudden sense of moral obligation. Even in Price's account of the successful international NGO campaign to ban landmines, these weapons are not central to the defence of most major states, though NGOs still failed to convince the US to sign up to the new pact. Similarly the nation-states that had their sovereignty 'reconstituted' by transnational advocacy networks were relatively weak states, such as Argentina, Mexico and South Africa. Yet even relatively weak states can bring NGO campaigns undone. William E. DeMars (2005: 30) contests Keck and Sikkink's boomerang model of transnational action by showing that governments have the ability to instigate a 'bungie cord effect' whereby they manipulate and constrain local NGOs in order to keep transnational NGOs at bay. This is discussed in relation to human rights abuses in Egypt where a number of factors have prevented local NGOs from 'throwing the boomerang', including Egypt's relations with other nation-states. In essence, constructivist scholarship is unbalanced: it highlights NGO agency in inter-national politics at the expense of structural factors such as the power and interests of nation-states and MNCs.

Second, constructivist scholarship emphasizes how NGOs hold states to account rather than how cooperative relations between NGOs and particular states might assist NGOs in achieving their goals (Klotz 1995; Keck and Sikkink 1998; Risse et al. 1999; Smith and Johnston 2002). This is curious given that nation-states and other intergovernmental organizations, including the European Commission and World Bank, are major sources of finance for NGO activity, especially in the areas of humanitarian aid, environmental issues and development projects (Uvin 2000: 15; Imig and Tarrow 2001; Risse 2002: 260; DeMars 2005; Cox 2007). Though Keck and Sikkink's boomerang model does involve states and international institutions as the 'international allies' of local NGOs, little is said about the factors underpinning the relation-ships between NGOs and supportive states. Will a state simply support a cause for its normative qualities, or because it aligns with (or at least does not run counter to) its own objectives? This is likely to depend upon the issue at stake and requires much more investigation. Many accounts of NGO norm entre-preneurship therefore provide little assistance in understanding how NGOs might foster relationships with nation-states in order to affect international decision-making. This aspect of NGO behaviour is likely to be especially important for NGOs contesting international trade policy at the WTO where only states are allowed to sit at the negotiating table.

The focus on human rights and environmental issues within the construc-tivist literature has also meant that scholars have viewed NGO and civil soci-ety activity as having a universalizing effect, whereby NGOs are primarily viewed as agents that create and disseminate universal norms and standards in these areas. In other issue areas, particularly international economic policy, it is equally if not more likely that NGOs will seek to defend national sover-eignty from the intrusions of multilateral economic agencies. Paul Nelson, who has examined NGO advocacy at the World Bank, concurs that a flexible model is needed to account for NGO advocacy in the area of international economic policy to allow for variations in the relationships that NGOs culti-vate with governments (and other political actors) in order to gain traction for their causes (2002: 389). International economic policy, particularly interna-tional trade policy, impacts a wide variety of other policy areas including human rights, the environment, development and economic equality. A vast number of different types of non-state actors, including those typically excluded from constructivist analysis on the grounds that they lack 'principled issue' mandates (such as MNCs and business associations), are involved in framing these policy problems in a myriad of ways and advocating solutions that can differ or complement those proposed by NGOs.

Overall the neglect of state power and the focus on norm construction and dissemination renders the constructivist approach a partial account of how NGOs work to exert influence in international politics. To understand the varied roles that NGOs undertake in the context of the international trade regime, the work of NGOs as 'norm entrepreneurs' should be understood as just one of the aspects of NGO activity and must be integrated with a focus on international trade policymaking processes and NGO relationships with member states.

GLOBAL SOCIAL MOVEMENTS: SUSTAINING TRANSNATIONAL CONTENTION

While they view non-state activists as agents of global norm diffusion and isomorphism, global sociologists have interpreted the growth in NGO advocacy and other types of activism as the 'scaling up' of domestic social movements beyond the level of the nation-state (Smith et al. 1997; della Porta, Hanspeter and Rucht 1999; Guidry, Kennedy and Zald 2001; Cohen and Rai 2001; Smith and Bandy 2005; della Porta and Tarrow 2005). Accounts of global social movements attempt to identify the factors, or more specifically, the 'mobilizing structures' (see Tilly 1984), that underpin the growth of social movements beyond the state. In doing so, writers such as Smith et al. (1997), Smith and Bandy (2005), and della Porta and Tarrow (2005) examine the stability and maintenance of global social movements, focusing upon the linkages between local and transnational social movement contention. Following the 9/11 terrorist attacks, a key concern has centred around the sustenance of global social movement activism while avoiding violent confrontations such as those witnessed at the 1999 'Battle of Seattle'. Some social movement theorists have broken off to focus on what they call the 'new' activism made up of networks of activists across multiple issue-areas, such as those that contested the US-led invasion of Iraq in 2003, rather than single issue-driven contention driven by professional NGOs (see Bennett 2005). Although this body of literature details transnational collective action in the form of transnational protest movements, mass mobilization and grassroots movements (rather than the activities of professional NGOs), it does offer some insights for understanding the role of NGOs at the WTO. These insights relate to the emphasis on the structures that underpin social movement activity at the international level.

Within the global social movement literature, a great deal of attention is paid to the divides among activists, especially between activists from wealthy industrialized nations and those from developing and under-developed nations. In regard to activism against economic globalization, Jackie Smith and Joe Bandy find that within coalitions of activist organizations, differences between groups of diverse sizes and types, as well as those spanning class differences, may also be problematic for maintaining coalitions across borders (2005: 13). This concern is quite distinct from the constructivist view that emphasizes the shared norms and values, common goals, and functional relations between local and international NGOs. Accordingly social movement scholars have criticized Keck and Sikkink's concept of the transnational advocacy network, which is said to obscure the level of contention among actors within the network, making them appear united and homogeneous. On the contrary, it is argued that all actors within a network are concerned about the relative strength of their organization, maintaining their independence and progressing their own agenda (Bandy and Smith 2005; Smith and Fetner 2007). In this respect the social movement perspective is much more aware of the power structures and material interests at play within activist movements themselves.

Though they differ in their views on the level of contention within and between activist groups, several social movement scholars share with constructivists an optimistic view regarding the impact of the transnational activity of 'principled-issue' actors. For example Robin Cohen and Shirin Rai state that the transnationalization of social movements has uncovered the potential for new forms of global politics with cosmopolitan dimensions (2000: 1). Smith and Bandy claim that activists are self-reflexive and may therefore avoid the replication of global inequalities within their networks; they are also said to have the potential to transform power inequalities between states (2005). In doing so, Smith and Bandy outline a normative research agenda focusing on the factors that contribute to creating and maintaining effective coalitions: 'research on transnational coalitions will allow us to identify strategies for managing internal tensions, building trust across borders, and developing strategies and organizations with greater global impact' (2005: 231–2). This focus has given rise to a body of work that attempts to understand the structures that facilitate and maintain global social movements across borders rather than how global social movements affect policymaking at intergovernmental institutions.

Contributors to the global social movement literature have put forward a range of factors to help understand how global social movements are constituted and maintained. Drawing upon domestic social movement theory, Chadwick F. Alger (1997) points to the way in which issues of concern are framed (issue-framing), the domestic structures facilitating the growth of a movement (mobilizing structures), the level of resources available, unity among activists and the types of strategies and tactics used for contesting the issue at stake, also known as 'repertoires of contention' (see Tilly 1984). Additionally Alger (1997) states that the presence of political opportunity structures including international economic conditions, access to intergovernmental institutions and relations between nation-states are significant structural factors that promote the consolidation of global social movements. Although Khagram et al. also discuss the international political opportunity structure as an important factor in constraining and enabling NGO networks in achieving their goals (2002), this concept is much more thoroughly investigated within the social movement literature (see also Kitschelt 1986; McAdam, McCarthy and Zald 1996; Tarrow 1996). For activists contesting international economic policy, Smith and Bandy contend that the presence of nationally-based movements and foreign movement allies (and the extent of their similarities), governments or corporations that are open to change, mass public dissent, and the absence of international political conflict, are also significant political opportunities (2005: 232–7). It is these types of structural conditions that are likely to be important, not just for the maintenance of global social movements, but also for professional NGOs seeking to realize their goals regardless of the policy issue at stake.

Though the global social movement literature usefully sheds light on the structural factors underpinning the development of social movements beyond the nation-state, it does suffer from a unit-of-analysis problem. 'Global social movements' are relatively cumbersome units for investigating non-governmental activism, resulting in some difficulties in operationalizing transnational activism. For example, in the Smith et al. (1997) volume, contributors discuss not just 'transnational social movements', but NGOs and transnational social movement organizations (TSMOs). Others, such as O'Brien et al. (2000), offer their work as a study of global social movements, yet focus on NGOs in their case studies. Quite often, the relationships between NGOs, TSMOs and global social movements are unclear. Further it is uncertain as to whether the term 'global social movement' accurately describes the activities of transnational activists. The social movement concept has been employed rather too freely: many social movement theorists have simply applied the social movement concept to transnational activities that 'would be more recognizable as lobbying, communication, and educational and service activity if they were observed at home' (Tarrow 2001: 10). Risse wades through this difficulty by distinguishing between formal organizations, like NGOs, groups of formal organizations like epistemic communities (see Haas 1990, 1992), and more loosely connected networks such as groups of individuals (2002: 255–6). Meanwhile, Tarrow (2001: 12) distinguishes between TSMOs and NGOs in regard to their behaviour, arguing that mass-based TSMOs tend to *rally against* particular states and international institutions while NGOs engage in *routine interactions* with these same actors (see also della Porta and Tarrow 2005: 235).

In summary, global social movement scholars are more concerned with the maintenance of social movements beyond national borders and their creation and dissemination of norms than how NGO activity affects international policy-making. As such, they focus more on loosely connected groups and individuals around particular issues, such as the Iraq War and neoliberalism in general, rather than professional NGOs that routinely engage with nation-states and international institutions. Nevertheless in pinpointing the factors that sustain social movements internationally, this perspective contends that structural factors enable and constrain activists in attempting to further their goals via international policy processes. In particular, the political opportunity structure provides a basis for understanding the external constraints and opportunities faced by NGOs in attempting to affect policy change at organizations such as the WTO, where decision-making procedures, rules and practices as well as states' interests and their domestic politics are all in play. As a consequence the social movement perspective offers a more balanced perspective than that of social constructivism, which focuses unduly on NGO agency. Ultimately both the constructivist and social movement perspectives share an overly optimistic view about the potential of activist networks to reconfigure power structures and state interests to achieve their goals.

Overall the constructivist and social movement perspectives are valuable for understanding how NGOs construct and disseminate norms, as well as the structures sustaining global social movements. But given this preoccupation, neither provides a comprehensive framework for understanding the role of professional NGOs in the international trade policy process. For the purpose of this book, only a governance approach that situates NGO activity in the context of the trend towards increasing international decision-making, taking into account both norms and interests, provides the scope to understand the roles that an increasing number of NGOs are playing in relation to the WTO and the operation of the international trade regime.

A governance-centred framework provides scope for an assessment of a range of agents (NGOs, states, international institutions) and structures (WTO decision-making processes, states' interests, and conflicts and alliances between states, for example) and how the interrelationships between NGOs and WTO member states might provide NGOs with leverage to affect WTO negotiations. With its roots in neoliberal institutionalism, this approach highlights cooperation (as opposed to anarchy) in international politics, which is achieved through rules, norms and institutions (Keohane and Nye 1977). It accounts for the role of norms that shape aspects of the policy process including the formal rules, informal practices and patterns of bargaining among actors over the issues at stake. It allows for the incorporation of some of the most important insights developed by constructivists (the role of NGOs in generating normative consensus) and the social movement scholars (the role of political opportunity structures) into a framework that centres the analysis on the institutional site of contention. Finally, it is essential, given the institutional characteristics of the WTO and the policy issues with which it deals, that NGOs are viewed not simply as entrepreneurs and diffusers of norms, but as strategic actors in the international trade policy process.

CONCLUSION

In concentrating on the democratizing potential of NGOs at the WTO and the inadequacies of the organization's current mechanisms for engagement with NGOs, much of the literature on NGOs in the WTO context overlooks the role that NGOs currently play in international trade politics and how this role might affect WTO decision-making. The rapid expansion of the NGO sector in recent decades, the increasing number of NGOs applying to attend WTO ministerial conferences, the growth of NGO-led campaigns directed at the WTO and the presence of NGOs on governmental delegations to ministerial conferences, all reveal the chasm between the academic literature and the current practice of international trade politics. In particular, little is known about the nature of relationships between NGOs and member states or the impact of NGO campaigns on WTO decision-making.

Given the limited nature of the WTO-NGO literature, this chapter explored the governance-centred, constructivist and social movement approaches to the study of NGOs in international politics in order to gain some insights about how NGOs contest international decision-making. Though offering important and in-depth accounts of how NGOs attempt to construct and disseminate norms at the international level, the constructivist and social movement approaches suffer from a number of limitations in terms of their applicability to NGOs at the WTO. The constructivist perspective does not account for the important role of interests and power structures within world politics and it more often highlights antagonistic, rather than cooperative, relationships between NGOs and governments. The implication is that NGOs, through the mobilization of transnational advocacy networks, can somehow rise above power politics 'to reconstruct, re-imagine and re-map world politics' (Lipschutz 1992: 391).

Meanwhile, global social movement scholars focus on specifying the 'mobilizing structures' that facilitate the globalization of social movements and examine the factors that may sustain and strengthen social movements on a global scale. Although they take into account power structures and potential sources of disunity among activists to a greater extent than constructivists, the objective behind much of the global social movement literature is to understand more about the impediments to and opportunities for entrenching moral values and new norms rather than how NGOs affect intergovernmental decision-making. Their interest in broad-based global social movement activism, rather than the activity of professional NGOs, means that (as with the constructivist literature) there is only a limited investigation of how NGOs might work cooperatively with nation-states. This is likely to be a prominent factor in understanding how NGOs affect the WTO as a 'states-only' institution.

While the work of NGOs in attempting to generate global normative consensus is a significant aspect of what NGOs actually do in international politics, it is only a *partial* account of the role in international politics. There is a general lack of specification about how normative consensus affects the decision-making processes and outcomes at international institutions. Governance-centred approaches in contrast emphasize the importance of intergovernmental institutions in promoting the involvement of NGOs in international politics and policymaking; it is argued that the growth of transnational non-state advocacy is largely due to 'the resources, incentives and opportunities of international institutions' (Tarrow 2001: 15). A governance-centred perspective provides a basis for an examination of the interrelationships, and even partnerships, between state and non-state actors – all are viewed as participants in international policy processes. The empirical accounts of Fox and Brown (1998) and DeMars (2005) highlight the significance of governments as political partners for NGOs in achieving their objectives. In contrast to constructivist accounts of NGOs, governance-centred perspectives also take into account the structures that NGOs must navigate in order to influence decision-making at an international organization, such as an institution's organizational culture, decision-making processes and the relations between nation-states (O'Brien et al. 2000). Though the global social movement literature also considers these structural constraints and opportunities, their work is directed at a different end – the sustainability of global social movements.

It is clear then that in understanding NGO advocacy in the context of the WTO, a governance-centred perspective that takes into account norms, interests and institutional structures provides a valuable framework to begin theorizing about the roles that NGOs play in the international trade regime. Based on the insights derived from the governance-centred perspective on NGOs in international politics, the following chapter sets out a framework for evaluating the roles of NGOs in international trade governance.

3. Conceptualizing NGO activity in the WTO context

INTRODUCTION

The increasing number of NGO campaigns on international trade issues, coupled with the number of NGOs attending WTO ministerial conferences, suggests that NGO activity in relation to the WTO has increased over the past decade in line with the international expansion of the NGO sector more generally (Boli and Thomas 1997, 1999; Katz 2008; Union of International Associations 2008–9). This has occurred despite the fact that the WTO does not allow NGOs to formally participate at the WTO and is unlikely to do so in the foreseeable future. Given that they cannot formally contribute to WTO decision-making, this raises some important questions:

(1) What strategies or tactics do NGOs employ in contesting international trade issues and WTO decision-making?
(2) What roles do NGOs fulfil in the international trade regime?

This chapter outlines the methodological framework for the study to ensure that evidence and assessment of NGO activity in relation to the WTO is dealt with in a systematic manner. This is an essential requirement for any examination of NGOs because, as Betsill and Corell make clear, there is an unfortunate tendency in this area of scholarship to 'look for any possible sign that NGOs made a difference in a given political process while ignoring evidence suggesting that NGOs had little effect' (2001: 69). In navigating these difficulties, I employ a comparative case study research design, drawing upon the insights of Alexander L. George (1979).

In the first part of the chapter, I establish the scope of the study and define the key concepts employed. I investigate the different ways in which non-governmental actors and NGO collective action has been conceptualized, arguing that a focus on the campaigns of what Scholte et al. (1999) refer to as 'reformer' NGOs is the most useful way in which to approach NGO advocacy directed at the WTO. The discussion includes a brief overview of some of the key reformer NGOs that feature prominently in the case study chapters.

Drawing upon the NGO literature, the middle section of the chapter explains that NGO campaign activity, for the purposes of this study, can broadly be understood as 'mobilizing support', which involves generating unity among relevant NGO communities and attracting various WTO member states to the NGO cause. NGO influence is conceptualized as *impact on the international trade policy process at the agenda-setting stage* rather than the decision-making or implementation stages of policymaking. This acknowledges that while NGOs are not permitted to formally contribute to WTO decision-making, their activities external to the WTO arena have a bearing on the positions of WTO members inside the WTO arena. The final section introduces the selected case studies of NGO campaigns in the key areas of labour standards, foreign investment rules and IP rules.

CONCEPTUALIZING NGOs IN INTERNATIONAL POLITICS

Civil Society and Global Civil Society

There are several ways in which to conceptualize and define non-governmental advocacy organizations in international politics. Over the past two decades, the term civil society has become increasingly well used in international relations and political science as an umbrella term to describe the sphere in which these actors are said to reside. Civil society is usually defined as a public realm of voluntary, not-for-profit civic association located above the level of the family and distinct from both the state and the market (Wapner 1995; van Tuijl 1999: 494; Anheier et al. 2001). From the early 1990s, the term *global* civil society, also known as international civil society or transnational civil society, emerged (Rosenau 1990; Lipschutz 1992; Falk 1995, 1999; Wapner 1995; Florini 2000; Anheier et al. 2001). Global civil society is generally understood as a social sphere 'above and beyond national, regional, or local societies' (Anheier et al. 2001: 3) consisting of a broad collective of more or less formal organizations (Scholte et al. 1999: 109).

Perhaps because of its broad definition, a significant problem has emerged with the way in which the concept of global civil society has been employed in much of the international politics literature. Many have treated civil society not only as an institution and a set of relationships, but an aspiration (Stiles 2000). As a result scholars have focused almost exclusively on groups that pursue noble or virtuous causes (Klotz 1995; Wapner 1995; Keck and Sikkink 1998; Price 1998; Kaldor 2003), while neglecting actors that pursue blander or manifestly instrumental objectives. But as Scholte et al.'s explanation of the civil society category makes clear, civil society groups possess diverse goals that may relate to either '*reinforcing or altering* existing rules, norms and/or deeper social structures' (1999: 109, emphasis added). Despite their minimal presence in the civil society literature, business associations and terrorist groups cannot be excluded from the sphere of civil society, even if they pursue their goals via 'uncivil' means (Keane, 2003). It is simply not theoretically or empirically sustainable to discriminate between actors in the manner so frequently encountered in the civil society literature: all actors are constituted by both their normative and instrumental goals (Sell and Prakash, 2004).

Another difficulty is the use of the global civil society term in opposition to nation-states. Many civil society scholars perceive civil society actors as challengers to nation-states and intergovernmental organizations, thus paying little attention to the ways in which civil society actors and states cooperate to achieve shared goals. As R.B.J. Walker summarizes, the nation-state is defined as the 'problem' and global civil society presented as the 'solution' (1994: 673–4). But civil society groups often support the activities of one state in a given issue area, while criticizing the activities of others. Anti-whaling NGOs such as Greenpeace lend support to the anti-whaling positions of states like Australia and the US, for instance, while condemning the whaling activities of Japan and Norway. Nation-states and intergovernmental institutions not only provide arenas and focal points for civil society activity, they facilitate their influence. The European Commission, for example, funds the activities of many NGOs in an attempt to boost civil society participation in regional governance (Cox 2007).

While it is useful to understand non-governmental activity as part of a broader 'third sector' distinct from government and the market, this discussion highlights that it is necessary to operationalize civil society in a way that avoids a restrictive focus on groups pursuing 'good' causes, and the tendency to view non-state advocacy in opposition to the state system. Below, I examine various conceptualizations of NGOs in the international studies literature and literature specific to the WTO.

NGOs

The existence of NGOs, and their networks, has been an enduring component of international politics for over a century (Boli and Thomas 1997, 1999). The term 'NGO' is commonly used to refer to voluntary, non-profit organizations that engage in governance activities as insider policymaking participants and/or outsider challengers. Given that NGOs are often active participants in policymaking, Hirst and Thompson argue that the specification of these groups as *non-governmental* actors is, in practice, a misnomer (1999: 276–7). Many NGOs are playing increasingly important roles in domestic and international governance but these activities are often not immediately apparent in the general definitions of NGOs in the literature. For example Khagram et al. view NGOs as 'private, voluntary, nonprofit, groups whose primary aim is to influence publicly some form of social change' (2002: 6). Weiss and Gordenker offer a similarly vague 'catch all' definition, stating that NGOs consist of 'durable, bounded, voluntary relationships among individuals to produce a particular product, using specific techniques' (1996: 18).

While Peter Willetts is correct when he states that 'there is no such thing as a typical NGO' (1996: 62), categorizations of the different types of NGOs nonetheless shed greater light on the governance activities in which NGOs engage. Weiss and Gordenker distinguish between government-organized NGOs (GONGOs), such as those set up by governments in the former Soviet Bloc, quasi NGOs (QUANGOs) like the International Committee of the Red Cross (ICRC), and donor-organized NGOs (DONGOs) such as those established by governments or the UN to carry out specific objectives (1996: 20–21). Additional categories include business NGOs (BINGOs), religious NGOs (RINGOs), and environmental NGOs (ENGOs).

Others prefer to avoid the amusing acronyms and instead categorize NGOs according to their geographical sphere, distinguishing between local grassroots NGOs, national NGOs and international NGOs (Boli and Thomas 1997, 1999; Khagram et al. 2002). International NGOs such as Amnesty International are generally considered to have greater power, financial resources and autonomy than nationally based NGOs, though many nationally based organizations are affiliated with international NGOs. The NGO Greenpeace, for instance, comprises Greenpeace International (Stichting Greenpeace Council) in Amsterdam, 41 Greenpeace national/regional offices around the globe and 2.8 million supporters worldwide that finance the organization (Greenpeace International).

Though there are interesting relationships between national and international NGOs and varying motivations underlying the establishment of certain types of NGOs (such as DONGOs, GONGOs, and BINGOs), in emphasizing their governance activities, I propose that NGOs are better and more simply conceptualized as *contributors* to international policymaking processes. The content of NGOs' normative and instrumental goals or whether they are national or international organizations is less relevant. Having discussed some prominent definitions of NGOs that highlight their status as private, non-profit organizations that seek to exert policymaking influence, I now turn to definitions and typologies of NGOs in relation to the WTO.

NGOs AT THE WTO: REFORMIST, NON-PROFIT ADVOCACY NGOs

Specific to the WTO context, a number of definitions and typologies of NGOs have been suggested. Bellmann and Gerster offer three categories according to *organizational type*: (1) non-profit organizations that engage in advocacy and lobbying, (2) umbrella professional associations such as trade unions and business associations, and (3) research institutions and universities (1996: 35). Though useful for descriptive purposes, these categories are difficult to sustain in practice. For instance, trade unions and business associations, which belong to the second category, may also be non-profit groups that frequently engage in advocacy and lobbying at the WTO thus additionally fulfilling the characteristics of the first category. O'Brien et al. (2000) instead distinguish between NGOs in terms of their *issue focus*. They examine the activities of environmental, gender equity and labour organizations in relation to the WTO (as well as the IMF and World Bank). But this categorization ignores the growing phenomenon of NGOs that focus on different issues joining together in common campaigns directed at the WTO. It is instructive to note that the ongoing campaign for fair trade has involved NGOs ranging from trade unions and human rights groups to religious and economic development organizations.

Scholte et al. alternatively categories NGOs according to their broad *objectives* in relation to the WTO, describing civil society organizations as 'conformers', 'reformers' or 'radicals' (1999: 112). Avoiding the distinction between the normative and instrumental goals of NGOs, this typology bypasses the focus in much of the literature on NGOs pursuing worthy causes, and the associated tendency to ignore business associations. Conformers are described as those who support the international trade regime and generally endorse the goals of the WTO. They are said to include business associations like the ICC who seek to ensure that their interests are served at the WTO (Scholte et al. 1999: 112–13). At the other end of the spectrum, radical NGOs such as Earth First! reject economic globalization and call for the WTO to be dismantled (Scholte et al. 1999: 115–16). These groups do so mainly as outsider challengers through protest and public mobilization activities. It is interesting to note that in spite of their longer term, radical stances toward the WTO, high-profile NGOs such as Greenpeace, Friends of the Earth International (FOEI), and TWN have all applied for and received recognition status to attend WTO ministerial meetings (Mason 2004). In practical terms, these groups are therefore better understood as reformers.

Scholte et al. contend that reformer NGOs work within existing institutional structures, seeking to inject issues and priorities that they consider to have been neglected in the trade liberalization process. Reformist NGOs such as the Institute for Agriculture and Trade Policy (IATP), Oxfam International, WWF and the ICTSD engage in policy advocacy and lobbying in addition to their public mobilization activities in order to achieve their goals. This category of reformer NGOs, comprising groups that accept, and are willing to work within, the existing international trade regime, aligns with the direction and goals of this book as outlined in the key research questions posed at the beginning of this chapter.

I therefore focus primarily upon reformer, non-profit advocacy NGOs with a formal legal status and paid staff rather than conformist organizations that represent business interests or radical organizations that fundamentally oppose the WTO. There are a great many national, regional and international NGOs comprising religious, development, environment, and economic justice organizations, as well as trade unions, research institutes, and agricultural unions that fit within this category.

Below, I list the major reformer NGOs on which this study focuses and provide a brief description of those groups that feature prominently in the case study chapters.

Of the NGOs listed in Box 3.1, Oxfam International is among the most high profile. The organization consists of 12 independent organizations based in developed nations around the world. It is well-known for its work on a number

---

BOX 3.1   MAJOR NGOs IN INTERNATIONAL TRADE POLITICS

American Federation of Labor and Congress of Industrial Organizations (AFL-CIO)
ActionAid
Catholic Agency for Overseas Development (CAFOD)
Center for International Environmental Law (CIEL)
Friends of the Earth International (FOEI)
Heinrich Böll Foundation
Institute for Agriculture and Trade Policy (IATP)
International Centre for Trade and Sustainable Development (ICTSD)
International Gender and Trade Network (IGTN)
International Institute for Sustainable Development (IISD)
Médecins Sans Frontières (MSF)
Oxfam International
Public Citizen's Global Trade Watch
Public Services International (PSI)
Quakers United Nations Office (QUNO)
South Centre
Third World Network (TWN)
Trades Union Congress (TUC)
World Wide Fund for Nature (WWF)
World Development Movement (WDM)

of development, environment and trade issues, and the high quality of its research over the past decade has granted it a great deal of respect as a non-governmental participant in international politics. In 2002, the Oxfam Geneva Advocacy Office was established specifically to increase the NGO's influence on the WTO (Interview, Oxfam 2006). Oxfam has played a key role in several international campaigns directed at the WTO and has spearheaded its own campaigns in relation to fair trade and the WTO's rules on trade in agriculture, frequently supporting the rights of developing countries in WTO negotiations.

TWN, another prominent NGO in international trade politics, is an international network of organizations dedicated to research and advocacy on development and North–South issues, with the aim of injecting Southern perspectives into international policy debates. The TWN international secretariat is based in Penang, Malaysia, with additional offices located in Geneva (Switzerland), New Delhi (India), Montevideo (Uruguay), and Accra (Ghana). TWN also has affiliated organizations in several developing nations including India, the Philippines, Thailand, Brazil, Bangladesh, Malaysia, Peru, Ethiopia, Uruguay, Mexico, Ghana, South Africa and Senegal. Though it cooperates with a range of international and Northern-based NGOs, TWN's longer term goals in relation to the WTO are more radical than reformist. However, for the purposes of this study it is considered a reformer NGO as it works within the WTO's existing structures and frequently cooperates with other reformer NGOs.

Another international NGO that straddles the reformer and radical categories is FOEI, which describes itself as 'the world's largest grassroots environmental network' (FOEIa). It consists of 69 national member organizations and 5 000 local groups with more than 2 million members globally (FOEIa). Contrary to its name, FOEI campaigns on social as well as environmental issues. In relation to its trade campaigns, FOEI states: '[w]e work with others to curb the power and scope of the World Trade Organization and other regional and bilateral trade liberalization agreements' (FOEIb).

The International Confederation of Free Trade Unions (ICFTU), an international federation of national trade unions, is a different kind of NGO. Though the ICFTU merged with the World Confederation of Labour (WCL) to become the International Trade Union Confederation (ITUC) on 6 November 2006, for the purposes of this study, which deals with the organization's activities in the 1990s, I refer to the ICFTU rather than ITUC. The ICFTU is among the oldest and largest global non-governmental networks and is regarded as professional, legitimate and pragmatic in its dealings with the WTO (Anner 2001: 54). Established in 1949, the ICFTU has 155 million individual members and 241 affiliated organizations in 156 countries (ICFTUa). The ICFTU was part of the Global Union Group, which also includes the International Trade Secretariats (ITSs) and the Trade Union Advisory

Committee (TUAC) to the OECD.[1] The ICFTU is highly respected for the quality of its research and has considerable informal access to the WTO secretariat (Interview, ICFTU 2006).

The Geneva-based ICTSD, established in 1996, plays an important role in monitoring and reporting on developments on the trade negotiations at the WTO, with a particular focus on environmental and developmental concerns. As its website declares, 'ICTSD plays a unique systemic role as a provider of original, non-partisan reporting and facilitation services at the intersection of international trade and sustainable development. ICTSD facilitates interaction between policymakers and those outside the system to help trade policy become more supportive of sustainable development' (ICSTD 2007). The work of the ICTSD has thus been an important source of information for stakeholders and WTO policymakers, especially those from developing nations.

Though not normally active on international trade issues, Médecins Sans Frontières (MSF) developed an interest in the work of the WTO due to the impact of the organization's IP agreement on access to medicines in developing and under-developed nations. Primarily involved in health service delivery in the developing world, this organization is a highly respected international medical humanitarian organization and won the Nobel Peace Prize for its work in 1999. MSF is discussed in this study in relation to the access to medicines campaign detailed in Chapter 5.

Among the other NGOs active on international trade issues, the Quaker United Nations Office (QUNO), with offices in Geneva and New York, is involved in several WTO campaigns and runs programmes aimed at assisting developing countries in trade negotiations such as the Trade, Intellectual Property and Development programme. Likewise, the Center for International Environmental Law (CIEL), with offices in Washington DC, Geneva, and San Francisco, runs a Trade and Sustainable Development programme that targets a number of international institutions including the WTO (CIEL 2008). Seeking to integrate the principles of sustainable development into international trade and investment rules, CIEL was a key NGO in the campaign opposing a comprehensive investment accord at the WTO. ActionAid International, an international development agency, which moved its head office from London to Johannesburg in early 2004, has also had a strong presence on numerous NGO campaigns directed at the WTO ranging from agriculture to IP.

In addition to the international NGOs outlined above, a number of nationally and regionally based groups are heavily involved in international trade politics and work alongside the international NGOs mentioned above. In the UK, these include CAFOD, the World Development Movement (WDM) and the Trades Union Congress (TUC). In the US, the Heinrich Böll Foundation, the American Federation of Labor and Congress of Industrial Organizations (AFL-CIO) (an ICFTU affiliate), and Public Citizen's Global Trade Watch, are among the most prominent North American NGOs that have campaigned on international trade issues.

UNDERSTANDING NGO COLLECTIVE ACTION: NGO CAMPAIGNS

A range of concepts has been developed to explain how NGOs work together across borders. As discussed in Chapter 2, attempts have been made to extend the social movement concept by viewing NGOs as transnational social movement organizations that work within transnational or global social movements. But the social movement term, used to capture a wide variety of protest activity (particularly in regard to anti-globalization protests), is simply too broad for the purposes of this study, which centres on NGOs willing to work within existing institutional structures to reform aspects of international trade policy.

International relations scholars have developed concepts of NGO collective action more specific to reformer NGOs in international politics. The concept of a 'transnational advocacy network' proposed by Keck and Sikkink (1998) is of an NGO network made up of local/national NGOs and international NGOs, along with other supportive, issue-relevant actors. According to Keck and Sikkink, all actors within a transnational advocacy network share a common discourse and 'a belief that individuals can make a difference' (1998: 17). They are also held together by their dense exchange and creative use of information as well as sophisticated political strategies (Keck and Sikkink 1998: 2). Khagram et al. distinguish two more forms of NGO groupings based on their key advocacy methods. These are 'transnational coalitions', whereby the NGOs involved coordinate their tactics, and the broader category of 'transnational movements' that are said to engage in 'joint mobilization' (Khagram et al. 2002: 9).

Though Khagram et al.'s framework usefully combines the terminology of social movement theorists with that employed in the international relations literature, it pre-determines the types of activities in which NGOs engage. NGOs active on trade issues are likely to not only share information, but also coordinate their tactics and engage in joint mobilization, thus straddling all three types of groupings identified. Along with Keck and Sikkink's transnational advocacy networks, these concepts are predicated upon the nature of the interrelationships between non-governmental actors. In contrast, the goal of this study is not simply to illuminate the extent to which they share a 'common discourse', but to shed light on the particular tactics that NGOs employ in order to influence what appears to be a rather unreceptive international arena: the WTO.

To circumvent the difficulties embodied in the above conceptualizations of NGO collective action, I instead employ the more straightforward notion of an *NGO campaign*. As Jordan and van Tuijl explain, a transnational NGO campaign involves 'the pursuit of loosely linked political objectives' that are 'named after the dominant concern or after the targeted object' (2000: 2053). Investigating NGO campaigns better captures the fluid nature of the NGO sector in the WTO context where a variety of NGOs, regardless of their primary issue orientation, join together in campaigns and use a range of tactics to target the WTO. The multifaceted nature of international trade policy does not lend itself to a specific issue: NGO campaigns directed at the WTO attract environmental, development, human rights, anti-globalization, labour, religious and aid organizations among others. For NGO campaigns directed at the WTO, statements of 'political objectives' are found in campaign documentation such as joint-NGO declarations and sign-on statements. It is the *pursuit* of these political objectives that this study seeks to shed light upon in order to evaluate the roles that NGOs play in the international trade regime. Understanding international NGO collective action in terms of NGO campaigns is thus a more specific, targeted conceptualization of NGO collective action on the WTO than those presented by social movement and constructivist scholars.

ASSESSING THE ROLES OF NGOs AT THE WTO

Because they do not possess hard power or formal authority, the study of NGOs is more methodologically complex than the study of nation-states. The behind-the-scenes activities typical of NGOs add to the difficulties in assessing their roles in the trade policy process at the WTO. One rather obvious but deficient approach to conceptualizing NGO roles within the international trade regime is to simply assess whether or not NGO activity impacts WTO decision-making. For example, in studies of NGOs in international environmental governance, Michael Lisowski (2005) looks at how NGOs 'tip the balance' towards particular decision-making outcomes. Similarly, David Humphreys (2004) assesses NGO influence in affecting the textual outputs from international forest negotiations. In the area of human rights, Joachim (2003; 2007) emphasizes the significance of NGO access to UN organizations, which she states is an important avenue for NGOs in influencing decision-making outcomes.

But international environmental governance and international discussions around human rights issues differ from international economic governance arenas in that NGOs have far less formal access to multilateral economic institutions like the WTO. In the area of multilateral economic governance, the work of Fox and Brown (1998) and O'Brien et al. (2000) attests that adopting a 'hard' test case such as this may prevent scholars from uncovering the more subtle ways in which NGOs affect the World Bank, WTO, and IMF through agenda-setting and the reshaping of institutional structures.

It is necessary to differentiate between the agenda-setting and decision-making phases in the international policy cycle in order to better capture the role of NGOs in international governance. As David Dery (2000) explains, while non-governmental groups can exert sufficient influence to get an issue on the policy agenda, they often have little or no influence over how decision-makers subsequently respond to the issue or problem raised. Nevertheless their role in getting an issue on the agenda for consideration in the first place, whether it is addressed in a manner they support or otherwise, is significant as it reveals that NGOs play important roles at earlier stages of policymaking processes. Understanding and assessing NGO influence in terms of the actual decision taken, which occurs towards the *end* of the policy cycle, is therefore misdirected as it fails to adequately capture the roles that such actors do play. Viewing NGO influence as the power to affect decision-making is better suited to studies of NGOs in international governmental arenas where they enjoy greater formal access than at multilateral economic institutions. At the WTO then, where formal NGO input is relatively limited, it is more likely that the activities of NGOs might be of significance at the agenda-setting stage rather than at the point of decision-making.

This study therefore conceptualizes the roles and influence of NGO activity in relation to the WTO as agenda-setting. The origins of the agenda-setting concept can be traced to public policy and media studies (see McCombs and Shaw 1972; Cobb and Elder 1983; Kingdon 1984; and Baumgartner and Jones 1993; Kerbel 1995; Cappella and Jamieson 1997; McCombs, Shaw and Weaver 1997). Cobb and Elder profess that agenda-setting concerns 'how issues are created and why some controversies or insipient issues come to command the attention and concern of the formal centers of decision-making, while others fail' (1983: 14). Agenda-setting may involve any type of political or societal actor promoting a particular issue that they wish to have addressed, in a particular way, by decision-makers. Reformer NGOs that operate internationally may be especially adept at exerting influence in this way due to their organizational flexibility, effective use of the media, lobbying skills, perceived legitimacy and supposed independence (from business actors and states). Conceptualizing the NGO role in terms of agenda-setting allows NGOs to be viewed as potential contributors to global policymaking and offers a way to avoid overly simplistic tests of whether NGOs 'matter' in international trade politics.

NGO AGENDA-SETTING: MOBILIZING SUPPORT

So far, I have explained that this study focuses on reformer NGOs that possess high levels of resources, knowledge, and expertise, and who periodically and temporarily join together in campaigns to target aspects of the international trade regime. But how should the particular *strategies* that NGOs pursue to affect WTO negotiations be categorized? The general literature on NGOs in international politics (as outlined in Chapter 2) pinpoints a range of campaign tactics that NGOs use in their attempts to exert influence on decision-makers. These include disseminating relevant information to specific political actors and the general public, engaging in public demonstration activities, hosting campaign workshops and issue-relevant conferences, organizing boycotts, lobbying at international organizations, and forging alliances with nation-states and issue-relevant non-state actors. Much of this activity can be described generally as *mobilizing support*; in essence, it involves NGOs working to gain agreement among a sufficient number of actors so that decision-makers are forced to respond to NGO demands.

There is some implication, particularly in constructivist contributions to the existing NGO literature, that decision-makers (and other targeted actors) simply capitulate to the normative demands of NGOs if sufficient normative support external to an intergovernmental organization is achieved (Klotz 1995; Wapner 1995; Keck and Sikkink 1998; Price 1998). This scenario is unlikely to ensue for campaigns directed at the WTO: nation-states are the only actors permitted to participate in decision-making and their goals revolve around realizing the economic gains to trade while minimizing domestic political fallout. As such, I suggest that in mobilizing support for policy change at the WTO, NGO campaign goals must resonate with the objectives of WTO member states. In other words, NGO campaign goals must be compatible in some way with the interests of at least a small section of WTO members in order to provide sufficient impetus for these states to actively support the introduction of an issue to the WTO discussion agenda. This involves NGOs demonstrating that a campaign issue is relevant to the core business of the WTO and highlighting to supportive states the aspects of an issue that, if resolved, could benefit these states. I therefore challenge the idea that NGOs and states are mostly 'opposing forces' in international politics and instead will attempt to show that in many circumstances, their goals and activities are complementary.

A key aspect determining the capacity of NGOs to mobilize consensus among both the NGO sector and amenable WTO member states are the constraints and opportunities facing NGOs in attempting to achieve their goals. Featuring in the social movement literature, the idea that political actors are embedded within *political opportunity structures* is extremely useful for beginning to understand the role of NGOs at the WTO (see Tilly 1984; Tarrow, 1996; McAdam et al. 1996). The political opportunity structure essentially refers to the institutional context in which actors operate. Taking account of the political opportunity structure offers a corrective to the constructivist focus on NGO agency by directing attention to the particular conditions that constrain and enable NGO campaigners.

For NGOs that conduct campaigns at the international level, a complex set of political opportunity structures affect their activities. NGOs must navigate the relations between nation-states (in terms of conflict, cooperation and power disparities), as well as the issue priorities and governance structures of international institutions. For NGOs waging campaigns against the WTO, the role and operations of institutions such as the ILO and the United Nations Conference on Trade and Development (UNCTAD) are important, as NGOs have greater formal access to these institutions than they do to the WTO. The activities of other non-state actors also present opportunities and risks for NGO campaigners. In regard to reformer NGOs that campaign on international trade issues, the most likely non-state challengers are MNCs (and other conformer groups) as well as more radical NGOs that hold opposing goals. But depending upon the campaign issue at stake, it may be just as likely that these other non-state actors have complementary objectives, with their presence more of an opportunity than a threat.

On top of international level factors, domestic political structures also affect NGO attempts to mobilize normative consensus for their goals (see Putnam 1988; Risse-Kappen 1995). These revolve around the problems and opportunities arising from the national implementation of international trade rules and domestic electoral cycles, especially in powerful states such as the US. These types of domestic political factors shape the preferences of WTO member states and thus their amenability to NGO goals. Altogether, a complex mix of international and domestic political factors profoundly shape the behaviour of NGOs (as well as states), structuring the way in which NGOs campaign for the WTO to address their particular issues. These political opportunity structures must be of prime consideration in understanding the strategies and tactics used by NGO campaigners to mobilize support and thus play roles in the international trade regime.

CASE STUDIES: OVERVIEW

As discussed in Chapter 2, there have been a number of NGO campaigns directed at the WTO, which gives us some idea of the universe of cases available. These campaigns can be separated into two groups: (1) campaigns that contest particular WTO agreements; and (2) campaigns that rally against new trade rounds and the WTO in its entirety. Given that this book seeks more information about the contribution of reformer NGOs to the international trade policy process, it is appropriate that cases of NGO campaigns are selected from the first category, that is, campaigns that seek to delete, expand or modify (in some other way) aspects of WTO agreements. Broadly speaking, campaigns of this type contest the impact of WTO agreements on the environment, labour rights, agricultural practices, and the economic development of LDCs.

Of the broad range of NGO campaigns directed at the WTO, I select three campaigns in the areas of labour standards, foreign investment rules, and IP rights through which to examine the strategies and tactics of NGO campaigners and the role that they play in international trade politics. These are:

(1)   the campaign for the incorporation of core labour standards into WTO rules;
(2)   the access to medicines campaign opposing the application of the WTO's TRIPS Agreement to generic essential medicines required in developing nations; and
(3)   the campaign against the development of a WTO foreign investment agreement.

In the first case, the campaign for the incorporation of a core labour standards clause into the WTO framework was led by the ICFTU and supported by a range of labour unions and NGOs from around the world. Campaigners lobbied the WTO to incorporate a 'social clause' into trade rules that would commit WTO member states to respect seven basic ILO conventions relating to freedom of association, the right to collective bargaining, the abolition of forced labour, prevention of discrimination in employment and a minimum age for employment. In doing so they attempted to draw attention to the link between increased trade liberalization and labour exploitation, arguing that the violation of labour rights in export sectors is an unfair trade practice. Though this campaign continues today, the case study focuses upon the campaign in the lead-up to the 1996 WTO ministerial conference in Singapore through to the 1999 Seattle conference. Though a labour standards clause was supported by a number of influential states, including the US, it was strongly opposed by most developing nations and attempts to institutionalize the link between trade rules and labour standards at the WTO ultimately failed.

The second case, the access to medicines campaign directed against the WTO's TRIPs Agreement, involved NGOs seeking to prevent WTO rules from curbing developing country access to affordable generic versions of patented medicines for diseases predominantly affecting those in the developing world. The major point of debate concerned whether (and exactly *how*) the in-built TRIPS 'safeguards' might be used by developing countries. The campaign tactics of the key NGOs, including MSF, Oxfam International and ActionAid, were aimed at exposing the support of wealthy WTO member states for maintaining high international IP standards with narrow recourse for using the safeguards. NGOs also worked closely with developing WTO member states including India, Brazil and the African Group, whose citizens were most affected by WTO rules in this area. Ultimately the NGO campaigners were successful in having this issue debated at the WTO, with member states agreeing upon the 2001 Doha Declaration on TRIPS and Public Health, which permitted developing countries to use the safeguard measures to meet public health objectives.

The final case study is the NGO campaign against the establishment of a WTO investment agreement. Although the NGO campaigners and most developing WTO members opposed all four new issues added at the Singapore conference, investment is chosen as the focus of the case study because it was the most contentious and divisive issue and attracted a greater level of attention from NGOs than the other issues.[2] Following the 2001 Doha Ministerial Conference, a vast array of NGOs and several developing countries were extremely unhappy with the consensus decision that members would begin negotiations on a WTO investment agreement. With the aim of having the investment issue removed from the WTO's agenda at the 2003 Cancún Ministerial Conference, a NGO campaign emerged to publicize the negative aspects of a WTO investment accord. According to the NGOs, these included greater economic volatility for developing and newly industrializing countries, a potential 'race to the bottom' in regulatory standards in areas such as labour standards and the environment, and increasing the power of MNCs *vis-à-vis* nation-states. At the Cancún Ministerial Conference, NGOs supported the G-90 developing nations in refusing to agree to the launch of negotiations on a WTO investment agreement. Following the collapse of the Cancún meeting, in July 2004, WTO members agreed to remove investment from the Doha agenda altogether as part of a broader initiative to salvage the Doha Round of trade negotiations. The removal of the investment issue from the Doha Round renders this NGO campaign another useful case study for examining the roles of NGOs in relation to the international trade policy process.

The three cases outlined above provide the opportunity to understand more about the roles played by NGOs in the international trade policy process across three separate issue-areas. The aim is to reveal the major campaign tactics and strategies used by NGOs and elucidate the important roles that they play at the beginning of policymaking processes at the WTO. While the case study selection represents a 'most similar' approach to case study selection – that is, all three campaigns managed to affect the WTO agenda in some way – they differ in a number of respects. Most importantly, they differ in terms of their goals for the WTO arena. The access to medicines campaigners attempted to modify an existing WTO agreement (TRIPS), the investment campaign worked to remove the proposed WTO investment agreement from the Doha Round agenda, while the labour campaigners sought to incorporate an entirely new accord into WTO rules. Put differently, both the medicines and investment campaigns aimed to *scale-back* the WTO's authority over nation-states, declaring that the application of 'one size fits all' international rules applied to all WTO members regardless of development status are inappropriate. These NGOs supported the autonomy of developing countries to make decisions about their economic development and social priorities independently of WTO rules. In contrast, the labour standards campaigners sought to *expand* the institution's authority over member states by seeking to integrate labour standards into WTO rules to be uniformly applicable to all states. The selection of these cases will allow for an analysis of how these different goals affect the strategies and tactics used and whether it is easier for NGOs to lobby for the WTO's jurisdiction to be curbed rather than expanded.

Another key difference between the selected case studies concerns the relations between NGO campaigners and particular WTO member states. For the medicines and investment campaigns, NGOs allied with developing WTO member states. In contrast, the ICFTU, the chief campaigner on labour standards, worked closely with a selection of the most influential WTO members: the US, Norway and a handful of EU states. The disparities in influence of the states with which NGO campaigners forged relationships allows for an examination of NGO relations with both developed and developing states. This will enable a comparison of the different roles played by NGOs according to the status of the WTO member states with which they share trade policy goals.

CONCLUSION

Based on the insights of Chapter 2, which found that existing WTO-NGO scholarship focuses on the democratizing potential of NGOs at the WTO rather than their real-world impact, the present chapter reiterated the research questions guiding this book regarding the current role of NGOs at the WTO: (1) what strategies or tactics do NGOs employ in contesting international trade issues and WTO decision-making?; and (2) what roles do NGOs play in the international trade regime? Adhering to the major guidelines of comparative case study method, I explained that this study will focus on reformer, non-profit, advocacy NGOs (as opposed to radical or conformer NGOs) and justified the conceptualization of NGO collective action in terms of NGO campaigns. Derived from the existing literature and preliminary evidence about NGO behaviour in regard to the WTO, I conceptualized NGO campaign activity in terms of 'mobilizing support'. This involves not only a focus on how NGOs work to generate consensus among the NGO community, but also how their campaign goals resonate with the objectives of particular member states. This understanding seeks to address the relative neglect of the role of relations between nation-states and NGOs in studies of NGO advocacy in international politics. I also examined the various ways in which NGO influence has been conceptualized, and contended that for the purposes of this study, it is best understood in terms of agenda-setting, which occurs at the beginning of the policymaking cycle.

The final part of the chapter introduced the case studies of NGO campaigns that have targeted the WTO in the areas of labour standards, IP rules and foreign investment. Two major differences among the cases studies of NGO campaigns were elaborated. First, by selecting cases that attempt to both minimize and expand WTO authority, the study will be able to examine how NGO campaign goals affect the types of strategies pursued. I posit that it is likely to be more difficult for NGOs who campaign for the establishment of new WTO accords to achieve their goals than it is for those lobbying for the removal of issues from the WTO's negotiating agenda. Second, the cases comprise campaigns where NGO goals have aligned with both developing countries (the medicines and investment cases) and those of more powerful states (the labour standards case). Therefore, the case selection also provides scope to examine how NGO strategies might differ in line with the various states involved, as well as the mechanics of the relationships between NGOs and member states with differing power capabilities.

In the three case study chapters that follow, I explore in detail how NGOs contest international trade issues by harnessing political opportunities and mobilizing support for their goals among the international NGO community and various amenable WTO member states. Drawing upon secondary and primary source material, including interviews with NGO personnel and a representative of the WTO, the case studies illustrate the strategies and tactics employed by NGOs to affect the WTO's agenda. Following the three case study chapters, the final chapter is dedicated to comparing and contrasting the insights gained from the case study research in order to build a theory about the roles of NGOs in the international trade regime and explain why power-based outcomes do not consistently prevail at the WTO.

NOTES

1. After 2001, the ITSs became known as the Global Union Federations.
2. In addition to investment, the Singapore Issues, which emerged at the WTO's 1996 Singapore Ministerial Conference, include competition policy, transparency in government procurement, and trade facilitation. WTO working groups were set up on each of these issues with a view to beginning negotiations at some future point.

4. The campaign for international core labour standards at the WTO

INTRODUCTION

The long-running campaign to incorporate internationally recognized core labour standards, also known as a 'social clause', into WTO trade rules has given rise to entrenched divisions among developed and developing member states, NGOs and scholars. The ICFTU, through its campaign on labour standards and trade, has been a major non-governmental advocate for WTO labour rules. In its campaign push, the ICFTU was strongly supported by sympathetic, influential states (including the US, Norway and France), which used their influence to have the issue of labour standards discussed by members at the WTO's 1996, 1998 and 1999 ministerial conferences.

Although the issue of core labour standards was repeatedly debated at the WTO, a number of factors contributed to the failure of NGOs and pro-labour member states – and conversely the success of the opposing developing countries – to enact a WTO social clause. These factors were the complex regulatory 'Baptist and bootlegger' nature of different coalitions involving moral values and economic interests with vastly different payoffs for different states (see Yandle 1983), as well as the WTO's decision-making process based on obtaining consensus among member states. Domestic politics in the US also played its part, since the 1999 Seattle conference was held in the lead-up to the 2000 presidential elections. While the bid to develop a WTO social clause was ultimately unsuccessful, it did contribute to progressive developments on labour standards at the ILO. These included the 1998 Declaration on Fundamental Principles and Rights at Work and its follow-up, and the inclusion of labour standards provisions in regional and bilateral free trade agreements involving the US, the EU and other pro-labour states.

This chapter assesses the role played by the ICFTU in lobbying for a WTO labour clause, the nature of relations between the ICFTU and sympathetic nation-states in this context, and how the issue was dealt with at the WTO. The linkage of international trade and labour standards is a complex international policy issue and together, these state and non-state labour standards advocates employed a number of arguments to support their case. These included arguments that labour standards are universal human rights, constitute 'fair' international trade rules, and can assist the economic development of the global South. Labour standards proponents also argued that the WTO, with its effective dispute system, was the most appropriate multilateral arena in which to enforce labour standards.

Most developing nations, along with some NGOs from developing nations, opposed the trade-labour linkage on the basis that it would constitute protection for wealthy WTO members and thus compromise the gains from trade for developing countries. Most of the existing literature on core labour standards at the WTO focuses on these for and against arguments and analyses various options for enhancing cooperation between the WTO and ILO on this issue (see Hughes and Wilkinson 1998; Hensman 2001; Thomas 2002; Leebron 2002; van Roozendaal 2002; Basu, Horn, Román and Shapiro 2003; Elliot and Freeman 2003; Guzman 2003; Mavroidis 2003; Staiger 2003; Trebilcock 2003; Winters 2003; Cho 2005).

Instead, this chapter explains how the multiple arguments contained in the labour standards debate facilitated a pro-labour linkage alliance between the NGOs and states supporting a WTO social clause. In contrast to the other two case studies outlined in Chapters 5 and 6, which concentrate on relations between NGOs and developing states, the labour standards campaign allows for an investigation of the relationship dynamics between NGOs and more powerful WTO members. It provides a basis upon which to compare and contrast the nature of these relationships, facilitating an understanding of some of the key differences in the roles undertaken by NGOs in the international trade regime according to the development status of the member states for whom their positions support. In Chapter 7, I synthesize this by noting – with specific reference to this campaign – that NGOs play key roles in enhancing the legitimacy of the negotiating positions of WTO member states by promoting normative rationales for policy change. Unlike the investment and medicines campaigners (see Chapters 5 and 6) the labour standards campaigners played less of a role in harnessing relevant political opportunities and mobilizing support internationally – instead they relied on their close links to influential pro-labour member states.

The first part of the chapter provides a brief history of international cooperation on labour issues at the ILO and GATT, which illustrates some of the power dynamics at play among nation-states on this issue. This is followed by an overview of conceptualizations of the trade-labour linkage within this issue's literature. I then turn to the WTO arena and investigate member state activity and NGO lobbying on the labour issue, focusing on the 1996 Singapore, 1998 Geneva, and 1999 Seattle ministerial conferences. Finally, I explain that the WTO's institutional characteristics obstructed progress on labour standards issues in this arena, despite the relative power of pro-labour

WTO member states. As such, these states (and NGOs) continue to progress labour standards through other international forums including the ILO and the UN Global Compact.

LINKING TRADE TO LABOUR STANDARDS: INTERNATIONAL COOPERATION AT THE ILO AND GATT

The notion that internationally recognized labour standards accompany international trade liberalization did not emerge with the establishment of the WTO, but has been subject to international discussion since the end of the First World War. The beginnings of the debate can be traced back to the establishment of the ILO by the Treaty of Versailles in 1919. In recognition of the interdependent nature of labour standards, the preamble of the ILO constitution states that 'the failure of any nation to adopt humane conditions of labour is an obstacle in the way of other nations which desire to improve the conditions in their own countries' (ILO 1919). In 1946, the ILO became UN-affiliated and is now considered the premier institution dealing with labour issues internationally (though this status has been threatened by the labour standards debate at the WTO). The organization has a membership of 183 states and is unique among international organizations in that it has a tripartite corporatist structure, where labour and business are represented alongside states.

The ILO administers a system of international labour standards, contained in almost 190 conventions, 'aimed at promoting opportunities for women and men to obtain decent and productive work, in conditions of freedom, equity, security and dignity' (ILO). Of these conventions, eight have been endorsed in a number of international arenas as 'core' labour standards. These are:

(1) C29 Forced Labour Convention, 1930 (concerning forced or compulsory labour);
(2) C87 Freedom of Association and Protection of the Right to Organize Convention, 1948;
(3) C98 Right to Organize and Collective Bargaining Convention, 1949 (concerning the application of the Principles of the Right to Organize and to Bargain Collectively);
(4) C100 Equal Remuneration Convention, 1951 (concerning equal remuneration for men and women for work of equal value);
(5) C105 Abolition of Forced Labour Convention, 1957;
(6) C111 Discrimination (Employment and Occupation) Convention, 1958;
(7) C138 Minimum Age Convention, 1973; and
(8) C182 Worst Forms of Child Labour, 1999.

Many of these conventions have become subject to international agreement in other arenas: the UN Universal Declaration of Human Rights (1948), the International Covenant on Civil and Political Rights (1966), the International Covenant on Economic, Social and Cultural Rights (1966) and the UN World Summit for Social Development (1995). The 1995 UN World Summit in Copenhagen helped pave the way for international consensus on seven of the conventions in the June 1998 ILO Declaration on Fundamental Principles and Rights at Work and its follow-up (C182 on child labour was not established until 1999).

While the ILO possesses a unique tripartite organizational structure, this has not helped alleviate the organization's limited capacity (beyond suasion) via monitoring and reporting on national compliance, to enforce its labour standards conventions. As these standards align with those in wealthy industrialized nations, it is primarily LDCs that are in violation of ILO conventions. But the ILO's limited enforcement capacity has rendered it an ineffective institution in the eyes of developed states and pro-labour civil society organizations, especially trade unions based in the global North, who view labour standards as basic human rights that should be internationally respected. Numerous efforts have been made on the part of these state and non-state actors to strengthen international labour standards by seeking to integrate them into international trade rules in order to force developing countries with low standards to improve their conditions for labour.

The efforts of wealthy states and trade unions to formally link labour standards to international trade began in the early 1940s. The failed International Trade Organization (ITO) was set up to incorporate labour standards (Blackett 1999). Article 7 of the Havana Charter, adopted at the 1947 United Nations Conference on Trade and Employment that proposed the creation of the ITO, contained a provision on Fair Labour Standards. It stated that all countries shared a common interest in respecting fair labour standards: '[t]he Members recognize that unfair labour conditions, particularly in production for export, create difficulties in international trade, and, accordingly, each Member shall take whatever action may be appropriate and feasible to eliminate such conditions within its territory' (UNCTAD 1948). However, the US did not ratify the ITO charter due to opposition from the US Senate and thus the ITO did not materialize. The parties to the agreement had been engaged in parallel negotiations on substantive tariff concessions, out of which the GATT was established in 1947 (Alben 2001: 1431; Howse, Langille and Burda 2006: 176). The GATT did not contain a provision on labour standards, although it did permit members to take measures relating to the products of prison labour (Article XX(e)), measures to protect public morals (Article XX(a)) and measures relating to human life or health (Article XX(b)). For pro-labour states, including the US and European states, these provisions were deemed insufficient for improving international respect for labour standards, especially given that developing states were not contracting parties to the GATT.

The complexity of the interests and moral values involved in the trade-labour linkage debate began to emerge with the US State Department's attempt to incorporate a labour clause into the GATT in 1952, which drew heavily upon Article VII of the ITO charter (Alben 2001: 1436). The US supported this measure not simply because it had a normative commitment to upholding labour standards, but because it wanted to ensure Britain's support for Japan's accession to the GATT. Britain considered the accession of Japan a major threat to its cotton textiles industry, and the US saw a GATT labour clause as a way to ease British concerns while gaining from increased trade with Japan (Alben 2001: 1433–7; Howse et al. 2006). The call for a GATT labour clause was supported by the British Trades Union Congress who, along with US trade unions, lobbied their governments to support a GATT labour clause to prohibit the movement of goods made in violation of labour standards. These included the right to organize, the prohibition on child labour, minimum wages, and maximum hours of work (Charnovitz 1987: 575).

Ultimately a GATT labour clause was a rather coarse instrument for alleviating British concern about Japan's accession. Instead the GATT contracting parties instituted a one-off safeguard clause for the cotton textiles industry only. In addition, several GATT parties employed a number of discriminatory tools to restrict Japanese imports (Alben 2001: 1438). One effect of the GATT labour clause debate was that during the period in which Japan's accession to the GATT was being considered, Japan ratified ten ILO conventions, while only ratifying two ILO conventions in the 15 years after its GATT accession (Alben 2001: 1438–9). Thus, via the GATT, wealthy contracting parties were able to exert their power to gain special instruments to maintain their interests. The follow-on effect was that Japan increased its commitments to the ILO in order to boost its application for entry into the GATT club.

From the late 1950s onwards, wealthy states and trade union groups from these states continued to push for a GATT social clause to integrate labour standards into international trade rules, though this did not result in any significant outcomes (Charnovitz 1987: 575). For example, in 1959, the ICFTU and TUAC argued for the resurrection of the ITO charter and for GATT contracting parties to enact permanent labour standards provisions (Charnovitz 1987: 575). And, during the Tokyo Round from 1973 to 1979, the Nordic countries promoted discussion on labour standards as a potential future issue for the GATT, though some contracting parties denied there was any connection between labour standards and international trade (Charnovitz 1996: 565; Hughes and Wilkinson 1998: 375).

During the Uruguay Round, pro-labour states made further attempts to get labour standards on the agenda (Hughes and Wilkinson 1998: 375). In preparatory meetings the US raised the issue of how the GATT parties might deal with workers' rights, and the European Parliament issued a resolution stating its support for a GATT social clause for the new round (Charnovitz 1987: 565; Howse et al. 2006: 177). Nonetheless these efforts were rejected by most developing countries. During the final phases of the Uruguay Round in late 1993, the US proposed the creation of a working group at the soon-to-be established WTO to examine the links between labour standards and trade. But again, this proposal failed to generate enough support from the membership (Stigliani 2000: 187). In April 1994 at the Marrakesh conference, almost every minister expressed a view on whether there should be a role for the WTO in regard to labour standards (WTO 1996b). The European Parliament proposed to expand GATT Article XX(e) (allowing for trade restrictions on products manufactured in prison) to encompass child labour and the principle of freedom of association and collective bargaining (Waer 1996: 31). Ultimately these calls for the integration of labour standards into WTO rules only managed to entrench divisions between wealthy and developing states over the issue.

Upon the conclusion of the Uruguay Round in 1994, having failed to get their way at the GATT/WTO, the US and EU developed labour standards provisions within their own trade legislation and attempted to exert their power in other international, regional and bilateral forums more amenable to their influence. In 1994 the US sought to establish a working group at the ILO entitled 'Social Dimensions of the Liberalization of International Trade' to examine labour rights and economic development in the context of international trade and investment (Stigliani 2000: 183). Even this attempt, like those within the GATT, was rejected by developing countries led by India and Pakistan (Stigliani 2000: 183). As a result, the ILO's governing body decided in 1995 that the issue of trade sanctions would not be addressed nor would the issue of the link between international trade and social standards (Trebilcock 2003: 290). One positive development that kept the issue of labour standards on the international agenda was the endorsement of basic workers' rights at the UN World Summit for Social Development in March 1995.

The US and EU also attempted to encourage developing states to comply with international labour standards by including labour rights conditionality in their Generalized System of Preferences (GSP) regimes.[1] In 1995 the EU revised its GSP provisions to allow the withdrawal of benefits to developing states if they violated core labour standards (Braithwaite and Drahos 2000: 235). In determining whether to extend GSP benefits to a nation, the US GSP law requires the US President to take into account whether a country has taken or is taking steps to uphold internationally recognized workers' rights (Office of the United States Trade Representative (USTR) 2000). The US has also unilaterally incorporated labour rights provisions into its region-specific trade legislation (such as the Caribbean Basin Initiative, the African Growth and

Opportunities Act, and the Andean Trade Preferences Act) as well as into the North American Free Trade Agreement (NAFTA) (Howse et al. 2006: 177; Kolben 2006: 230).

In parallel to the attempts to strengthen compliance with labour standards in bilateral and regional forums, the linkage debate at the GATT/WTO continued to have a significant impact on the ILO during the 1990s, despite the failure of the US to establish an ILO working group on the matter. This was partly in response to concern that the ILO was being sidelined on the issue of core labour standards (Hughes and Haworth 1997; O'Brien et al. 2000; Haworth and Hughes 2004) but also because it served pro-labour standards states, particularly the US, to keep the issue on the international agenda. In 1997 the ILO membership debated but rejected the ILO director-general's proposal for the ILO to administer a certification and labelling programme of products from countries that respect core labour standards, as it was deemed too close to institutionalizing a linkage between international trade and labour (Trebilcock 2003: 291). In the same year, however, work began at the ILO on what became the Declaration on Fundamental Principles and Rights at Work, adopted on 18 June 1998. The declaration privileged four core areas: freedom of association and right to collective bargaining, the elimination of child labour, the freedom from discrimination, and freedom from forced labour (ILO 1998). It asserted that all member states have an obligation to implement the core conventions, even if they have not yet ratified them. On 17 June 1999 the ILO adopted Convention 182 on the Prohibition and Immediate Action for the Elimination of the Worst Forms of Child Labour. US officials played key roles in the development of both documents (Stigliani 2000: 183).

Despite their relative power, the long held goal of the US and other wealthy states to engender greater international compliance with core labour standards has been a difficult undertaking. This has occurred due to the lack of authority of the ILO and the consensual multilateral decision-making processes in place for GATT trade rounds. The establishment of the WTO and the increasing importance of international trade heightened the sense of purpose of pro-labour states, which led to this protracted debate continuing at the WTO (the major topic of this chapter). Thus far I have only hinted at the complexity of the interests and moral values at stake in the linkage issue, and I now explore these in more detail by examining the ways in which the linkage debate has been conceptualized in the literature on labour standards and the WTO.

CONCEPTUALIZING THE TRADE–LABOUR LINKAGE

The proposed WTO social clause has been debated as a human rights issue and in terms of its impact on economic efficiency and domestic policy autonomy.

The institutional capacity of the WTO to administer such a provision has also been examined in the literature. I choose to focus on the economic and human rights arguments as these are most relevant for explaining the complementary goals of the ICFTU and states in advocating a WTO social clause. Appreciating the complexity and cross-cutting nature of the instrumental and normative motivations for the linkage provides a basis to understand the relationship between the NGOs supporting the social clause and pro-labour states. Ultimately the multi-sided alliance was insufficient to convince developing states to acquiesce to demands for a WTO social clause, simply because these standards were harmful to their competitiveness in the global economy.

Labour Standards as Human Rights

For human rights advocates of a WTO social clause, all workers, regardless of nationality, are said to share 'universal and inalienable rights', some of which are specific to the workplace (Kolben 2006: 227). The particular labour standards that most proponents agree should be tied to WTO rules are the internationally endorsed core ILO conventions. These include the abolition of prison labour, discrimination in employment and child labour; the right to organize and collectively bargain; and equal remuneration for men and women, as listed above. Having received endorsement in a number of international arenas as *the* core labour standards, these conventions were also the basis of the ICFTU's campaign for core labour standards at the WTO.

Though they claim to support labour standards, developing countries and some NGOs from developing countries have rejected the human rights arguments. Southeast Asian nations in particular have argued that core labour standards are not universal norms but 'western legal-philosophical constructs' (Stigliani 2000: 184). Deepmala Mahla of the Indian NGO CUTS, for instance, has stated that while demands for improved regulation of labour standards are supported, 'regulation must be introduced domestically in order to do justice to cultural differences' (CUTS International 2000). These critics have thus contended that the *international* enforcement of these standards through the trade regime would constitute an intrusion into their sovereign affairs.

This has generated an impassioned response from labour standards proponents and other commentators, who have accused governments and NGOs that peddle this view as elitist. Hughes and Wilkinson, for example, state that opposition to labour standards draws on 'relativist arguments constructed to protect political elites in the face of growing demands for democratisation' (1998: 376). Similarly, Hensman claims that shunning universal values will only result in 'backward, dependent econom[ies] in which the mass of the population cannot even dream of possessing the commodities produced for export to developed countries' (2001: 442). In regard to India, Hensman also points out that human and labour rights are not foreign concepts, but gave rise to the nation's independence movement and are enshrined in the Indian constitution (2001: 442).

Economic Growth, Comparative Advantage and International Labour Standards: Coalescing Norms and Interests

The most hotly contested aspect of the trade-labour linkage debate revolves around economic arguments and its costs and benefits for different WTO member states (see Salazar-Xirinachs and Martínez-Piva 2003; Trebilcock 2003; Kucera 2004; Howse et al. 2006). Social clause opponents argue that the promotion of a WTO social clause is a thinly disguised bid for greater trade protection for wealthy nations. The push for the WTO to take a role in the enforcement of labour standards internationally is closely linked to growing concern about cheaper labour costs in developing WTO member states and efforts to reduce trade deficits and high unemployment in G-7 nations among others (Charnovitz 1987: 565; Hughes and Wilkinson 1998: 376). As Braithwaite and Drahos suggest, the US was seen by linkage critics as simply attempting to get the GATT/WTO to do its 'dirty work' (2000: 235).

Espousing this view, prominent economist and scholar Jagdish Bhagwati (2001) has stated that all trade linkage issues, including labour and environmental standards, are essentially discriminatory tools that do not belong at the WTO due to their potential to harm developing countries. According to this argument, a WTO social clause would reduce the comparative advantage of most developing states in the area of low labour costs, reducing overall economic efficiency (Fields 1994). Such provisions are also said to impose administrative costs on developing countries attempting to adhere to standards that are already well established and upheld in wealthy member states (Panagariya 2000).

Critics assert further that a WTO social clause would benefit only privileged wage workers in the formal sector in developing countries while neglecting those working in informal, unregulated sectors, thereby demonstrating that labour standards supporters from the global North are only concerned about those developing country workers with whom they must compete. In this vein, Kolben (2006) contends that only workers in export sectors might experience any improvement in working conditions. Even worse, Hernández (1998) argues that a social clause would drive additional workers into the informal sector, which cannot be easily monitored and regulated. A WTO social clause might also reduce the overall level of employment in developing countries by potentially driving up the costs of employing labour.

For these reasons, it is claimed that the enforcement of higher labour standards would make little difference overall in the developing world. The increased cost of labour would reduce trade from developing countries to developed countries, leading to a decline in economic growth (Singh and Zammit 2000). This in turn would result in capital flight and increases in unemployment, thereby making workers in developing countries worse off (Summers 2001; Kolben 2006: 244). This line of argument against a WTO social clause is part of a larger argument frequently used by developing countries: that 'one size fits all' approaches to international trade rules are inappropriate due to differing levels of development.

Linkage proponents have responded to accusations that a WTO social clause is protectionist (and would thus adversely affect the economic growth of developing states) by referring to empirical evidence. In 1996 an Organisation for Economic Co-operation and Development (OECD) study entitled *Trade, Employment, and Labour Standards: A Study of Core Workers' Rights and International Trade* found that trade liberalization was largely unaffected by the enforcement of core labour rights. Instead it found that in the long term, adherence to core labour standards could boost economic performance:

> The view that argues that low-standards countries will enjoy gains in the export market share to the detriment of high-standards countries appears to lack solid empirical support. These findings also imply that any fear on the part of developing countries that better core standards would negatively affect either their economic performance or the competitive position in world markets has no economic rationale. On the contrary, it is conceivable that the observance of core standards would strengthen the long-term economic performance of all countries. (Delechat and OECD 1996: 105)

The greatest competition over cheap labour is said to be not between developing and developed countries, but between developing countries themselves (Hensman 2001: 437–8). This is evident in developing countries' apprehension over China's accession to the WTO, a nation that has an abundance of cheap labour. If then, according to the OECD, there is 'no economic rationale' to resist labour standards and labour competition is primarily between developing nations, a set of enforceable international rules might promote a 'race to the top' rather than a 'race to the bottom', which could serve the long-term interests of developing WTO members. The ICFTU argues that the push for core labour standards is actually *anti*-protectionist because it would strengthen rule-driven trade liberalization and reduce unfair competition or 'social dumping' (ICFTU 1996).

Linkage proponents have additionally pointed out that two of the core labour standards, freedom of association and the right to collective bargaining, are enabling human rights. As Dessing (2001) explains, enabling rights set process standards that seek to realize the conditions reflected in the assumptions underlying neo-classical economic models, including freedom of choice, equal bargaining power, and full information. They therefore have little bearing on production costs. In addition, none of the core labour standards encompasses substantive standards that set wage levels or detail the specific content of health and safety standards. As the ICFTU affirmed, '[w]e do not advocate global minimum wages and working conditions – what we seek to stop is governments trying to gain competitive advantage through the repression, discrimination, and exploitation of workers, and instead to ensure that globalization does result in gains for all workers' (ICFTU 1998).

Given the complex nature of the arguments surrounding the labour standards issue, the labour standards debate has not found an easy resolution at the WTO, having essentially divided both states (and to a lesser extent, NGOs) into opposing camps, mostly along developed/developing country lines. Though linkage proponents present some evidence that a WTO social clause would not economically impair developing member states in the long run, these arguments have been completely ineffective in blunting the opposition of developing WTO members and some civil society groups. As a result the issue has remained prominent in discussions within and outside the WTO since the establishment of the organization. Having now examined some of the arguments over the incorporation of core labour standards at the WTO, the following section details the campaign activities of the ICFTU and other NGOs and outlines developments on the issue at the WTO's Singapore, Geneva and Seattle ministerial conferences.

CAMPAIGNING FOR CORE LABOUR STANDARDS AT THE WTO

Key Actors

Following the many previous attempts to have labour issues recognized at the GATT, the establishment of the WTO in 1995 offered both state and civil society actors a new opportunity to establish a formal link between labour standards and international trade rules. The ICFTU, the chief NGO proponent, is regarded as one of the most professional, legitimate and pragmatic NGOs that the WTO deals with (Anner 2001: 54). This is due to the representative nature of the organization and the quality of its research output. As such, the ICFTU (now ITUC) has enjoyed a level of informal access to the WTO secretariat often exceeding that granted to other NGOs, which has been a major advantage for the organization in helping to get the core labour standards issue put on the WTO's agenda (Interview, ICFTU 2006).

In addition to the ICFTU, a number of other labour and non-labour NGOs were involved in the campaign, including the WCL, Union Network International, the European Trade Union Confederation (ETUC) and the International Trade Secretariats (ITSs). By directly targeting MNCs through developing and monitoring corporate codes of conduct the work of aid and development NGOs Solidar, Oxfam, and Christian Aid had the effect of supporting the campaign (Anner 2001: 15). For example, Oxfam's 'Make Trade Fair' campaign promoted workers' rights through fair trade, while Solidar's development education campaign 'Globalisation of rights: justice and equity in the global market', funded by the European Commission, was linked to the ICFTU campaign. Some national ICFTU affiliates also played prominent, high-profile roles, particularly the AFL-CIO, the German Union Federation, the Congress of South African Trade Unions (COSATU), and Central Única dos Trabalhadores (CUT) in Brazil.

Among WTO members, the US, Norway and France were the strongest supporters of the linkage. During the Uruguay Round, and in the lead-up to the WTO's Singapore Ministerial Conference, these WTO members, along with several other supportive European countries, urged all WTO members to provide a role for the WTO in commanding respect for core labour standards (O'Brien et al. 2000: 89). South Africa, one of the few developing countries with a strong and influential union movement, was also in favour. The support of the UK and Germany was only moderate, even following the 1997 election of the Blair Labour government in the UK and the 1998 election of Chancellor Schröder's Social Democrats in Germany. Under their previous Conservative governments, the UK and Germany had strongly opposed the incorporation of core labour standards into WTO rules. For all pro-labour states mentioned above, a major driving force behind their support of a social clause at the WTO was the significance of the labour movement as an interest group to the governments in power.

Underpinning the push for a social clause at the WTO were very close ties between the ICFTU and the states supporting a WTO labour standards clause. The Norwegian foreign ministry for example provided substantial funding for the ICFTU campaign via the Norway Labour Office (LO-Norway), an ICFTU affiliate (Anner 2001: 10). This was considered special funding that was not subject to the same rigorous supervision to which other projects were held, which gave the ICFTU a great deal of flexibility to pursue their objectives with little interference or constraint (Anner 2001: 4). As one ICFTU official stated, the alliance with Norway was extremely important for the campaign and meant that resources could be fully devoted to the campaign itself rather than diverted to fundraising activities (Interview, ICFTU 2006).

There were also strong links between the US government and the ICFTU's US affiliate, the AFL-CIO. During the 1990s President Clinton promoted

Table 4.1   *Core labour standards at the WTO: opposition and support*
           among selected states and NGOs

	Supporters	Opponents
States	Belgium United Kingdom post-1997 Canada France Germany post-1998 Italy Norway South Africa United States	Australia United Kingdom pre-1997 G-77 Germany pre-1998 India Indonesia Pakistan
NGOs	American Federation of Labor and Congress of Industrial Organizations (AFL-CIO) Central Única dos Trabalhadores (CUT) (Brazil) Christian Aid Congress of South African Trade Unions (COSATU) European Trade Union Confederation (ETUC) German Union Federation Global Union Group: comprising the International Confederation of Free Trade Unions (ICFTU) Norwegian Confederation of Trade Unions Oxfam International International Trade Secretariats (ITSs) Trade Union Advisory Committee (TUAC) Solidar World Confederation of Labour (WCL)	Consumer Unity and Trust Society (CUTS) Eurocommerce Hind Mazdoor Sabha (HMS), India Indian National Trade Union Congress (INTUC) International Chamber of Commerce Third World Network (TWN) Union of Industrial and Employers' Confederations of Europe

closer ties between the USTR and the AFL-CIO, appointing AFL-CIO president, John Sweeney, to the President's Advisory Committee for Trade Policy (Stigliani 2000: 180–83; Frutiger 2002: 69). At an ICFTU preparatory workshop prior to the WTO's 1996 Singapore conference, acting USTR Charlene Barshefsky told unionists that the USTR was 'fighting your fight' (O'Brien et al. 2000: 90).

Further trade union representatives have also been granted places on official government delegations to WTO ministerial conferences. At the Singapore conference for instance, ICFTU affiliates were accredited to the delegations of the US, Canada, New Zealand, Denmark, Norway, Egypt, Tunisia, Burkina Faso and South Africa, giving them important access to government briefings and government officials (O'Brien et al. 2000: 89).

Most developing nations, especially in Asia, opposed the integration of core labour standards at the WTO. Led by the Indian government, the Group of 77 (G-77) developing nations has been a vocal critic of the social clause and its economic impacts on the global South. A number of NGOs from developing nations, even including some ICFTU affiliates, also opposed the social clause. Among these were the Indian National Trade Union Congress (INTUC) and Hind Mazdoor Sabha (HMS) (both ICFTU affiliates), as well as the international NGO, TWN, and the Indian NGO, CUTS. Organizations representing the international business sector also opposed a WTO social clause, for example, the ICC, Eurocommerce, and the Union of Industrial and Employers' Confederations of Europe (O'Brien et al. 2000: 91). Table 4.1 lists the key states and NGOs that supported and opposed the trade-labour linkage.

Campaign Goals

For state and civil society trade-labour linkage supporters, the major catalyst for the WTO campaign was the ongoing frustration with the weak enforcement capacity of the ILO and the new opportunities presented by the establishment of a strengthened international trade organization. The strength of the WTO's DSB and the organization's broad membership comprising developed and developing nations meant that linkage proponents viewed it as a far more attractive arena than both the ILO and GATT in which to enforce core labour standards. As the ICFTU elucidated: '[t]here is no doubt that the WTO represents a real opportunity for a workers' rights clause campaign … Both the "package deals" and the way the WTO operates as an organization mean that the ICFTU and our affiliates can target our lobbying campaigns much more clearly' (ICFTU 1998). The ICFTU and other civil society supporters were also spurred on by the fact that they had been consulted very little during the Uruguay Round on the mandate of the WTO. In contrast business representatives had been closely involved via the US and EU and had achieved many of their goals in relation to the incorporation of agreements on services liberalization and IP rights (see Ostry 2000).

The ICFTU and its supporters argued that a strong relationship existed between trade liberalization and labour exploitation and that the violation of labour rights in export sectors was an unfair trade practice that should be addressed at the WTO (ICFTU 1999; O'Brien et al. 2000: 77; Seidman 2004: 111). The ultimate goal of the ICFTU and the other groups involved in the campaign was to have the WTO adopt a social clause that would commit states to respect the seven basic ILO conventions with violations to be punishable with trade sanctions. The ICFTU proposed that these standards be attached to all WTO accords, with the ILO retaining responsibility for monitoring compliance and the WTO's DSB to be used as the enforcement mechanism.

Though the interpretation of labour rights violations as unfair trade practices helped qualify the issue as suitable for being dealt with at the WTO, the ambiguity surrounding the definition of an *unfair* trade practice was destined to be a sticking point. Furthermore the trade regime principles of national treatment and most-favoured nation (MFN) do not permit trade discrimination in production methods (including labour standards). These issues ensured that the issue would not find an easy resolution at the WTO.

Campaign Strategies

The first step taken by the core labour standards campaigners was to lobby for the establishment of a WTO working group on trade and labour standards. As the ICFTU put it, this working group would discuss how 'the rules of the WTO can ensure that the mutually reinforcing relationship between core international labour standards and the multilateral trading system are enhanced' (ICFTU 1996). Both the US and Norway shared this goal. In 1994 AFL-CIO lobbying resulted in the US Congress demanding that the President establish a working group on labour issues at the WTO as part of its approval of the Uruguay Round (van Roozendaal 2002: 100). Norway's provision of funding to the ICFTU was also directed at boosting the legitimacy and support for the shared goal of establishing a labour standards working group (Interview, ICFTU 2006). Both state and NGO linkage supporters thus began promoting their goals in preparation for the first WTO ministerial conference.

The WTO's inaugural ministerial conference in Singapore in December 1996 was the first opportunity for supporters of the linkage to advance their goals. In preparation, the ICFTU organized meetings with affiliated unions (and with the TUAC, ETUC, and representatives of the ITSs) to inform them of their intention to press for the incorporation of labour standards into WTO rules. They also briefed them on their campaign strategy, which was primarily based around lobbying WTO member governments to support the issue rather than embarking on an international public education and mobilization campaign. For a pre-ministerial workshop on labour standards for ICFTU affiliates and other unions, the ICFTU invited other non-trade union NGOs to attend, though invitations were only extended at the last minute on a casual basis (O'Brien et al. 2000: 86). During the workshop, a number of the non-trade union NGOs, including the Washington-based International Labor Rights Fund, the International Centre for Human Rights and Democratic Development, and Solidar, urged the ICFTU to form a Workers' Rights Caucus in order to bring together NGOs and labour unions to strengthen their case in preparation for the Singapore conference (O'Brien et al. 2000: 86). The ICFTU agreed to the formation of the caucus and provided representatives from its Geneva office, TUAC and the ITSs.

In the two years preceding the WTO's first ministerial meeting, outright opposition to the social clause proposal solidified among developing countries and a small number of NGOs. In May 1994, the Association of South East Asian Nations (ASEAN) expressed their opposition at the ASEAN Labour Ministers Meeting. In their joint communiqué they stated

> that they are not opposed to the application of labour standards and are committed to improving the economic and social well-being of workers. However, they are concerned with the rigid imposition of labour standards and the use of rigid standards to stifle free trade and economic development which constitutes a new form of protectionism. (ASEAN 1994)

This sentiment was also expressed by developing nations at UNCTAD and at a 1994 meeting of the United Nations Economic and Social Commission of Asia and the Pacific (ESCAP) (van Roozendaal 2003: 135; Kolben 2006: 237). The Indian government was particularly active in mobilizing support against the linkage among developing countries and in the media (Kolben 2006: 238–9). In January 1995 at the labour ministers conference of the Non-Aligned and Other Developing Countries group in Delhi, India helped organize the participants to issue the 'Delhi Declaration', proclaiming their unanimous opposition to a WTO social clause (Non-Aligned and other Developing Countries 1995). In November 1995 at the Group of 15 (G-15) summit in Buenos Aires, Indian Prime Minister Narasima Rao rallied developing countries to oppose a social clause and instead lobby for development assistance from industrialized countries (Kolben 2006: 240). The final joint communiqué from this meeting declared that '[t]he current and potential comparative advantages of developing countries and the benefits resulting from the Uruguay Round should not be impaired by new forms of protectionism in the guise of labour or environmental standards' (G-15 1995).

The positions of some developing country NGOs hardened during this period. In March 1995 the Centre for Education and Communication (CEC), a

prominent Indian NGO closely aligned with independent trade unions, organized a forum on the social clause with participants from NGOs, trade
unions and academia (Kolben 2006: 238). Though participants argued about
the benefits of a WTO social clause, they echoed the Indian government in
agreeing that the clause was motivated by protectionist Western goals
(Kolben 2006: 238). Immediately prior to the Singapore conference, TWN
organized two workshops entitled 'The WTO, trade and development' held
in Penang, Malaysia on 30 November to 4 December, and 'The WTO: key
issues and prospects' in Singapore on 6–8 December (TWN 1996). Based on
the discussions at these meetings, the TWN outlined its rejection of any
discussion of 'new issues' including labour standards in the 'Joint NGO
statement on issues and proposals for the WTO ministerial conference',
which was released on the first day of the conference (TWN 1996). By
December 1996 then, the debate about the trade-labour linkage had well and
truly intensified.

The 1996 Singapore Ministerial Conference

The 1996 Singapore Ministerial Conference saw WTO members clearly
divided into two camps: those that sought to have labour standards integrated
into WTO rules, and those who opposed it, fearing that the issue would
adversely affect developing countries and become a stumbling block for
progress at the new institution. As a result, the conference, held from 9–13
December 1996, was dominated by the labour standards debate.

The key point of discussion concerned the suitability of the WTO as an
institution for enforcing labour standards and the impact of labour standards
on the comparative advantage of developing countries with low labour costs.
As the Indonesian Minister of Industry and Trade argued in his statement,
'to link labour standards and trade will easily run the risk of creating a new
form of protectionism which does not help in meeting the ultimate objective
of the WTO' (WTO 1996c). The representative of Pakistan also highlighted
protectionist concerns:

> [o]ur resistance to inject the issue of labour rights into the WTO stems from the fact
> that there is no proven relationship between trade and observance of core labour
> standards. A discussion of this issue in the WTO will merely encourage protection-
> ist lobbies in the developed countries to resist the competitive advantage of low-
> wage countries through self-serving campaigns disguised as concern for the
> promotion of labour standards in the developing countries. (WTO 1996d)

In support of developing members, a number of developed nations also
opposed the labour linkage including the UK, Germany and Australia. For
instance, Australia's Minister for Trade contended that:

[w]e need to be clear about which new issues are core WTO business. For Australia, the test of what is WTO business is whether an issue is potentially trade liberalizing. On this test we, like most WTO Members, do *not* support a working role for the WTO on labour standards or human rights. This is something for the ILO. (WTO 1996e, original emphasis)

Despite intense opposition, the US and EU remained committed to their goal of establishing a working group on the matter. As acting USTR Barshefsky argued:

[w]e must do more to acknowledge that there is a mutually reinforcing relationship between an open trading system and respect for core labour standards. That is why we hope to have an agreement that the WTO should, in cooperation with the International Labour Organization, examine in greater detail the important nexus between trade and labour standards. (WTO 1996f)

It quickly became evident from these statements delivered on the first day of the conference that the intensity of opposition from developing countries, especially the South Asian bloc of India, Pakistan and Sri Lanka (backed up by the TWN-led coalition of NGOs) had rendered the possibility of establishing a working group on labour standards very unlikely. Instead the debate shifted to whether there should even be a mention of labour standards in the final ministerial declaration, and if so, what form this might take.

While WTO member states battled each other over this issue on the conference floor, on the sidelines, NGOs that had been accredited to attend the conference supplemented the debate. Each morning of the ministerial, the ICFTU and the Workers' Rights Caucus held meetings following the ICFTU's briefings. The Workers' Rights Caucus issued press releases, attended other NGO meetings and hosted a workshop for all NGOs on workers' rights. But the release of the joint statement from the TWN-led coalition of NGOs on the first day of the conference ('Joint NGO statement on issues and proposals for the WTO ministerial conference'), supported by 34 NGOs, dented the push for progress on labour standards. The statement from the TWN-led group mirrored the views of developing countries, especially regarding claims that labour standards would be used as a protectionist tool. The overarching goal of the TWN was to restrict, not expand, WTO powers:

[c]ountervailing measures imposed unilaterally by powerful countries on weaker nations (and hardly conceivable, the other way around) would lack legality, moral authority and effectiveness to lead to any effective improvement in workers' conditions or human rights situations in poor or rich countries ... We therefore reject the idea of introducing labour standards or a 'social clause' in the WTO system. (TWN 1996)

Though TWN and its supporters were sympathetic to the overall goal of improving compliance with core labour standards, they agreed with developing WTO members and other linkage opponents that the ILO, not the WTO, was the appropriate body to deal with the issue.

Following the release of the TWN statement, the ICFTU and TWN held a closed-door meeting at which the ICFTU argued that the work of the ILO needed to be supplemented by the WTO's enforcement powers (O'Brien et al. 2000: 87). But their differences could not be bridged: TWN perceived the issue in the context of broader inequalities between the developed and developing world, while the ICFTU was more pragmatic in seeking to improve workers' rights regardless of the institutional venue.

While the proposal to form a labour standards working group at the WTO's Singapore meeting ultimately failed, linkage supporters managed to secure a mention of core labour standards in the final text, largely due to the role of South Africa in influencing other developing states to support this outcome (O'Brien et al. 2000: 100). The final ministerial declaration reads:

> We renew our commitment to the observance of internationally recognized core labour standards. The International Labour Organization (ILO) is the competent body to set and deal with these standards, and we affirm our support for its work in promoting them. We believe that economic growth and development fostered by increased trade and further trade liberalization contribute to the promotion of these standards. We reject the use of labour standards for protectionist purposes, and agree that the comparative advantage of countries, particularly low-wage developing countries, must in no way be put into question. In this regard, we note that the WTO and ILO Secretariats will continue their existing collaboration. (WTO 1996g)

In exchange for accepting this text, developing nations requested that the Singaporean Chairman of the conference, Yeo Cheow Tong, provide an interpretation of the text to clarify that the WTO was not mandated to undertake new work on the issue, and nor did it set up the WTO to establish a trade-labour link in the future. In response, the Chairman issued a strongly worded concluding statement:

> there is no authorization in the text for any new work on this issue ... [s]ome delegations had expressed the concern that this text may lead the WTO to acquire a competence to undertake further work in the relationship between trade and core labour standards. I want to assure these delegations that this text will not permit such a development. (WTO 1997: 14)

This was interpreted by the UK, India, Malaysia and several other Asian states to mean that the issue would not be revived at the WTO. As Malaysian Trade and Industry Minister Rafidah Aziz declared, '[t]here will be no more talk of labour standards in the WTO. Nobody will in future make us discuss labour standards here' (Khor 1997). In contrast, at a post-conference press briefing, acting USTR Barshefsky said that the chairman's closing statement did not reflect the US position, stating that: '[w]e must recognize that issues of workers' welfare and worker rights are absolutely part of the trade debate, whether we like it or not ideologically ... When we have such an important subject, it will always remain an important subject in the WTO' (Khor 1996). The Vice President of the European Commission, Sir Leon Brittan, concurred: 'we regard core internationally recognized labour standards as essential human rights ... This dialogue must now be taken further' (Khor 1996).

The events at the Singapore conference represented a mixed outcome for linkage proponents. On the one hand, the final declaration recognized the importance of the issue, but stated that the WTO was not the appropriate international body to deal with it, and thus did not take any steps towards instituting a social clause. As Howse et al. have remarked, '[n]o one believed that there had been a mass conversion at Singapore' (2006: 184). Other commentators have argued that the outcome was a strong rebuttal for the labour standards campaigners because the text did not specify how the cooperation between the WTO and ILO might proceed, nor how members' observance to core labour standards might be achieved (Griffin et al. 2003: 470; Haworth and Hughes 2004: 131).

Linkage supporters nevertheless avoided the worst possible outcome of not getting any mention of labour into the final declaration, which would have limited opportunities for future discussion on the matter at the WTO. The outcome allowed the US and Europe to be seen to achieve some progress on the issue without disaffecting business interests (O'Brien et al. 2000: 90). For the ICFTU, the Singapore ministerial statement represented a 'small, but significant step forward. It is not the Havana Charter; but it is the first time in the fifty-year history of GATT that a commitment to core labour standards had been made' (ICFTU 1998).

The 1998 Geneva WTO Ministerial Conference

The differing interpretations of the Singapore text ensured that the issue would continue to be discussed at the WTO. For the ICFTU, the Singapore conference highlighted the need to alter aspects of the campaign strategy, in particular to increase communication with ICFTU affiliates in developing nations with a view to persuading developing country governments to support the social clause. To do so, the ICFTU established the Task Force on Trade, Investment and Labour Standards (TILS) comprising representatives of ICFTU affiliate organizations, the ITSs, ETUC, and TUAC (ICFTU 2004: 118). TILS, financially supported by the Norwegian foreign ministry via LO-Norway (Anner 2001: 45), set up an email network and an information database that provided updates to all campaign affiliates. Meanwhile, during 1997, the ICFTU sought to pressure individual WTO member states by reporting on their adherence to core labour standards (ICFTUb). The ICFTU timed the submission of its reports to coincide with the WTO's own trade policy reviews of member states.

In preparation for the Geneva conference, the ICFTU forged a close working relationship with the NGO Solidar, provided key campaign information to other NGOs and launched a targeted campaign highlighting child labour issues. Given the ceremonial purpose of the Geneva conference (celebrating the fiftieth anniversary of GATT) the ICFTU simply aimed to keep labour standards on the agenda. In attempting to do so, TILS organized a three-day pre-ministerial workshop to prepare unionists to lobby their governments to express their support for the core labour standards issue at the WTO meeting (Anner 2001: 49). Significantly the director-general of the WTO, the director-general of the ILO, as well as the secretary-general of UNCTAD addressed the TILS conference. At the conference, South African and Brazilian affiliates suggested that the ICFTU broaden its engagement with the WTO to include issues facing developing countries, as well as environmental issues and NGO participation in the WTO's DSB. Their rationale was that this approach would demonstrate that the ICFTU was not just about furthering its own interests but genuinely cared about the problems developing countries faced and the other issues on which major NGOs were campaigning. But with the exception of its work with Solidar, the ICFTU did not adopt this suggestion. The organization maintained its top-down approach to information sharing and did not substantially alter its engagement with other international NGOs.

At the Geneva conference (18–20 May 1998), labour standards gained a prominent place in the discussions. Several heads of state, including US President Bill Clinton, EU director-general for trade Sir Leon Brittan, British Prime Minister Tony Blair, USTR Barshefsky, Norway's Prime Minister Kjell Magne Bondevik and South African President Nelson Mandela all made formal statements in which they expressed support for core labour standards. Clinton voiced his desire to see the WTO and the ILO convene a special meeting to address the labour standards issue, which was essentially a joint US/EU proposal:

> the WTO and the International Labour Organization should commit to work together, to make certain that open trade lifts living conditions, and respects the core labour standards that are essential not only to workers' rights, but to human rights everywhere. I ask the two organizations' Secretariats to convene at a high level meeting to discuss these issues. (WTO 1998a)

Norway's Prime Minister Kjell Magne Bondevik also conveyed his government's support for increased cooperation between the WTO and ILO:

'Although ILO has the main responsibility, labour standards should also be an issue for the WTO. By working towards continued improvements, in the rules concerning these issues, we will strengthen the credibility of the system and demonstrate the need for international cooperation in these areas' (WTO 1998b). Meanwhile, South African President Nelson Mandela urged other developing nations to consider the proposal:

> There can be no refusal to discuss matters such as labour standards, social issues and the environment, but equally all must be prepared to listen carefully before judgments are made. If developing countries feel that there is nothing to gain except further burdens, then it will prove difficult to deal with these crucial matters. (WTO 1998c)

Despite the presence of several heads of state and the high profile of the TILS pre-ministerial conference, little was achieved at the WTO's second ministerial meeting, primarily due to its ceremonial nature. The meeting did however foreshadow the ILO's International Labour Conference in June 1998 at which members agreed upon the Declaration on Fundamental Principles and Rights at Work, the most concrete international statement on labour standards and trade to date (ILO 1998). Ultimately the Geneva conference is noteworthy in that it paved the way for the 1998 ILO statement and revealed that the issue still occupied a high place on the agenda of several WTO members. In this respect it provided a stepping-stone for the discussion of the issue not only at the ILO but also at the WTO's Seattle conference the following year where intense discussions on the matter were held.

The 1999 Seattle WTO Ministerial Conference

Following the Geneva conference, there was a shift in the international debate away from the idea of a social clause backed up by trade sanctions, to a more general appeal for core labour rights to be respected. In December 1998 the ICFTU held a three-day seminar in Geneva to engage in campaign strategizing for the WTO's Seattle Ministerial Conference. The background document for the seminar, 'Globalisation, investment and labour standards', detailed many of the campaign activities to be pursued, which revolved around harnessing greater support among affiliates and NGOs in developing nations (Anner 2001: 49). The ICFTU published its own proposal for a workers' rights clause entitled 'Building workers' human rights into the global trading system', which was used as a key educational and organizing tool (ICFTU 1999a). In toning down its language regarding trade sanctions, the booklet focused on amending laws rather than imposing trade measures, and suggested that the ILO work with the WTO to determine whether a country is in violation of core labour rights (ICFTU 1999: 44–6; Anner 2001: 14).

In early 1999 the ICFTU organized a number of campaigning activities in developing countries to increase support for the campaign. It hosted regional and sub-regional workshops at which affiliates were informed about the ICFTU's campaign goals in relation to labour standards. A large proportion of the campaign budget was devoted to hosting regional meetings: seven seminars were held during 1999, in South Africa, Brazil, Sri Lanka, Tunisia, the Czech Republic, Ghana, and Jamaica (Anner 2001: 12). The ICFTU encouraged participants to lobby their governments on the issue and request that they be allowed to join official government delegations to the Seattle conference. In September 1999 a three-day meeting of trade unionists from several Asian nations was held in Malaysia. Its purpose was to allay fears among unionists in these countries that the campaign was to impose a global minimum wage and explain why the WTO (not just the ILO) needed to be involved in the issue (Anner 2001: 13).

Despite the ICFTU's attempts to smooth discord among the NGO community over a WTO social clause, the TWN-led coalition of NGOs remained a vocal critic. In September 1999 TWN issued a public statement, 'Enough is enough: Third World intellectuals and NGOs' statement against linkage', expressing their opposition to the WTO taking on new 'non-trade' issues, including labour standards (TWN 1999). Supported by over a hundred academics, the statement conveyed 'unambiguous opposition' to any linkage between labour and trade at the WTO. Echoing developing country governments, the statement argued that protectionists from the global North would use a labour standards clause to decrease developing country imports regardless of the goals of 'the morally-driven human rights and other groups' (TWN 1999). The statement also accused labour standards proponents of highlighting labour rights abuses in the global South while ignoring violations in the North (Griffin et al. 2003: 477). For example, sweatshops in the textiles apparel industry and the rights of migrant labour in developed countries were not dealt with, while issues such as child labour 'where the developing countries are expected to be the defendants rather than plaintiffs' were in focus (TWN 1999). For these reasons, the statement argued that the ILO, not the WTO, should deal with the issue.

In response to the TWN statement, the ICFTU issued its own statement entitled 'Enough exploitation is enough: a response to the Third World intellectuals and NGOs' statement against linkage' (ICFTU 1999b). The statement contended that the conclusions drawn in the TWN statement were flawed and that it offered nothing to address current abuses of labour rights. The ICFTU pointed out that the chosen labour standards were far from arbitrary, since they had been repeatedly endorsed by UN member states. The ICFTU further accused the TWN-led coalition of NGOs of lending support to corporate interests and governments that abuse labour rights: 'there are far too many such interests and governments opposing core labour standards at the WTO for it to be a coincidence. It is those parties which have most to gain from the perpetuation of a status quo which enables them to continue their exploitation of workers without any constraints' (ICFTU 1999b). Moreover Griffin et al.'s analysis of the TWN statement casts doubt on the legitimacy and representativeness of the groups involved and their links to workers, especially compared to the ICFTU whose membership is put forward as evidence that it represents working people:

> an examination of the TWIN-SAL statement reveals that, of the 99 signatories, 57 are associated with universities or research centres; 31 are professionals associated with NGOs in the areas of aid and development, consumer protection and the environment; three are lawyers, two are public servants, two are from church organizations, one a retired foreign secretary, one a judge and two unknown. In short, those who signed the document opposing the introduction of instruments designed to protect the fundamental human rights of workers did not include any workers or worker representatives. (2003: 477)

The exchange of NGO statements exposed the sharp divide that still existed between NGOs on the issue, which had the effect of weakening the legitimacy of the ICFTU's position going into the Seattle conference.

Renewed discussion among member states on core labour standards began in the preparatory meetings for the Seattle conference held in Geneva. In October 1999 the US announced its key priorities for Seattle: to establish a 'Trade and Labor' working group at the WTO (to monitor the observance of internationally recognized core labour standards) and make the ILO an observer to the WTO (WTO 1999a). But the US did not call for the enforcement of labour rights with trade sanctions. Instead it pitched the working group proposal as a mechanism for the realization of the Singapore commitment and the 1998 ILO Declaration (WTO 1999a; Stigliani 2000: 189). In signalling the importance of the issue to the US, and with the US presidential elections looming, Clinton used his State of the Union address in January 1999 (as well as his January 2000 address following the Seattle meeting) to press the necessity of a firmer link between labour standards and the international trading system (Clinton 2004; see also Clinton 1999). The prominence given to the issue was reflected in the bolstering of the US Department of State's labour function: an Advisory Committee on Labor Diplomacy and a new high-profile position entitled Special Representative for International Labor Affairs were created (Stigliani 2000: 181).

Though highly supportive of labour standards, the EU was unwilling to back the US call for a WTO labour standards working group. This was due to their recognition of the opposition among developing countries and resultant slim chance that a WTO working group could be achieved. In early November the EU informed the WTO director-general of its decision to support a joint standing forum between the WTO and the ILO on trade, globalization and labour issues instead (WTO 1999b). The EU suggested the use of positive incentives in the form of additional trade benefits to developing countries that respect core labour standards. In the meantime developing countries in the G-15 and G-77 separately announced that they remained opposed to discussing the issue at the WTO (Anner 2001: 53; ICTSD 1999).

Once the Seattle conference began on 30 November, the US, the EU (with strong support from France, Italy and Norway) pressed for a joint WTO/ILO forum to investigate the issue, while developing nations reiterated their opposition. From the outset, the G-77 informed members that 'developing countries are firmly opposed to any linkage between labour standards and trade ... the question of labour standards should be dealt with by the competent international organizations and not by the WTO' (WTO 1999c). Malaysia made the point that the linkage contradicted Most-Favoured Nation (MFN), a cornerstone operating principle of the organization (WTO 1999d). Among NGOs, the ICFTU again had an active presence both inside and outside the conference and a number of nations, including Norway, Canada and the US, had allowed trade unions and other NGOs onto their official government delegations (Anner 2001: 48). Significantly, President Clinton also met with AFL-CIO president John Sweeney during the ministerial conference (Knowlton 1999).

Outside the ministerial meeting, 30,000 street protesters congregated to rally against the major goal of the ministerial conference: the launch of a 'Millennium Round' of trade negotiations. The AFL-CIO sponsored the main protest on the opening day of the conference (Knowlton 1999). The protests, which attracted a diverse mix of environmentalists, human rights advocates, protectionists, and regular citizens, were not limited to the city of Seattle; they were part of a global day of action against neo-liberalism, involving 111 protest events in 22 countries in 97 cities across the globe (Wood 2004: 86). The morning inaugural session on 30 November had to be abandoned because of the protests, while the plenary session, which was to start in the afternoon on the same day, was held under police protection. The Seattle protests, which became known as the 'Battle of Seattle', received extensive media coverage, heightening public awareness of the impact of international trade negotiations and the WTO. As Stigliani surmises, 'many people who had previously been unaware of, or paid little attention to the WTO now have some sense of the purpose of the organization and of the debate over the relative benefits and costs of the worldwide free trade that it seeks to promote' (2000: 178).

On 1 December 1999, day two of the conference, the *Seattle Post-Intelligencer* published an article detailing an interview with President Clinton in which he infamously commented:

What we ought to do first of all is to adopt the United States' position on having a working group on labor within the WTO, and then that working group should develop these core labor standards, and then they ought to be a part of every trade agreement, and *ultimately I would favor a system in which sanctions would come for violating any provision of a trade agreement.* (Paulson 1999, emphasis added)

This comment resulted in instant, widespread anger from developing countries, reigniting their accusations that a WTO social clause was a protectionist drive. Clinton's remarks were also said to have stunned US negotiators as they compromised the softer approach that had been adopted by labour standards proponents in the lead-up to the conference (Burgess 1999; Greenhouse and Kahn 1999).

On 2 December, despite Clinton's comments to the media regarding trade sanctions, the discussion on trade and labour standards chaired by Vice-Minister Anabel González of Costa Rica proceeded (WTO 1999e). From the outset it was clear that the US proposal for a working group lacked support and was not even considered. Members instead discussed the EU proposal for a joint ILO/WTO standing forum that was to sit outside the WTO structure. But even this proposal invoked strong opposition from several developing countries. The Indian Minister of Commerce Murasoli Maran, for example, responded by declaring '[n]o, I cannot drink a drop of poison' (Pani 1999 in Kolben 2006: 242).

Some African and Latin American delegations did not perceive the EU proposal as threatening as a working group inside the WTO and attempted to help develop a compromise proposal, while some Southeast Asian nations were even willing to consider a 'one off' meeting at the WTO on labour issues (Stigliani 2000: 190). But others contended that the texts put together by the green room chairpersons did not accurately reflect the debate on the floor, thereby making the labour standards discussion appear more positive than it actually was (Raghavan 1999). In any case the EU compromise proposal was far less than the US was willing to consider.

On 3 December, day four of the conference, 35 countries attended a final meeting on the labour issue. At the meeting the Costa Rican chairperson proposed the establishment of a discussion group on the matter that would not report to the WTO and for which the WTO would not be responsible establishing (Anner 2001: 54). The text of this proposal, a lesser version of the EU proposal for a joint ILO/WTO standing forum, became known as the 'Costa Rica Document' (Anner 2001: 54; Haworth 2002: 175) and was apparently viewed in a relatively positive light by most members involved in the discussions. As Griffin et al. note, '[d]espite the publically voiced opposition, and the fact that while no transcripts are available, it is reported that, in this private domain, developing country governments were much more willing to explore the possibility of trade-offs that could render a trade-labour rights link acceptable' (Griffin et al. 2003: 471). It is now widely accepted that a fragile consensus had been reached on the Costa Rica document, though this was ultimately overshadowed by debates on other issues at Seattle.

In addition to labour standards, the Seattle conference was notable for its intense discussions on agriculture, anti-dumping subsidies and the Singapore Issues, which led to the collapse of the meeting. While it is often commented that the 'Battle of Seattle' protests brought an end to the meeting (it did indeed make it difficult for some delegates to access the conference venue), it is more accurate to see the protests as emblematic of the intensity of debate inside the conference. Thus, with agreement allegedly within reach on the Costa Rica document, the labour standards issue was not the straw that broke the camel's back. Likewise Clinton's comments to the press regarding trade sanctions to enforce labour standards were not the fatal blow, as suggested by commentators such as Trebilcock (2003: 293). There was nevertheless still debate over whether the conference had been positive for the labour standards cause. While the AFL-CIO was optimistic that Seattle had highlighted labour issues (Stigliani 2001), others charged that it represented a backwards step for the labour linkage issue given the 'angry "in house" confrontation' that occurred at the meeting (Haworth and Hughes 2004: 132).

Following Seattle, a number of factors conspired against progress on the linkage issue at the WTO. Most significantly the ICFTU effectively lost a key ally when a Republican administration hostile to the labour linkage took office in the US. Regardless, the ICFTU campaign for core labour standards and other NGO proponents continued targeting the WTO. In 2001, at the WTO's fourth ministerial conference in Doha, WTO member states reaffirmed their commitment to respect core labour standards, as originally pledged at the 1996 Singapore Ministerial Declaration on 14 November 2001: '[w]e reaffirm our declaration made at the Singapore Ministerial Conference regarding internationally recognized core labour standards. We take note of work under way in the International Labour Organization (ILO) on the social dimension of globalization' (WTO 2001a).

To date this is the last mention of labour standards at a WTO ministerial conference. Though the ICFTU pushed for discussion of core labour standards at the 2003 Cancún conference (ICFTU 2003), this did not amount to any progress because, like Seattle, the meeting collapsed over disagreements over agriculture and the Singapore issues. At the 2005 Hong Kong conference, there was no substantial discussion of core labour standards, though an ICFTU representative considered paragraph 56 of the Hong Kong Ministerial Declaration concerning WTO cooperation with relevant UN agencies a step forward (Interview, ICFTU 2006; see WTO 2005b). The view of WTO officials at this time was that any foreseeable chance of the linkage being realized had been put on the backburner (Haworth and Hughes 2004: 133).

COMMANDING INTERNATIONAL RESPECT FOR CORE LABOUR STANDARDS: STRATEGIC ARENA SHOPPING

Despite not achieving their goals at the WTO, the ICFTU and pro-labour states did contribute towards developments on the issue in other international arenas. As recognized by some union advocates, pursuing the trade-labour linkage issue at the WTO helped keep the issue of compliance with international labour standards alive and generate debate in other international arenas (Interview, ICFTU 2006). Perhaps as a result of the sustained campaign directed at the WTO, a number of other international organizations were compelled to respond to the issue. The UN developed the Global Compact, a global corporate citizenship initiative to encourage businesses to respect universally accepted principles in the areas of labour, human rights, the environment and anti-corruption (UN Global Compact 2007). There has also been increased emphasis on labour rights issues at the World Bank and at Asia-Pacific Economic Cooperation (APEC) meetings.

Most significantly, the WTO labour standards campaign created the environment for greater action at the ILO, as the organization stepped up efforts to remain the dominant institution in regard to labour issues (O'Brien et al. 2000: 102). For example, following the WTO's Singapore conference in 1996, the governing body of the ILO began monitoring compliance of all ILO members with core labour standards regardless of whether they had ratified the conventions. The WTO campaign was also a major force behind the ILO's adoption in 1998 of the Declaration on Fundamental Principles and Rights at Work (Anner 2001: 44). The events at Seattle additionally created conditions that made approval of the ILO's maternity clause possible in June 2000. Most interestingly, in their attempts to keep the labour issue out of the WTO, developing countries that had rallied against the trade-labour linkage at the WTO supported these ILO accords and participated in discussion over labour issues in these alternative arenas. In this respect then, the ICFTU campaign targeting the WTO resulted in some positive developments on core labour standards.

Another consequence of the ICFTU campaign was that it provided a normative rationale for the US and EU to incorporate labour standards clauses into their regional and bilateral trade agreements (Wilkinson and Hughes 2000: 272). In the US, Congress inserted language into the 2002 Bipartisan Trade Promotion Authority Act directing the US President to include labour standards provisions in all bilateral trade agreements. Rules regarding labour standards now exist in a number of US bilateral trade agreements including those with Australia, Cambodia, Jordan, Chile, Singapore, Bahrain, Argentina, Morocco, and in the Central America Free Trade Agreement (CAFTA) (Brathwaite and Drahos 2000; Griffin et al. 2003: 471 and 491). The provisions in the majority of these agreements, however, require each trading partner to enforce their own labour laws. In addition the ICFTU campaign provided the impetus for the US and EU to modify their GSP benefits to give preference to developing nations that uphold ILO conventions (Griffin et al. 2003: 492). The EU's GSP system now includes an incentive system that offers additional tariff concessions to developing countries that comply with ILO conventions 87, 98 and 138 (Tsogas 2000).

The ICFTU campaign and the increasing number of NGOs dedicated to monitoring the activities of MNCs resulted in the business sector paying greater attention to codes of conduct on workers' rights. Following the Singapore Ministerial Conference, labour unions and NGOs renewed their campaigns to address the exploitation of workers in the global garment and sportswear industries (Interview, Oxfam Community Aid Abroad Australia 2005). These campaigns include the Clean Clothes Campaign, the Australian FairWear campaign, the US Campaign for Labour Rights, and the UK-based Labour Behind the Label network (see URLs for Clean Clothes Campaign; Fairwear; Campaign for Labor Rights; Labour Behind the Label). The Clean Clothes Campaign, for example, comprises a vast number of organizations working to put pressure on various MNCs to adopt ILO core labour standards and adhere to Article 23 of the Universal Declaration on Human Rights (Clean Clothes Campaign). In attempting to improve compliance with core labour standards therefore, trade unions and other NGOs have adopted a multi-pronged approach targeting international institutions, states, and particular industries and MNCs.

CONCLUSION

The ICFTU's campaign on labour standards and trade played an important role in the international debate about the trade-labour linkage in the WTO context. The campaigners repeatedly helped get the issue on the WTO agenda for discussion among member states. While the general literature on NGOs in international politics emphasizes the importance of unity and shared goals among activists (Klotz 1995; Price 1998; Khagram et al. 2002), for this case, weaknesses in the ICFTU's top-down campaign style did not hamper their ability to get the issue onto the WTO agenda. The ICFTU's chief mechanism of influence was the use of its close ties to the governments of the US and Norway.

Despite their capacity to get the issue on the WTO's agenda at successive ministerial conferences, the ultimate goal of the ICFTU and pro-labour states – to achieve progress on linking labour standards to trade rules at the WTO – met with little success. A key factor was the complexity of the labour standards issue itself: it involved normative values in regard to universal human rights as well as competing economic interests among states, particularly in relation to the enforcement of labour standards through trade sanctions. The economic interests at stake made it extremely difficult for the ICFTU to successfully project their interpretation of the issue as one of fundamental human rights, a recognized source of leverage for NGOs in waging transnational campaigns (Keck and Sikkink 1998). The ICFTU and pro-labour WTO member states were completely ineffective at masking some of the instrumental motivations underpinning their objectives. In this respect the opposing NGO campaign led by TWN that questioned pragmatic approaches to tackling the issue, served to undermine the efforts of the ICFTU. The flaws in the ICFTU's campaign and the links between pro-labour states and the ICFTU (and its affiliates) are explored in greater depth in Chapter 7.

Perhaps the key factor inhibiting progress on the trade-labour linkage issue was the WTO's consensus decision-making procedures combined with its single-undertaking approach. Unlike the campaigns on investment and access to medicines (detailed in Chapters 5 and 6 respectively), these procedures were unreceptive, even obstructive, for labour standards proponents. They neutralized the power of the developed members advocating the labour clause, essentially preventing the will of a minority of wealthy states to trump that of the majority of developing members. This case study confirms that powerful states do not always dominate multilateral policymaking arenas, especially those in which decisions are taken by consensus.

Since the intense discussions over the issue at Seattle, the WTO's position is that the trade-labour linkage is outside its competencies, and that the ILO, not the WTO, is the appropriate institution for dealing with labour standards. Though the debate at the WTO has stalled for now, the controversy over labour issues in the context of international trade is likely to remain a simmering issue in international trade governance. In addition to positive developments at the ILO, pro-labour states are insisting that labour standards provisions are built into bilateral and regional free trade agreements where they have greater influence. Meanwhile the ICFTU and other NGOs are continuing to press for change by monitoring and reporting on states and MNCs that violate core labour standards.

NOTES

1. GSP laws are recognized as exceptions to WTO non-discrimination rules that permit developed countries to extend preferential and differential treatment to developing countries.

5. Safeguards pending: TRIPS and the access to medicines campaign

INTRODUCTION

Through their access to medicines campaign that began in the late 1990s, NGOs such as MSF, Oxfam International and Health Action International (HAI) significantly contributed to the international debate over the application of IP rules to essential pharmaceutical products required in developing nations. In highlighting the problems faced by developing nations in implementing the WTO's TRIPS agreement, NGO campaigners used numerous political opportunities to mobilize supporters and engage developing country governments to contest the issue in the WTO arena, thereby playing a role in the re-evaluation of the agreement itself. Specifically the NGO campaign helped unleash a series of developments at the WTO on the issue, including the 2001 Doha Declaration on TRIPS and Public Health, the '30 August temporary waiver' in 2003, and most significantly, the *first ever amendment* of a core WTO agreement in the form of the '6 December Decision' in 2005 (WTO 2005c).

In exploring the relationship dynamics between NGOs and developing states in the context of the international trade regime, this case study illustrates that NGOs can play a role in the international trade policy process at the agenda-setting stage, despite their lack of formal status at the organization. In contrast to the labour standards case study (see Chapter 4), it also provides the opportunity to examine the different roles that NGOs play in the international trade regime when their objectives align with less powerful states.

The WTO's TRIPS agreement, which came into force with the establishment of the WTO, is the first multilateral accord to link IP rights with international trade. It defines the minimum standard of IP protection for all WTO members and requires the establishment of effective national patent regimes to uphold internationally agreed standards for IP rights for all types of goods, including pharmaceutical products. The WTO's adoption of an IP regime has meant that for the first time, international disputes over IP rights can be adjudicated in an effective multilateral forum: the WTO's dispute settlement system. In comparison to most developed nations, where IP protection is already well established, many developing countries have few procedures in place for administering and enforcing IP rules and are mostly importers, rather than producers, of patented technology. The implementation of TRIPS has therefore imposed serious costs on developing countries, and for this reason, its intended application to all members by 2006 was highly contentious. At the same time, corporations that hold IP rights, especially in the area of medical technology, have been concerned about the protection of their patented innovations in foreign markets and the potential loss of returns on their substantial investments.

The greatest source of concern for developing countries has been in regard to the application of the TRIPS agreement to patented medicines required in developing countries. The controversy has centred on the circumstances under which a member state may invoke the in-built TRIPS safeguards or 'flexibilities' to override patents for pharmaceutical products in order to provide citizens with access to affordable generic versions of essential medicines for HIV, tuberculosis and other life-threatening diseases. The ambiguity over the appropriate use of the TRIPS safeguards revolves around whether a public health crisis constitutes a 'national emergency', one of the few circumstances under which the TRIPS agreement allows a nation to override a patent. As the major creators of new technology, wealthy industrialized nations, especially the US, have used this ambiguity to pursue the interests of US-based pharmaceutical companies, pressuring nations such as South Africa, Thailand and Brazil to uphold their patents and refrain from employing the TRIPS safeguard measures.

Although a number of scholarly accounts recognize the NGO role in the outcome of the TRIPS and public health issue, most highlight other aspects of the case. For example, Frederick M. Abbott (2002) investigates the international negotiations leading to the Declaration on TRIPS and Public Health, with a focus on the legal effects of the text. Kenneth Shadlen (2004) explores the divisions between developing and developed nations over the rules of global IP governance, demonstrating that developing countries are best served by multilateral rules that minimize their vulnerability to the demands of powerful states. And Susan Sell and Aseem Prakash (2004) employ the TRIPS and public health debate to compare and contrast the relative influence of the pharmaceutical business network and the NGO network in the US, viewing them as competing interest groups.

There are also several accounts of the case written by NGO personnel, most notably Ellen 't Hoen (2002, 2003) and Nathan Ford (2004) from MSF. These contributions publicize the real-world impacts for developing country citizens of TRIPS implementation problems and appeal for more to be done to solve the issues around access to medicines in LDCs. Although it is clear that NGOs did not achieve all their goals in relation to TRIPS and public health, contributions from NGO personnel tend to undervalue the significance of the NGO role at the WTO, perhaps due to their unwavering commitment to resolve these issues in full. This chapter instead seeks to provide a basis to comprehensively understand and evaluate how NGOs were able to achieve as much as they did, given the constraints and the interests of powerful states opposing them.

In bringing about a review of the TRIPS agreement, the NGO campaigners took into account political constraints and opportunities, including policy crises, domestic political cycles, the activities of private actors and particular national interests. The NGOs used these to construct the TRIPS safeguards issue as an urgent policy problem that had to be dealt with by the WTO. In undertaking various campaign activities such as hosting international conferences and working through alternative intergovernmental arenas, NGOs were able to demonstrate that their TRIPS agreement objectives were compatible with the interests of the African Group and other developing countries such as Brazil. As such they provided a basis for NGOs to enhance the negotiating resources of LDCs in order to tackle the issue within the WTO arena.

The first part of this chapter examines the negotiation of the TRIPS agreement during the Uruguay Round of trade negotiations, which began in 1986 and concluded in 1993. I then explore the 'for' and 'against' arguments concerning the establishment of international IP rules and technology transfer in the context of pharmaceuticals. Turning to the contention surrounding the TRIPS agreement following the establishment of the WTO in 1995, I explain how 'creative ambiguity' and power-based outcomes in the negotiation stage resulted in problems and controversies between developed and developing countries over the interpretation and implementation of the agreement once it had been enacted.

The second part of the chapter focuses on the NGOs' access to medicines campaign. I detail the key actors involved and outline their campaign activities and strategies. These include mobilizing support through hosting international workshops, campaigning in both national and international policy arenas, exposing and challenging the behaviour of private actors such as research-based pharmaceutical MNCs, highlighting the bullying tactics of wealthy nations directed against LDCs, and significantly, informing a key set of developing countries to contest the issue at the WTO. In evaluating the NGO campaign, I trace the key developments at the WTO from the 2001 TRIPS Council Special Sessions to the Doha Declaration, to the decision of members to permanently amend the TRIPS agreement in 2005.

INTERNATIONAL COOPERATION FOR THE PROTECTION OF IP: A BALANCING ACT

Dating back to the Paris Convention of 1883, international cooperation among the advanced industrialized nations for the protection of IP rights has a relatively long history. Following the Paris Convention, which protects industrial property through patents and trademarks, a number of additional international IP accords were enacted. These include the 1886 Berne Convention (rules on copyright); the 1891 Madrid Agreement (trademark rights); the 1893 establishment of the United International Bureaux for the Protection of Intellectual Property; the 1925 Hague Agreement (the registration of industrial designs); the Universal Copyright Convention administered by United Nations Educational, Scientific and Cultural Organization (UNESCO); and the Rome Convention (rules for the protection of broadcasters, performers and sound recordings).[1] In 1967 the World Intellectual Property Organization (WIPO) was established to administer many of these agreements, which itself became a specialized agency of the UN in 1974. As of 2009 WIPO has 184 signatories and a membership, staff and budget greater than that of the WTO (WIPOa).

Despite the number of international accords and agreements relating to IP rights in existence prior to the WTO, they did not constitute a coherent international IP regime: some aspects of IP protection were not covered and governments had a great deal of flexibility over which agreements to uphold (Croome 1995: 131). As a result the TRIPS agreement signified a new era in the protection and enforcement of IP rights. It not only linked IP with international trade, but also backed up the work of WIPO with significant enforcement powers in the form of the WTO's DSB.

There are two major arguments for increasing protection for holders of IP rights internationally. First, it is claimed that IP rights are no different to more tangible property rights and therefore should be protected. As explained by IP Australia (the Australian government agency responsible for administering IP rules): '[i]ntellectual property represents the property of your mind or intellect. It can be an invention, trade mark, original design or the practical application of a good idea. In business terms, this means your proprietary knowledge – a key component of success in business today' (2008). Second, a well-structured system for protecting IP rights can promote technological innovation and advancement from which society as a whole may benefit. In enacting IP laws, governments typically confer monopoly production rights to the holder of the IP to enable them to recuperate the investment made developing a new technology. Without some form of IP protection, there may be little incentive to invest research in new technology as other producers may 'free ride' by using the new technology to produce and sell generic versions of a product more cheaply, thereby capturing the market. While this outcome is seemingly preferable for consumers, in practice, it means that there would be little, if any, inducement to invest in new technology. Consequently governments typically enact and administer IP rights regimes to promote investment, economic growth and technological advancement. The key issue for governments is maintaining a balance between encouraging investment and the development of technology with the need to promote competition in the market and ensure that important technological advancements are available to citizens. This balancing act is even more difficult to achieve in the international context.

The issue of balancing technological advancement with equitable access to technology is perhaps no more clearly illustrated than by the international multi-billion dollar pharmaceuticals industry. The cost of developing new medicines is extremely high. According to the Pharmaceutical Research and Manufacturers of America (PhRMA), discovering and developing a new medicine involves between 12 and 15 years of research, development, testing, patent application and approval, drug production and marketing, all of which costs in excess of $US1 billion (2005: 2). Most of this activity is undertaken in industrialized nations with well established IP rights regimes. Increased global economic integration through international trade and foreign investment has exposed the divides between the established systems of IP rights in industrialized nations with the often poorly enforced patent protection legislation in many developing countries. It is important to note that this is not simply a case of poor governance.

Several developing countries have compelled pharmaceutical companies to offer their medicines for reduced prices, often using the threat of allowing generic production as a bargaining chip. In fact states such as India and Brazil actively encourage the production of generic versions of patented medicines, viewing the generic medicines industry as an important component of their economies. In many developing nations then, generic versions of patented medicines, either produced locally or in other developing countries, are available relatively quickly, well inside the 20-year monopoly period, which is the standard in developed nations. While this level of availability enables developing country citizens suffering from life-threatening diseases, such as HIV and malaria, to access comparatively cheap medicines, the producers of the medical technology are deprived of revenue to reimburse their substantial initial investment. And without adequate remuneration for their investment, little incentive is provided for investment in new technology. At the same time, diseases such as HIV, tuberculosis and malaria are suffered disproportionately by citizens of developing countries who cannot afford the price of patented drugs. Clearly an international IP regime that could adequately balance these issues was always going to be difficult to achieve, especially given the range of interests at stake.

THE DEVELOPMENT OF THE TRIPS AGREEMENT

The impetus for the inclusion of a trade-related IP accord at the WTO emerged during the Uruguay Round of trade negotiations. Given that US-based MNCs were among the most significant contributors to investments in new technologies, the US was the major advocate of a WTO IP accord (Sell 1998, 2003; Drahos 1995). With profits dependent upon IP protection, these firms convinced the US government that the nation's declining international competitiveness was directly linked to the inadequate protection of IP in developing countries (Sell 2003; Sell and May 2005). As such they argued that greater international patent protection was necessary to restore flagging US economic growth and trade competitiveness.

On top of promoting an international IP accord linked to trade, US MNCs additionally lobbied for an amendment to Section 301 of the 1974 US Trade Act. In 1988 this resulted in the creation of the 'Special 301' provision enabling the USTR to unilaterally pressure nations that failed to protect patents for US-held IP (Sell 2003: 119). The US was not alone in enacting legislation in an attempt to protect its patent holders internationally. In 1984 the European Community (now EU) instituted a similar policy entitled the 'New Commercial Policy Instrument', which deemed the failure to uphold a European firm's patent an 'actionable offence' (van Bael and Bellis 1990, cited in Shadlen 2004: 82). The US Special 301 provisions and EU's New Commercial Policy Instrument essentially mandated unilateral punitive action against nations (mostly LDCs) without adequate IP laws.

Though the threat of unilateral pressure from both the US and EU made the constitution of a multilateral IP agreement at the WTO appear more attractive to developing nations, the Uruguay Round negotiations concerning the TRIPS agreement were exceptionally long and hard-fought. Reminiscent of previous unsuccessful attempts to institute an international IP accord at UNCTAD and WIPO, deep divides between developed and developing countries emerged over the nature of the mandate for establishing an IP accord at the WTO. The absence of any existing rules within the GATT in relation to IP that might guide how an IP accord could be incorporated into the international trade regime bolstered doubts among developing countries (particularly India and Brazil) as to whether IP was within the competence of the GATT/WTO system (Croome 1995: 132–3).

The major stumbling block in the TRIPS negotiations was the uneven spread of costs and benefits resulting from an IP accord across WTO member states. Given their comparative advantage in the development of new technology, industrialized nations had a great deal to gain from the constitution of an IP accord linked to trade (Croome 1995: 135). Conversely the piecemeal, loosely enforced system of IP protection in many developing nations, combined with the need for access to new innovations and technology to fuel economic development, meant that most developing nations faced considerable costs in signing up to a WTO accord (Abbott 2002: 470). While developing countries contended that pharmaceuticals and other technologies were necessities for meeting national public health and economic development objectives, EU and US negotiators pointed out that they bore the costs involved in developing new technology (Abbott 2002: 470). In the later stages of the negotiations, the issue of the base standard of IP protection required, along with the types of special arrangements that might be provided for developing nations, were key debating points. The developing countries made it clear that they wanted TRIPS to recognize their special needs by containing flexibilities to pursue important national policy objectives (Croome 1995: 253).

In eventually agreeing to a multilateral IP accord linked to international trade under the auspices of the WTO, developing countries were granted three concessions: increased market access, technology transfer, and the TRIPS safeguards. The market access provisions, which applied to agriculture and textiles, were also part of the deal for developing countries in agreeing to other new issues including trade in services. In regard to technology transfer, developed nations were required to provide incentives for their companies to transfer technology to LDCs. Meanwhile the safeguard provisions were to deal with the negative consequences of patent protection in special circumstances such as 'national emergencies'.

In 1995 the TRIPS agreement came into force with the establishment of the WTO. The agreement outlines the minimum standard of protection for IP in regard to copyright and related rights, trademarks, service marks, geographical indications, industrial designs and patents for all types of goods (including pharmaceuticals) to be upheld by all member states. The penalties for violating TRIPS commitments are considered a strong deterrent to non-compliance, with the WTO's DSB able to order the disposal or destruction of pirated or counterfeit goods (WTOh).

In terms of timeframes, developed nations were given one year to become TRIPS compliant (by 1996), developing nations were allowed until 2000, and LDCs were granted an 11 year period (until 2006) to ratify TRIPS. LDCs were also granted the possibility of an extension while transition economies could also benefit from the same delay as developing nations if they met certain additional conditions (see WTOi). In addition, developing countries were given ten years to introduce patent protection if they did not already provide it in a particular area of technology (WTOj). But for pharmaceuticals and agricultural chemical products, it was agreed that developing nations would accept applications for patents from the start of the transition period, even though a patent would not actually have to be granted until the end of the transition period (WTOj).

In spite of the transition periods for developing countries, discord over TRIPS continued. This was largely because many of the market access and technology transfer provisions for developing countries were not forthcoming and the exact interpretation of the appropriate use of the safeguard measures became subject to creative ambiguity. Moreover developing countries found that they were under increasing pressure from Europe and the US to comply with TRIPS prior to the agreed deadlines (Croome 1995: 283; Sell and Prakash 2004: 160). This pressure, combined with emerging health crises in developing countries and the uncertainty surrounding the appropriate use of the TRIPS safeguard measures, led to a pervasive conflict between developed and developing countries over access to patented essential medicines.

THE TRIPS SAFEGUARDS: CREATIVE AMBIGUITY

Despite the inclusion of flexibilities in the TRIPS agreement to deal with the negative consequences of patent protection, there was considerable uncertainty amongst developing nations about exactly how and under what circumstances to invoke these safeguards. This was a particular issue in instances where pharmaceutical patents stood in the way of maintaining public health objectives, such as providing affordable access to essential medicines. The relevant articles of the TRIPS agreement, Article 30 'Exceptions to the Rights Conferred' and Article 31 'Other Use Without Authorisation of the Right Holder', did not adequately clarify the circumstances under which the TRIPS safeguard provisions could be used. Article 30 simply states: '[m]embers may provide limited exceptions to the exclusive rights conferred by a patent, provided that such exceptions do not unreasonably conflict with a normal exploitation of the patent and do not unreasonably prejudice the legitimate interests of the patent owner, taking account of the legitimate interests of third parties' (WTOg). The uncertainty for developing countries in activating the TRIPS flexibilities for public health reasons lies in the statement that the exceptions to providing a patent must not 'unreasonably' interfere with a patent, the interpretation of which is unspecified. Meanwhile Article 31 essentially outlines the conditions under which governments may issue what are known as 'compulsory licenses' to allow the production of generic versions of patented products. Issuing a compulsory license involves a government forcing a patent holder to allow either the government or others to use the IP. The TRIPS agreement states that in doing so, governments must normally have attempted to seek permission from the patent holder first. But it also stipulates that '[t]his requirement may be waived by a Member in the case of a national emergency or other circumstances of extreme urgency or in cases of public non-commercial use … the right holder shall, nevertheless, be notified as soon as reasonably practicable' (WTOg). Importantly, Article 31 states that compulsory licensing must be 'predominantly for the supply of the domestic market of the Member authorising such use' and that appropriate remuneration be provided to the patent holder

(WTOg). Article 2.1 of TRIPS incorporates Article 5.4 of the Paris Convention, which also allows for compulsory licensing if there is 'a failure to work a patent' (WIPOb). Despite this, Article 31(i) significantly casts doubt on the legal security of a nation using compulsory licensing as a safeguard measure. It explains that 'the legal validity of any decision relating to the authorisation of such use shall be subject to judicial review or other independent review by a distinct higher authority in that Member' (WTOg).

For developing countries then, the passage of the TRIPS agreement into international trade law and the uncertainty about how to interpret Articles 30 and 31 cast a significant level of doubt on the legality of their normal practices in relation to pharmaceutical products. These normal practices included regularly issuing compulsory licenses (also known as 'other use without the authorisation of the patent holder') to authorize the production of generic versions of patented medicines, and parallel importing (taking advantage of different prices in different countries for a patented product by importing the cheaper good without the patent holder's permission). These policies had been important bargaining tools for ensuring relatively stable and affordable access to medicines by inducing pharmaceutical companies to lower medicine prices in developing nations. As Shadlen explains, the 'post-Uruguay Round problem for developing countries was not just that many of the expected substantive concessions were not forthcoming, but that the stability and predictability to be produced by a multilateral agreement [TRIPS] did not materialize either' (2004: 84). Developing countries, notably South Africa, India, Thailand, Brazil and others that have attempted to employ the TRIPS safeguard provisions for public health purposes (especially by issuing compulsory licenses), have faced legal sanctions and diplomatic pressure from industrialized WTO members, particularly the US and the EU, as well as legal action from pharmaceutical MNCs that own patents.

Following the establishment of the TRIPS agreement in 1995, the USTR continued to apply unilateral pressure on developing countries to accelerate their implementation of TRIPS, and in many cases to institute levels of IP protection *greater* than that required by TRIPS. These 'TRIPS-plus' measures included limiting the circumstances in which compulsory licences on pharmaceutical products could be issued, extending patent terms beyond the 20 years required by TRIPS, and prohibiting the export of medicines produced under compulsory licence. TRIPS-plus standards have been included in bilateral trade agreements, including the 1977 Bangui Agreement, which is the IP agreement for former French colonies in Africa, updated in 1999 to ensure TRIPS compatibility ('t Hoen 2003: 57). US pressure has also led to the constitution of patent regimes that go beyond TRIPS requirements in Nigeria, Uganda and Cambodia, and in the Free Trade Agreement of the Americas (FTAA), which covers 34 nations (Ford 2004: 143).

On top of attempts to encourage IP protection greater than that required by TRIPS, the USTR pressured developing countries to become TRIPS compliant prior to their designated transition periods. The USTR produced an annual Special 301 Report on IP rights placing offending nations on either the Special 301 'Watch List' or the 'Priority Watch List'. In 1996, one year after the establishment of the WTO, the USTR created the Office of Monitoring and Enforcement (OME) to oversee trade agreement implementation and compliance with the WTO agreements, as well as other regional and bilateral trade agreements. OME findings have been the basis upon which the US has pursued legal action against nations failing to uphold IP rights or attempting to use the ambiguous TRIPS safeguards (Shadlen 2004: 91–2). Furthermore the US business lobby requested that the USTR sanction governments that employ the TRIPS safeguards while also initiating their own legal action against developing countries (Sell and Prakash 2004: 146). Where the USTR deemed a nation to be in violation of TRIPS, the US presented its case at the WTO. In 1996, for example, the US initiated separate proceedings at the WTO against Pakistan, Portugal and India, while the EU initiated proceedings against India in 1997. In 1998 the US successfully pressured Thailand to amend its pharmaceutical patent law. Thailand removed its provisions for granting compulsory licenses and parallel importing and abolished its Pharmaceutical Patent Review Board, a body set up to control the price of medicines (CPTech 2000a). To exert pressure on developing countries the US drew on its power at alternative multilateral economic institutions: developing nations placed on the Special 301 watch lists became subject to the risk of having their requests for funds from the IMF and World Bank rejected (Shadlen 2004: 91). As a result, at the height of the Asian economic crisis when Thailand desperately required IMF financial assistance, the country was beholden to US pressure over its patent regime.

US and EU unilateral pressure on developing countries, combined with the uncertainty surrounding the TRIPS safeguards, led to an entrenched debate involving developing countries, NGOs, MNCs and industrialized nations. I now turn to the role of the NGO campaign in this debate. The activities of NGOs were crucial in not only publicizing the TRIPS and public health issues but also helping to generate momentum to have them addressed at the WTO. As I will argue below, NGOs also played a significant role in empowering developing nations to contest the issue in the WTO arena, which ultimately resulted in the decision to permanently amend the TRIPS agreement.

TRIPS AND THE ACCESS TO MEDICINES CAMPAIGN

The access to medicines NGO campaign arose from the perception of an emerging crisis in maintaining access to affordable essential medicines in developing countries to treat diseases such as HIV, malaria and tuberculosis. This was viewed as a particular problem in Africa where it is estimated that NGOs provide 40 per cent of health services (UNAIDS 2000). Though access to medicines in the developing world is dependent upon a range of factors, including adequate production levels, supply management, correct storage and appropriate use, the NGO network contended that a major cause of declining access from the mid-1990s was a reduction in affordability brought about by the constitution of TRIPS. Specifically the implementation of TRIPS in developing countries was pinpointed as the cause of reduced local manufacturing capacity, minimal technology transfer and lack of encouragement for research and development in developing nations (Ford 2004: 139). NGOs also highlighted the ambiguity surrounding the use of the TRIPS safeguard measures in terms of the national emergency provisions and the pressure on developing nations from the US and EU to enact IP protection in shorter timeframes and at levels exceeding those specified by TRIPS. These issues were brought into sharp focus by the legal action brought against South Africa by a group of pharmaceutical MNCs (supported by the US and EU), which served as a major catalyst for the development of the NGO campaign.

During 1998 South Africa faced increasing pressure from a number of quarters to repeal its 1997 Medicines and Related Substances Control Amendment Act, which allowed for generic substitution of off-patent medicines, transparent pricing, and parallel importation of patented medicines. In February 1998 the South African Pharmaceutical Manufacturers Association and 40 predominantly multinational pharmaceutical corporations (later 39 due to a merger) brought a suit against the South African government alleging that the amendment act violated the South African constitution and South Africa's commitment to the TRIPS agreement.[2] Adding to the pressure on South Africa was the successful request of PhRMA to the USTR to place South Africa on the Special 301 Watch List. The US suspended South Africa's GSP benefits and threatened further trade sanctions (Barber 1998). In turn the European Commission pressured South Africa to retract the amendment act on behalf of European pharmaceutical companies. In a March 1998 letter to Thabo Mbeki (then Vice-President of South Africa), Sir Leon Brittan (then Vice-President of the European Commission) stated that 'Section 15c of the law in question would appear to be at variance with South Africa's obligations under the TRIPS and its implementation would negatively affect the interest of the European pharmaceutical industry' (see CPTech 2000b).

The legal action and unilateral pressure on South Africa from the US and EU provided strong impetus for an NGO campaign that sought to clarify the TRIPS safeguards in a manner that would allow developing countries greater flexibility in making essential medicines more affordable. The campaign strategy revolved around publicizing the negative impact of the IP rights/international trade linkage on public health, the bullying tactics of the wealthy industrialized nations and MNCs, and lobbying at policy-relevant intergovernmental institutions. The NGOs also sought to highlight the link between the HIV epidemic and TRIPS implementation, looking at access to patented antiretroviral medication in developing nations (Sell and Prakash 2004). The campaign activated a broad range of NGOs, from public health advocates and development NGOs to HIV activists, not to mention those organizations focused on the social impacts of international trade liberalization more generally.

Key Actors

Though the campaign did not get underway officially until 1999, its origins can be found in an October 1996 workshop organized by HAI, an informal network of more than 200 consumer, health, development and other public interest groups concerned with IP and pharmaceutical access issues (HAI a). The HAI workshop, held in Bielefeld, Germany, brought together health and IP experts, academics, and activists to discuss the potential impact of the new WTO accords (especially TRIPS) on the affordability of medicines and national public health policies (Tellez). The workshop paved the way for a host of influential international NGOs to lend their resources and support to the campaign. Among the most prominent international NGOs involved was MSF with its 'Campaign for Access to Essential Medicines' that began in 1999 (Ford 2004: 138). Prior to this campaign, MSF had devoted most of its resources to service delivery, supplying medicines and providing medical care in developing countries rather than international trade issues. However, the nature of its work led to its involvement in campaigning on IP and access to medicines issues. As noted in one campaign document, 'we grew more familiar with pharmaceutical patents, the TRIPS Agreement and the WTO in the process – not because we wanted to, but because we had to' (Boulet, Garrison and 't Hoen 2004: 3).

The well-known international NGO, Oxfam International, joined the campaign network in October 2000, launching its 'Cut the Cost Campaign' in February 2001 (Oxfam 2001). With the launch of the organization's 'Make Trade Fair' campaign directed at the WTO, the 'Cut the Cost Campaign' was renamed the 'Patents and Access to Medicines Campaign'. Similarly another prominent international NGO, QUNO, ran a programme entitled 'Trade, Intellectual Property and Development'. In the US, among the most active NGO contributors to the campaign were Consumer Project on Technology (CPTech) created by consumer advocate and former US presidential candidate, Ralph Nader (the organization is now known as Knowledge Ecology International), the Health Gap Coalition, and AIDS Drugs for Africa. The major European NGOs involved in the campaign included the Berne

Declaration, Intellectual Property Watch (both of Switzerland), the Wemos Foundation (the Netherlands), Misereor (Germany), Voluntary Service Overseas (VSO) and CAFOD (both based in the UK).

A number of NGOs involved in awareness campaigns for the recognition of the rights of people living with HIV contributed to the campaign, undertaking both lobbying and grassroots activism. These included several organizations that are part of the transatlantic ACT UP network, notably ACT UP Paris, ACT UP Philadelphia and ACT UP New York. In the developing world, several NGOs working on HIV issues were also involved, such as the Thai NGO Coalition on AIDS (TNCA) consisting of a network of over 160 Thai NGOs working on prevention, treatment and care of people living with HIV. In Brazil, where the government has been relatively successful in providing medicines to people living with HIV and had stood firm in the face of US pressure for TRIPS-plus measures, a number of NGOs lent their support, such as the Brazilian Network for Peoples' Integration (REBRIP) and the Brazilian Interdisciplinary AIDS Association (ABIA). In South Africa, the Treatment Action Campaign (TAC) was established in 1998 with the objective of campaigning for equitable access to medicines and treatment for people living with HIV (TAC). TAC also formed an important alliance with COSATU (the federation of South African Trade Unions) known as the Alternative Alliance (Lethbridge 2004). Given their focus on access to care and medicines, HIV organizations formed an important part of the campaign network.

A great many more NGOs from developing countries were also part of the access to medicines campaign. In India, NGOs and national generic pharmaceutical firms have long worked together to lobby the government to resist changes to India's patent system. India is the world's leading supplier of generic medicines: 67 per cent of the total produced is exported to other developing nations (Barton 2004; Oxfam, Make Trade Fair). The Affordable Treatment and Action Campaign, among the most prominent of the Indian organizations involved in the access to medicines campaign, was launched in 2001 by a broad group of public health NGOs. It aimed to create both national and international awareness of the public health and access to medicines problems in India. Focus on the Global South, an NGO whose trade campaign activities include lobbying WTO members in Geneva, producing research on various trade issues, forging links with national social movements in Asia, and organizing public demonstrations (Focus on the Global South a), has also been an important organization in the campaign network (Focus on the Global South b).

Together, the international and national NGOs, trade unions, and HIV activists listed above constitute the most prominent organizations contributing to the access to medicines campaign targeting the WTO's TRIPS agreement (Table 5.1). Though this case study does not delve into the internal relationship

Table 5.1   Major international and national NGOs involved in the access to medicines campaign

Location	NGO
International	Health Action International (HAI) Health Global Access Project (Health GAP) Médecins Sans Frontières (MSF) Oxfam International Quaker United Nations Office (QUNO) Third World Network (TWN)
North America	ACT UP Philadelphia AIDS Drugs for Africa Center of Concern Consumer Project on Technology (CPTech) (now known as Knowledge Ecology International) Essential Action Health GAP Coalition Institute for Agriculture and Trade Policy (IATP) Public Citizen Treatment Action Group (TAG)
Europe	ACT UP Paris Berne Declaration (Switzerland) Catholic Agency For Overseas Development (CAFOD) Dutch HIV Association (The Netherlands) European Public Health Alliance (EPHA) European Generic medicines Association (EGA) Evert Vermeer Foundation (The Netherlands) Intellectual Property Watch (Switzerland) Misereor (Germany) Netherlands Institute for Southern Africa (NIZA) Voluntary Service Overseas (United Kingdom) Wemos Foundation (The Netherlands)
Africa	Congress of South African Trade Unions (COSATU) Kenya Coalition for Access to Essential Medicines (Kenya) Treatment Action Campaign (TAC) (South Africa)
India	Affordable Treatment and Action Campaign (AMTC) Centre for Trade and Development Drug Action Forum

Table 5.1   continued

Location	NGO
India (*cont.*)	Federation of Medical Representatives Association of India (FMRAI)
	Jana Swasthaya Abhiyan (JSA)
	Lawyers' Collective HIV/AIDS Unit
	National Working Group on Patent Laws (NWGPL)
	Public Health Movement
	Research Foundation for Science, Technology and Nature Resource Policy (led by Vandana Shiva)
Thailand	Aids Access Coalition
	Alliance of Democratic Trade Union, Alternative Agriculture Network
	Coordinating Committee for Primary Health Care of Thai NGOs
	Focus on the Global South
	Thai Network of People Living with HIV/AIDS
	Thai NGO Coalition on Aids
South America	Brazilian Interdisciplinary AIDS Association (ABIA)
	Brazilian Network for People's Integration (REBRIP)
	Centro Debate de Accion y Ambiental (Colombia)
	Latin American Institute for Legal Service Alternative (ILSA)

dynamics between the NGOs involved in the campaign, it should be noted that there was a high level of collaboration amongst activists and consumer groups involved in the issue (Ford 2004: 139). Specifically developing country NGOs, as well as those international NGOs providing services in developing countries, acted as information providers within the campaign network. This fortified the legitimacy of the claims being made about access difficulties and the effects on developing country citizens (see Keck and Sikkink 1998 on the boomerang model).

The NGOs undertook a range of campaign activities in their attempt to improve access to essential patented medicines in developing countries. They mobilized support at NGO-organized international workshops and conferences; publicized the issue at relevant international policy arenas other than the WTO; sought to expose the pressure tactics of the US and EU; and worked alongside other private actors such as generic pharmaceutical firms and technology developers. Significantly, NGOs also informed the negotiating positions of developing country WTO members affected by the TRIPS safeguards controversy. In doing so they aimed to have the TRIPS safeguards clarified in a manner that would provide for greater technology transfer and allow developing countries to continue their use of compulsory licensing and parallel importing to provide affordable access to essential medicines. I now examine these strategies in detail alongside progress on the issue at the WTO from 1999 through to the eventual amendment of the TRIPS agreement in December 2005.

Generating Support: NGO Workshops and Conferences

Though the issue of access to medicines and IP had been on the radar of public health and development NGOs since the establishment of the WTO, it was not until 1999 that a dedicated campaign on the matter was launched. In March 1999 MSF, CPTech and HAI together sponsored the first series of international NGO meetings to discuss the viability of compulsory licensing as a policy tool for increasing access to essential medicines in developing nations. Justifying the intensified involvement of NGOs, Bas van der Heide of HAI argued that 'the issue of compulsory licensing is too important to leave to patent officers and trade officials' (CPTech 1999a). As the workshop invitation explained: 'although specifically allowed in international agreements on intellectual property, compulsory licensing of patents is a topic of some controversy. The purpose of this meeting is to begin a dialogue among stakeholders on several important factual, legal and ethical questions that will provide a context for policymaking' (CPTech 1999b).

Held in Geneva at the Palais des Nations, the high-profile March 1999 meetings involved approximately 60 public health and consumer NGOs from around the world, government representatives from both developed and developing countries, representatives of pharmaceutical companies, and international organizations including the WTO and WHO (CPTech 1999a; Williams 1999). According to news reports of the event, the US government representative came under sustained pressure at the meetings to stop pressuring developing nations over their lack of patent protection for pharmaceuticals (Richwine 1999). In effect, this first series of meetings provided an arena in which the key issues surrounding access to medicines and IP were established. The meetings also helped create a broad campaign platform upon which a core group of NGOs agreed and were willing to commit their resources to (Tellez).

On 25–26 November 1999, immediately prior to the WTO Ministerial Conference in Seattle, 350 NGO representatives from 50 countries met in Amsterdam for a conference jointly organized by MSF, CPTech and HAI. Entitled 'Increasing Access to Essential Drugs in a Globalised Economy:

Working Towards Solutions', the meeting produced the Amsterdam Statement. One of the core tenets of this joint NGO statement was the proposal for the establishment of a 'TRIPS and Public Health' working group within the WTO ('t Hoen 2003: 46). Such a working group, it was argued, could address the ambiguity surrounding the use of TRIPS safeguards including the circumstances under which compulsory licensing and parallel importing may be used to increase access to medicines in developing countries.

As 't Hoen explains, the Amsterdam Statement was significant in that it essentially 'served as a guide for the work of NGOs and other advocates on TRIPS and public health' (2003: 46–7). It also helped mobilize a great many international and national NGOs who subsequently added their weight to the campaign network including Oxfam International, the Health Gap Coalition, ACT UP Paris and TAC in South Africa (Interview, MSF 2006). Together, the March and November 1999 NGO-sponsored meetings helped to spearhead the international campaign on TRIPS and public health by generating consensus around the idea that the ambiguity surrounding the TRIPS safeguards was in large part responsible for the declining access to medicines in developing nations.

Working Through Alternative International Policy Arenas

Just prior to the NGO-sponsored meetings outlined above, NGOs like MSF had begun to play important roles in getting the issues of affordable access to medicines, TRIPS implementation and the HIV crisis on the agenda at policy-relevant international organizations, particularly the WHO. At the 1998 meeting of the WHO's World Health Assembly (WHA), NGOs participated in updating the WHO's drug strategy, attempting to focus attention on the effect of IP rules on access to essential medicines in developing nations. One of the important outcomes was that the WHA adopted the Revised Drug Strategy (Resolution WHA52.19), which called upon WHO member states to review their options to maintain equitable access to medicines in the face of international trade agreements (WHO 1998). The resolution also requested that the WHO 'report on the impact of the work of the World Trade Organization (WTO) with respect to national drug policies and essential drugs and make recommendations for collaboration between WTO and WHO, as appropriate' (WHO 1998).

In addition to pinpointing the role of international trade rules in complicating access to medicines, the WHA resolution resulted in the WHO publishing a guide containing recommendations for member states about how to implement TRIPS in a manner that maintains the equitable availability of essential medicines (WHO 2001). Not surprisingly, the US and EU strongly resisted the role played by the WHO in advising and assisting developing country members over TRIPS and they unsuccessfully attempted to pressure the WHO to cancel the publication of the guide (Abbott 2002: 475; 't Hoen 2003: 48). Overall the WHO's involvement in international trade issues has been contentious. According to Frederick Abbott (2002: 475), the WTO secretariat has been less than cooperative with the WHO in TRIPS matters, with WHO representatives not granted observer status at the WTO's TRIPS Council until July 2000 (WTOk).

For the May 1999 meeting of the WHA, both the NGOs and the US were prepared to contest the WHO's involvement in the TRIPS issue, with the US sending its trade officials (Sell 2003: 149). Immediately prior to the meeting, HAI and CPTech hosted a workshop for NGOs and member states to brief NGO-friendly negotiators on some of the key controversies surrounding the TRIPS and access to medicines issue (Sell 2003: 149). At the WHA meeting itself, the South African representative, Dr Olive Shisana (director-general of the South African Department of Health) used information provided to her by the NGOs to present extensive evidence of the US government granting compulsory licenses for pharmaceutical products as well as in the areas of biotechnology, aviation, and nuclear power (Sell 2003: 149). She thereby exposed the hypocrisy of the US in pressuring developing countries over their use of compulsory licenses for pharmaceuticals. The USTR, caught off guard by South Africa's presentation, was unable to respond effectively (Sell 2003: 149). Thus the NGO workshop, at which important information was provided to developing country representatives, worked to boost the claims of developing countries in this arena, thereby undermining the legitimacy of the hard line stance taken by the US on TRIPS implementation.

Beyond the WHO, other international institutions and forums were also useful for the NGOs in progressing the TRIPS and public health debate. Like the WHO, UNCTAD researched the impact of the implementation of TRIPS and provided advice to developing country members. Similarly the UN Commission for Human Rights (UNCHR) investigated the impact of TRIPS implementation on human rights. In August 2000 the UN Sub-Commission for the Protection and Promotion of Human Rights adopted Resolution 2000/7 entitled 'Intellectual Property Rights and Human Rights', which noted that the implementation of TRIPS has the potential to impact the right to enjoy the benefits of scientific progress and its applications; the right to health; the right to food; and the right of self-determination (UN Sub-Commission on the Promotion and Protection of Human Rights 2000).

From 25–27 June 2001, the UN General Assembly Special Session (UNGASS) on HIV/AIDS, the first ever to address a health issue, was held in New York City. This meeting was partly a result of the UN Secretary-General's call for action on the issue of HIV:

> The Secretary-General noted, based on his recent meeting with leaders of six of the world's largest pharmaceutical companies, that they are now ready to sell life-saving drugs to developing countries at greatly reduced prices. Some 95% of the world's 36 million HIV-infected people live in developing countries, and fewer than 25,000 people in sub-Saharan Africa currently have access to anti-retroviral therapy. (UNGASS 2001)

This conference received a substantial amount of publicity and again devoted attention to the role of IP rights in obstructing access to medicines in developing countries. The UN declaration from UNGASS emphasized both prevention and treatment of HIV, and there was a call to generate $US9 billion for a global AIDS and health fund (subsequently established in January 2002 as the Global Fund to Fight AIDS, Tuberculosis and Malaria).

Though motivated by its own budgetary considerations, the support of the World Bank nonetheless strengthened NGO claims about the issue. The World Bank provides funds for the supply of essential medicines to developing nations, spending approximately $US800 million on pharmaceuticals annually (Vick 1999). As such the World Bank, despite its neoliberal agenda, supported the use of policy measures such as compulsory licensing and parallel importing of pharmaceuticals in developing countries as the purchase of generics would significantly reduce the Bank's costs (Vick 1999).

In addition to these multilateral institutions, the European Commission served as a strategically important regional theatre for the NGOs to gain traction on the issue, especially given the EU's support for the MNC legal action in South Africa. Europe-based and international NGOs worked intensively to convince the European Commission to modify its opposition to the use of the TRIPS safeguards by developing country governments. In 2000, having become aware of the European Trade Commissioner's 1998 letter to then South African Vice-President Thabo Mbeki that rebuked South Africa over its medicines control amendment act, NGOs pointed out that this hard line position defied the common European practice of using parallel importing for accessing less expensive pharmaceuticals (HAI b). In early 2001, Dutch NGOs, led by the Wemos Foundation and the Netherlands Institute for Southern Africa (NIZA), lobbied the European Commission to formally withdraw the 1998 letter and support the South African government's amendment act (HAI b). These organizations also sent their own letter of support to the South African President Thabo Mbeki (CPTech 2000c).

In response to the ongoing international debate about TRIPS and public health within Europe, the European Commission set up an issue group on access to medicines as part of the European Commission's broader civil society dialogue (European Commission 2001a; Smith and Smythe 2003: 205). The issue group met on a number of occasions during 2000 and 2001 to discuss Europe's position on the TRIPS agreement and public health. Several organizations participated including representatives of the research pharmaceutical industry, the generic pharmaceutical industry and NGOs such as MSF, Oxfam International, HAI, ACT UP, and the Wemos Foundation (European Commission 2001c). The NGO network lobbied the European Commission to promote support for policy measures such as tiered pricing; increased local production through compulsory licensing; and technology transfer to increase access to medicines in developing countries (European Commission 2001c). In addition to their participation in the issue group meetings, the NGOs submitted a number of formal statements to the European Commission seeking to have Articles 31 and 39 of TRIPS clarified. They also lobbied EU Commissioners Pascal Lamy and Poul Nielson to get EU support for the creation of a working group on access to medicines in the WTO (CPTech 2000c). Furthermore they requested that the European Commission support a formal clarification of the TRIPS safeguards within the WTO arena (CPTech 2000c).

One positive outcome of the issue group meetings was the NGO contribution to the European Commission's 'Programme for Action: Accelerated Action on HIV/AIDS, Malaria and Tuberculosis in the Context of Poverty Reduction' endorsed by the Council of Ministers on 14 May 2001 (European Commission 2001a). The objective of the programme was to increase the affordability of medicines for diseases prominent in developing nations including HIV, malaria, and tuberculosis:

> The European Community will seek to increase the affordability of key pharmaceuticals through attention to issues related to taxes and tariffs in developing countries. The European Community will work towards the introduction of tiered pricing as the norm for the poorest developing countries, while seeking to prevent re-importation to the EU market. Investment will build capacity within developing countries on health and trade-related issues, including implementation of the TRIPs Agreement. (European Commission 2001a)

Combined with several European Parliament resolutions supporting a public health approach to TRIPS implementation in developing nations, the 'Programme for Action', paved the way for the European Commission to agree that compulsory licensing was indeed one of the safeguards provided for within TRIPS and that the EU should not demand TRIPS-plus measures (European Parliament 2001; 't Hoen 2003: 49). Moreover individual European governments also played an important role by promoting discussion within international arenas, including the WTO, the July 2000 Group of 8 (G-8) meeting in Okinawa and the EU-US summit, to generate consensus about relaxing the position towards developing nations on the use of TRIPS safeguards. Several European governments and the European Parliament even requested that the pharmaceutical companies withdraw the case against the South African government's amendment act ('t Hoen 2003: 44).

In combination with the discussions, activities and public statements of the WHO, UNCTAD, UNCHR, UNGASS and the World Bank, the establishment of the European Commission's Access to Medicines Issue Group and the Programme of Action were important advances for the NGO campaigners, helping to perpetuate the link between the HIV crisis, access to medicines and the TRIPS agreement. Though the EU ultimately stated that it was acting as an honest broker during the Doha negotiations (thereby not taking a clear-cut stance on the issue) this marked a significant turnaround from the 1998 position when the Directorate General for Trade of the European Commission stated that 'no priority should be given to health over intellectual property considerations' (European Commission 1998; 't Hoen 2003: 49).[3]

Shaming Tactics: 'Big Pharma', Al Gore, and the US Presidential Elections

On top of mobilizing consensus about the nature of the TRIPS and public health issue in various international and European policy arenas, the NGO campaigners held public demonstrations to highlight the TRIPS implementation problems for developing nations. In both developed and developing country locations, NGOs engaged the media by staging public demonstrations and holding press conferences. As part of a month long protest action against US pharmaceutical companies, ACT UP Philadelphia held a demonstration at PhRMA headquarters in Washington DC on 12 March 2001 to protest the lawsuit against South Africa's Medicines Act and the stalling of the trial (Health GAP 2001a). The demonstration involved hundreds of activists with giant puppet effigies of 'big pharma'. Other publicity stunts included a 'die-in' and the decoration of PhRMA headquarters with tombstones representing South African people who had died from AIDS-related illnesses whilst the implementation of the South African amendment had been delayed (Health GAP 2001a).

NGOs attempted to pressure pharmaceutical MNCs by seeking information about the true cost of manufacturing HIV medicines in order to highlight the extent of their profits. They consulted developing country governments and generics manufacturers including the Thai Government Pharmaceutical Organization, the US generics industry advocate William Haddad, and Dr Yusuf Hamied, chairman of the generic pharmaceutical company Cipla. Cipla subsequently offered to sell HIV medicines to MSF for as little as $US350 per yearly dose for countries facing HIV epidemics, as opposed to $US10,000 that research-based pharmaceutical companies charged (MSF and Cipla 2001). In response, the research-based pharmaceutical industry attempted a counter-attack, publishing a study illustrating that upholding patents is vital for the development of new medicines (see Attaran and Gillespie-White 2001). This study failed to gain traction with the interested public.

In early 2001 the NGO network successfully mobilized students and staff of Yale University in the US, which holds the patent for d4T, an important HIV medicine. Yale University had licensed the pharmaceutical company Bristol-Myers Squibb to produce the medicine from which it derived $US40 million a year in licensing fees (McNeil 2001). MSF requested that Yale University allow South Africa to import generic versions of d4T, but the university initially refused, claiming that Bristol-Myers Squibb had an exclusive license. A group of Yale University law students responded by organizing campus demonstrations and other protest activities with the support of Yale University Professor William Prusoff, one of the medicine's developers. The publicity generated ultimately resulted in Bristol-Myers Squibb announcing that it would reduce the price to 1.5 per cent of the cost to an American patient (McNeil 2001). By engaging the producers of the original medical technology, as well as generics industry figures, NGOs aimed to discredit the pharmaceutical companies' claims about production costs for medicines and therefore the need for high levels of IP protection to ensure investment into new medical technology.

In the lead-up to the US presidential elections in 2000, a number of US affiliates of the organization ACT UP, along with HIV awareness campaigners, targeted presidential candidate and US Vice President Al Gore in an attempt to publicize the US government's role in pressuring South Africa over its Medicines Act. Al Gore was targeted due to his close personal ties to individuals within the research-based pharmaceutical industry, receipt of campaign funds from this industry, and his pivotal role in threatening the South African government with trade sanctions.[4] In highlighting the US role in the South African court case, the activists staged publicity stunts at the announcement of Gore's bid for the presidency and his subsequent campaign rallies with banners that said, among other things, 'Gore's greed kills' ('t Hoen 2003: 44). NGOs also attempted to reinvoke anti-apartheid sentiment, arguing that only affluent South Africans (predominantly white citizens) could afford the cost of patented pharmaceuticals (ACT UP Philadelphia 1999). This in turn attracted negative attention from the US Congressional Black Caucus, a key pillar of support for President Clinton and Vice President Gore. Meanwhile Ralph Nader, founder of CPTech and presidential candidate in the US elections for the Green Party of the United States, contributed to the debate claiming that both Republicans and Democrats had 'sold out' to big business (Sell and Prakash 2004: 149).

The confrontation with Gore at election campaign rallies and the additional publicity generated by Nader supporters had an impact on the US government's eventual decision to reform its practices in regards to IP protection in developing countries (Morrison 2001: 199–200; Thomas 2002: 257). Clinton's desire to see Gore become the next US president and his close ties to the Black Congressional Caucus provided NGO campaigners with a great deal of leverage, and as a result, the Clinton administration changed its view. In June 1999 the US withdrew its objections to the new South African law, removing South Africa from the USTR's Special 301 watch list. In November 1999, at the WTO's ministerial conference in Seattle, US President Bill Clinton in his speech referred specifically to South Africa and the HIV crisis, stating that 'the United States will henceforward implement its health care and trade policies in a manner that ensures that people in the poorest countries won't have to go without medicine they so desperately need' (Clinton 1999). The US government also agreed to exercise restraint in the use of the Special 301 provision in cases where vital pharmaceuticals are involved. Clinton went on to forge institutional collaboration between the USTR and the US Department of Health and Human Services on trade cases involving public health issues (Sell and Prakash 2004: 166). In May 2000 this change of course in US policy was reflected in Clinton's issue of an Executive Order entitled 'Access to HIV/AIDS Pharmaceuticals and Medical Technologies', which supported the use of compulsory licensing to increase access to HIV medicines in sub-Saharan Africa (Clinton 2000).

But in June 2000, only one month after Clinton's Executive Order, the US broke the truce by lodging a 'request for consultation' with the WTO over Article 68 of Brazil's IP law, which allows for compulsory licensing (WTO 2000m).[5] The US argued (perhaps not convinced that Brazil qualified as a 'poorest of the poor' country) that Brazilian laws reduced patent owners' rights as specified in the TRIPS agreement under Article 27.1 and Article 28.1. In reply Brazil claimed that Article 68 was consistent with the objectives of the TRIPS safeguard provisions. But in January 2001, under the new Republican administration led by President George W. Bush, the US went on to request the establishment of a dispute panel at the WTO (WTO 2001m).

The issue of Brazil's protection of IP rights had long been a source of tension between the US and Brazil. Several MNCs had been in dispute with Brazil over its patent laws since the early 1980s, and on several occasions the USTR had threatened or applied unilateral trade sanctions against the country. Brazil had been active in a number of international forums advocating that developing countries ensure that they protect their rights to access medicines. In April 2001 Brazil presented a resolution to the UNCHR linking the HIV crisis to the TRIPS agreement in an attempt to repel challenges by the US and EU to patent regimes in developing countries. The UN Sub-Commission on the Promotion and Protection of Human Rights subsequently adopted Resolution 2001/33 'Access to Medicines in the Context of Pandemics such as HIV/AIDS', which condemned the US over its application of unilateral pressure on developing countries over TRIPS implementation (UN Sub-Commission on the Promotion and Protection of Human Rights 2001). Brazil also controversially offered support in the form of cooperation agreements comprising technology transfer provisions, to other developing countries seeking to increase their manufacturing capacity for generic HIV medicines ('t Hoen 2003: 45).

Meanwhile, the legal action taken by pharmaceutical MNCs against South Africa continued to be fought in the courts, even though the MNCS had effectively lost the support of the US government and the European Commission had distanced itself from the case ('t Hoen 2003: 44). During the course of the hearing, it was discovered that the most contentious section of the Medicines Act had been developed not by the South African government, but derived from a draft legal text constructed by the WIPO Committee of Experts ('t Hoen 2003: 44). As a result, by March 2001, the pharmaceutical companies could no longer feasibly continue to claim that the amendment was counter to South Africa's international legal commitments ('t Hoen 2003: 44). In the interim, NGOs stepped up the pressure on the MNCs. Through March 2001 COSATU and TAC staged protests outside the Pretoria High Court against the pharmaceutical companies, which were attended by thousands of people from trade unions, churches, NGOs as well as those living with HIV (TACb). These demonstrations were staged at a critical point in the legal proceedings, which culminated in the MNCs withdrawing their case unconditionally in April 2001.

Following this success in South Africa, NGO campaigners turned their attention to pressuring the US government over its action against Brazil in the WTO. Concerned that this dispute would have a detrimental effect on Brazil's successful HIV programme, which served as a model to other developing countries ('t Hoen 2003: 45), NGOs held a number of demonstrations to support Brazil. In April 2001 protests were held in Washington DC outside the offices of US trade officials. This was supplemented by an NGO press conference jointly held by ACT UP affiliates and Brazilian Consulate officials, at which they defended Brazil's use of compulsory licensing and highlighted the pressure tactics of the US government (Health GAP 2001b). At the same time MSF and TAC began importing HIV medicines from Brazil into South Africa and, in doing so, infringed patents held by MNCs in South Africa. But following the negative publicity generated by the South African court case, the industry was effectively hamstrung and thus unable to take any action. In May 2001 the work of the NGOs resulted in further payoff with US President Bush making the founding pledge of $US200 million for a disease fund, which later became the Global Fund to Fight AIDS, Tuberculosis, and Malaria. And in June 2001, on the first day of the UNGASS on HIV/AIDS, the US issued a joint statement with Brazil announcing that it was officially withdrawing the WTO case against Brazil (Bermudez and Oliveira 2004).

Three months prior to the Doha conference, the 9/11 terrorist attacks led to a softening of the US position on compulsory licensing for pharmaceuticals. The US government recognized that it might need to issue compulsory licenses of its own for national emergencies resulting from bio-terror threats such as anthrax (Abbott 2001: 486–7; Sell and Prakash 2004: 196). In mid-October 2001, in response to the terrorist threat, despite having stated its opposition to the use of TRIPS safeguards by developing nations, Canada overrode Bayer's patent by granting a compulsory licence to a generics manufacturer for the antibiotic Ciprofloxacin, considered the most effective treatment for anthrax (Harmon and Pear 2001). Similarly the US government announced that it had demanded Bayer reduce the price for Ciprofloxacin by threatening to issue a compulsory license (Carroll and Winslow 2001). These events allowed NGOs to further press the hypocrisy of the US stance on TRIPS. They served to highlight that 'no responsible government with a choice would place the public health of its citizens below the interests of a few patent holders' (Abbott 2001: 488).

TOWARDS DOHA: NGOs, DEVELOPING COUNTRIES AND THE WTO

During 2001 in the lead-up to the Doha Ministerial Conference, NGOs worked alongside developing countries to clarify the proper use of the TRIPS safeguards at the WTO. Having campaigned on the issue for over two years, NGOs had demonstrated that their objectives on TRIPS and public health were compatible with those of many developing country governments. NGOs went on not only to provide moral support to developing countries contesting the issue at the WTO, but to influence their negotiating strategy for clarifying the rights of developing countries in regards to the TRIPS agreement.

In April 2001, the WTO and WHO met in Norway for their first ever joint workshop that provided an important opportunity for NGOs to contribute to the WTO debate. In their joint statement 'Differential Pricing and Financing of Essential Drugs' endorsed by over 100 NGOs, CPTech, HAI, MSF, Oxfam International and Treatment Action Group (TAG) proposed that the WTO's TRIPS Council adopt a seven-point strategy, including a moratorium on dispute settlement action; an agreement not to put pressure on developing countries to forgo their right to TRIPS safeguards; and an extended deadline for TRIPS implementation in LDCs (CPTech, HAI, MSF, Oxfam International and TAG 2001). NGOs especially emphasized the need for policy instruments such as compulsory licensing and parallel importing to encourage generic competition in order to lower medicine prices. The statement argued that '[d]iscussions on schemes such as "differential pricing" or a global fund for

AIDS should not distract from, or be a substitute for, the need for action on patents and the TRIPS Agreement' (CPTech et al. 2001).

During the same month, Zimbabwe, which held the chair of the TRIPS Council, proposed a TRIPS Council Special Session on access to medicines on behalf of a coalition of more than 50 developing nations led by the African Group. In doing so Zimbabwe stated that the WTO could not remain silent on this issue, which was being widely debated outside the WTO ('t Hoen 2003: 49). In preparation for the TRIPS Council Special Session in June 2001, NGOs worked closely with governments of the African Group, Brazil, India and others to arrive at a common position. The lead paper submitted at the first TRIPS Council Special Session entitled 'TRIPS and Public Health', heavily drew upon the concerns raised by NGOs at other international institutions including the WHA, UN General Assembly and the UNCHR (Abbott 2002: 482). It was supported by the African Group, Barbados, Bolivia, Brazil, Dominican Republic, Ecuador, Honduras, India, Indonesia, Jamaica, Pakistan, Philippines, Peru, Sri Lanka, Thailand and Venezuela.

In addition to their contribution to the lead paper, NGOs provided LDCs with much needed financial and legal support in their shared endeavour to clarify the TRIPS agreement safeguards (see Tuerk 2003: 190 and 201). The QUNO website put it like this: '[r]epresentatives from developing countries have much at stake in international agreements, yet they are often ill-equipped for the negotiations which lead to these agreements. QUNO provides vital expertise and support, helping delegations to consolidate positions and back their arguments with research and analysis' (Quakers in Britain). In providing this assistance, the NGOs helped inform the developing countries' negotiating strategy for the TRIPS special sessions. Specifically NGO assistance helped transfigure the issue from one of policy (balancing technological innovation with equal access to medicines) to procedure (legally clarifying the 'terms of use' of the TRIPS safeguards) (Shadlen 2004: 95).

At the first TRIPS Council Special Session, developing countries sought official confirmation that measures to protect public health would not make them subject to dispute settlement procedures at the WTO. The discussions centred on the requirements of the TRIPS agreement, in particular how these might be aligned with public health needs in developing countries. As a result of NGO assistance, the developing countries insisted on a ministerial declaration on the use of TRIPS safeguards. With reference to the HIV crisis in Africa, Zimbabwe stated that a declaration was required to clarify the issues and in particular, to affirm 'that nothing in the TRIPS Agreement should prevent Members from taking measures to protect public health' (WTO 2001b). The session resulted in a degree of consensus among WTO members (including the EU) that TRIPS should not interfere with the protection of public health. Members also requested that the WTO secretariat prepare a checklist of the articles referred to and schedule a further informal session of the TRIPS Council for 25 July to consider the issues in more detail.

But at the second meeting in July little was achieved and, as a result, another two-day meeting was planned for late September 2001. At this third meeting, the African Group, with 19 other countries, presented a draft text for a ministerial declaration on TRIPS and public health, which included provisions for clarifying the use of compulsory licensing, parallel imports and the exportation of generic pharmaceuticals ('t Hoen 2003: 50). NGOs had helped design and draft this text at meetings at Quaker House Geneva (Quakers in Britain). But the US, together with Australia, Canada, Japan and Switzerland, circulated their own draft, highlighting the importance of upholding IP rights for promoting research and development into new medicines. In a particularly sanctimonious statement, the USTR argued that developing countries seek 'to justify use of protectionist measures by associating these measures [compulsory licensing and parallel importing] with the AIDS crisis when no such linkage exists' (Crossette 2001). In the meantime the EU had developed an alternative draft declaration addressing the exportation of medicines produced under compulsory licenses.

Alongside the TRIPS Special Sessions, NGOs held press conferences and issued public statements of their own to add weight to the claims made by developing countries inside the WTO arena. Prior to the opening of the September TRIPS Council meeting, for instance, NGOs held a press conference in Geneva on 17 September 2001 to highlight their concerns about the implications of TRIPS on access to medicines, as well as other issue areas affected by IP rules like food security and bio-piracy. They released a joint statement entitled 'Re-thinking TRIPS in the WTO – NGOs demand review and reform of TRIPS at Doha Ministerial Conference' (TWN 2001). Oxfam additionally promoted its petition (signed by 32 000 people in 163 countries) calling on the WTO to change its patent rules (Oxfam International 2001).

Despite opposition from the US and its supporters, the efforts of the NGO network in publicizing the issue and the developing countries in presenting a unified position at the TRIPS Council Special Sessions resulted in TRIPS and public health becoming a key agenda item at the November 2001 Doha Ministerial Conference (Interview, WTO 2006). Immediately prior to the conference, an NGO statement issued on 11 November 2001 called on WTO members to endorse an interpretation of the TRIPS agreement that protects public health: '[w]e support the leadership declared by the 71 countries of the African, Pacific, and Caribbean Countries, that the Ministerial Declaration on the TRIPS Agreement and Public Health must state that "nothing in the TRIPS Agreement shall prevent governments from taking measures to protect public health"' (Health GAP 2001c). The NGO statement again called for the right to issue compulsory licences, parallel importing and an extension for the implementation deadline of TRIPS for developing nations.

THE DOHA DECLARATION ON TRIPS AND PUBLIC HEALTH

Discussion of TRIPS and public health dominated the Doha Ministerial Conference. On the opening day of the conference, WTO Director-General Michael Moore stated that the TRIPS and public health issue could be a deal breaker for a new round of trade negotiations ('t Hoen 2003: 55). After a great deal of debate among members including the African Group, Brazil, India, and the US, members finally issued a declaration that was mostly a result of a compromise between the US and Brazil (Abbott 2002). The Doha Declaration on TRIPS and Public Health clarified the right of WTO members to use the TRIPS safeguards, thereby affirming the sovereign right of governments to take measures to protect public health:

> [w]e agree that the TRIPS Agreement does not and should not prevent Members from taking measures to protect public health. Accordingly while reiterating our commitments to the TRIPS Agreement, we affirm that the Agreement can and should be interpreted and implemented in a manner supportive of WTO Members' right to protect public health and, in particular, promote access to medicines for all. (WTO 2001c)

Paragraph 5(b) of the declaration additionally clarifies that '[e]ach Member has the right to grant compulsory licences and the freedom to determine the grounds upon which such licences are granted', while paragraph 5(c) explains that '[e]ach member has the right to determine what constitutes a national emergency or other circumstances of extreme urgency, it being understood that public health crises, including those relating to HIV/AIDS, tuberculosis, malaria and other epidemics, can represent a national emergency or other circumstances of extreme urgency' (WTO 2001c).

As well as clearly stating that members may use the TRIPS safeguards for public health reasons, the LDCs were given an extension of ten years, until 2016, to implement pharmaceutical patent protection (for which the TRIPS Council completed the legal drafting in mid-2002). The declaration also allows member states to appeal to the declaration and its negotiating history in the event that a member's legislation, particularly relating to patents for pharmaceuticals, is challenged on the grounds that it is incompatible with TRIPS. As Oxfam International declared, '[t]he final deal reaffirmed that public health is more important than patents. This was an important step forward in making medicines affordable for developing countries' (Oxfam International 2001; see also Banta 2001).

THE 'AUGUST 30 SOLUTION'

Despite the important advances achieved at Doha, the issue of the production and export of pharmaceuticals (either patented or made under compulsory licenses) to poor countries without the manufacturing capacity was not resolved. The TRIPS Council was accordingly assigned to find a solution and report to the General Council on the matter by the end of 2002 (WTO 2001c). In an attempt to meet the 2002 deadline to finalize the issue, WTO member states proposed, debated and rejected a number of different texts. The major point of contention was between developed and developing members over the scope for admitting parallel importation as a TRIPS safeguard ('t Hoen 2003: 58–61).

Throughout 2002 the NGO campaigners contributed to the debate over the text to deal with the parallel importation issue. On 19 December a coalition of NGOs comprising CPTech, Essential Action, MSF, Oxfam International, Health GAP Coalition, and TWN wrote to WTO members with their own proposal for the legal text. This read:

> [u]nder Article 30 of the TRIPS agreement, Members may provide an exception to the exclusive rights conferred by a relevant patent to permit all acts associated with the production for export to a third country of a patented product or a product produced by a patented process; where the export addresses health needs in the third country; and the product and/or process is either (a) not patented; or (b) a compulsory license has been granted or government use made of the relevant patent in the third country. ('t Hoen 2003: 59)

WTO member states finally reached a consensus on the export issue in August 2003 immediately prior to the WTO's Cancún Ministerial Conference. The August 30 Decision (also known as the Paragraph Six Solution) provided a temporary waiver for developing nations to allow them to import generic medicines made under compulsory license if they are unable to manufacture the medicines themselves (WTO 2003b). The decision temporarily set aside the obligations of exporting countries under Article 31(f). Provided certain conditions are met, any member country may export generic pharmaceutical products made under compulsory licences to meet the needs of importing countries. The decision includes provisions on transparency (giving a patent owner some opportunity to react by offering a lower price), special packaging and other methods to avoid medicines being diverted to other markets. An annex to the decision outlined the steps that a member state must take in order to declare itself unable to produce pharmaceuticals domestically.

It should be noted that the August 30 temporary waiver has been criticized by several NGOs as complex and unwieldy (MSF 2006). As Ford explains: '[t]he concerns of MSF and others is that the deal insists on such a high level of proof and gives such a heavy administrative burden that it is legally and politically unworkable' (2004: 144). Despite these claims, commentators such as Shadlen have noted that the August 30 solution did provide developing countries with a clear set of rules and thus a greater level of predictability and stability in using TRIPS safeguards for importing and exporting medicines produced under compulsory licenses (2004: 97). Certainly it represented a great advance over the uncertain situation prior to the Doha meeting in 2001.

THE PERMANENT AMENDMENT OF THE TRIPS AGREEMENT

The WTO's General Council set a deadline of June 2004 by which to convert the August 30 temporary waiver into a permanent amendment of the TRIPS agreement. But again a lack of consensus among developed and developing countries over how this should be achieved resulted in the deadline being missed. This time the disagreements revolved around exactly how to handle the text, in particular the proportions that should be placed within Article 31 and in an annex to the TRIPS agreement, as well as how to incorporate the chairperson's statement that had been issued when the General Council adopted the decision. Developing members argued that the waiver had been so difficult to negotiate that it should simply be translated directly into an amendment to avoid further delays.

Eventually on 6 December 2005, immediately prior to the WTO's Hong Kong Ministerial Conference, WTO members agreed to transform the 2003 temporary waiver into a permanent amendment of the WTO's TRIPS agreement (WTO 2005c). This decision was to be formally incorporated into the TRIPS agreement when two thirds of WTO member states had ratified the change, for which the initial deadline was 1 December 2007. (However, in December 2009, WTO members agreed to postpone this deadline until the end of 2011.) WTO members also agreed to extend the transition period for LDCs to enact protection for trademarks, copyright, patents and other IP to 1 July 2013 (LDCs had already been given until 2016 to protect pharmaceutical patents at Doha). The permanent amendment of the TRIPS agreement, designed to match the 2003 waiver as closely as possible, completed a process that began with the Doha Declaration on TRIPS and Public Health in

November 2001. Significantly it represents the first ever amendment to a core WTO agreement.

CONCLUSION

This chapter demonstrates that NGOs' access to medicines campaign played an agenda-setting role in the TRIPS and public health issue, which was eventually debated inside the WTO in 2001. NGOs used a number of key political opportunities including the pharmaceutical MNCs' legal action against the South African government, the 2000 US presidential elections, the global HIV epidemic, and US and EU pressure on developing nations to build their strategy for challenging and clarifying the right of developing nations to employ the TRIPS safeguards. Drawing upon the morbidity rates from HIV-related illnesses and other disease epidemics in developing nations to invoke the public anxiety that HIV had created in developed nations since the 1980s, NGOs projected the TRIPS and public health issue as an urgent matter of life and death. As Keck and Sikkink explain, campaigning on bodily harm and life and death issues can be a particularly potent strategy for NGOs, 'especially when there is a short and clear causal chain (or story) assigning responsibility' (1998: 17). NGOs argued that the legal uncertainty surrounding the use of TRIPS safeguards exploited by 'profit-hungry' pharmaceutical companies, and used as the basis for US and European 'bullying' of developing nations, was the major cause for the decline in access to essential medicines in developing nations. The simplicity of this causal link attracted a large range of organizations, including development, aid, and religious NGOs to lend their support to the campaign.

With broad consensus on the nature of the problem generated at NGO-sponsored meetings and workshops, NGOs worked through prominent international organizations, in particular the WHO and European Commission, to garner international support for action to clarify the TRIPS safeguards. Simultaneously, in the US the NGO network publicized the coercive tactics used by the Clinton administration against developing countries over the TRIPS safeguards. In doing so they targeted Al Gore's presidential campaign, lobbied the US government directly, and held numerous public demonstrations to pressure the US government to allow developing countries to employ the TRIPS safeguards. The staging of public events such as these not only worked to broadcast the urgency of the health crises associated with TRIPS implementation in developing countries, but laid the groundwork for closer relations between the NGOs and developing countries on the issue. As Coulby and Ndrangu note, through their campaign activities, NGOs demonstrated that 'they had a pragmatic approach to TRIPS that reflected a common understanding with the Africa Group' (2001: 7).

Further to the widespread support for the campaign amongst the relevant international NGO community, and the attempts to progress the issue at alternative international forums, the most potent strategy employed by the NGO campaigners in affecting the WTO were their attempts to influence the negotiating strategies of developing countries. Exploiting the divisions between developed and developing nations at the WTO, NGOs played a role in assisting developing nations to arrive at a unified position for negotiating the use of TRIPS safeguards at the WTO. With their financial resources and technical expertise, NGOs helped African nations to reorient the terms of the debate from one of policy substance to one with greater currency in the WTO arena: legal procedure and appropriate interpretation of legal text. As Shadlen states, the nature of the WTO as a rules-based institution renders it a prohibitive arena for debating substantive policy issues, while debates about procedural and legal matters are far more amenable to debate at the WTO (2004: 95). NGOs also assisted developing countries with their textual inputs to WTO negotiations. In the interim NGOs continued to host meetings and issue joint statements on the sidelines of WTO conferences thereby contributing to the debate involving the African Group, Brazil, India, the US and Europe inside the WTO. Following the release of the Doha Declaration on TRIPS and Public Health, the NGO network informed the debate in the lead-up to the August 30 decision, which member states eventually agreed to make permanent in December 2006.

In sum, the activities of the NGO campaigners were fundamental in leading the debate, through mobilizing the NGO sector concerned with international trade issues and assisting developing countries with negotiating strategies to bring about these changes at the WTO. The role of NGOs in harnessing political opportunities and using a range of strategies to mobilize support to do so is explored in more detail in Chapter 7. While it is important to note that many NGOs were opposed to the policy detail of the August 30 solution (and thus the 2005 permanent amendment of TRIPS), this does not negate the significance of their role at the outset of the WTO policy process that dealt with the TRIPS safeguards. Actors at this level of governance, whether states or non-state actors, very rarely achieve their goals in full. Perhaps a more pressing concern for NGOs in this area is the increasing number of bilateral and regional free trade agreements (especially those between the US and LDCs) that contain TRIPS-plus measures prohibiting the use of compulsory licensing and parallel importing measures. NGOs such as MSF and Essential Action hold concerns that the US aims to establish TRIPS-plus provisions as the international standard for IP, which may eventually be ratified at the WTO.

NOTES

1. For more detail about these agreements and conventions, see the WIPO website. URL: <http://www.wipo.int/about-wipo/en/gib.htm#P23_2347>.
2. Pharmaceutical Manufacturers' Association of South Africa v President of the Republic of South Africa. Case No 4183/98, filed 18 February 1998.
3. This comment was in response to the WHA resolution on the Revised Drug Strategy.
4. On Vice President Al Gore's links to the industry, see ACT UP New York 1999.
5. The Brazilian Patent Law. Industrial Property Law No 9 279 of 14 May 1996, requires patent owners to manufacture their products in Brazil. If this requirement is not met, a patent is subject to compulsory licensing after three years. An exception is made if the patent owner can demonstrate that it is not economically viable to produce in Brazil or that the requirement is, in some particular way, unreasonable. If the patent owner is permitted to use its patent by importation instead of production within Brazil, parallel importation by others is also permitted.

6. The NGO campaign against a WTO investment agreement

INTRODUCTION

Following the WTO's 2001 Doha Ministerial Conference, international debate over the launch of negotiations on a WTO foreign investment agreement polarized WTO member states and elicited strong opposition from a broad range of NGOs. In late 2002 in preparation for the Cancún Ministerial Conference, an international NGO campaign emerged to publicize the negative aspects of a potential WTO investment framework, especially for developing countries. The arguments put forward by NGOs significantly informed the anti-investment position of developing WTO members, including the ACP countries, the LDC group and the African Group. Some of these member governments even invited NGO representatives to sit on their official delegations at the 2003 Cancún Ministerial Conference. During the conference, a new coalition of developing countries emerged – the G-90 – that flatly refused to agree to the launch of negotiations on a WTO investment agreement and the other Singapore issues until progress was made on issues of importance to developing members. This stance contributed to the collapse of the Cancún conference. The following year WTO members agreed on the 'July package' to get the Doha Round back on track, which saw the removal of the investment issue from the agenda altogether.[1] This outcome is seen as a major victory for developing countries and their NGO supporters.

Like the medicines campaign outlined in Chapter 5, this case study detailing the NGO campaign against a WTO investment agreement seeks to shed light upon relations between NGOs and developing states. It thus provides another point of comparison with the labour standards case in which NGOs aligned with developed WTO members. The present chapter also allows for a further examination of NGO campaign tactics and the way in which NGOs highlight normative arguments for policy changes that serve to bolster the complementary interests of WTO member states. In working to consolidate opposition to a WTO investment agreement, NGOs produced research and analysis on the impact of a potential WTO investment agreement that highlighted the potential loss of domestic policy flexibility, especially for developing countries. These resources were disseminated widely amongst the trade-related NGO community, developing country governments and relevant international institutions. NGOs also hosted a series of international conferences and workshops at which NGOs, governments, international organizations and academics discussed the costs and benefits of a WTO investment agreement. These NGO activities, which publicized the pitfalls of a WTO investment accord, were crucial for informing and enhancing the negotiating position of developing countries. NGOs worked closely with nations from the African Group, providing them with analytical research and technical assistance to oppose an investment agreement within the WTO arena. This assistance helped unite and consolidate the negotiating position of the G-90 developing nations, which strongly opposed the launch of investment negotiations at the Cancún meeting.

While a number of accounts detail the breakdown of the WTO negotiations in Cancún (Alpert 2003; CAFOD 2003; Khor 2003b; South Centre 2003; van de Ven 2003; Cho 2004; Hurrell and Narlikar 2006), few examine the roles played by NGOs in this context. Narlikar (2003) and Narlikar and Tussie (2004), for example, explain how developing countries managed to maintain their unity during the Cancún conference when past attempts had proved difficult. Narlikar and Tussie do not explore the contribution of NGOs to this outcome, instead crediting the 'structural features' of developing country coalitions for maintaining their unity (2004). Other authors such as Jurgen Kurtz (2002) provide detailed accounts of the history of the WTO investment negotiations issue, starting with the establishment of the WTO's Working Group on Trade and Investment (WGTI). Kurtz devotes his attention to the potential role and benefits of multilateral and bilateral investment accords, examining the work to date on rules for foreign investment in the international arena. This chapter instead provides an account of the NGO campaign against a WTO investment agreement, assessing the tactics and strategies used in order to uncover more about the agenda-setting roles of NGOs in international trade policymaking.

The chapter is structured as follows. First I detail the contention surrounding the development of multilateral rules for foreign investment before briefly investigating attempts to establish such rules in a number of intergovernmental arenas. The development of the issue at the WTO is then examined, starting with the inaugural Singapore Ministerial Conference in 1996 through to the 2001 Doha Ministerial Declaration, which stated that members would work towards launching an investment agreement following the 2003 Cancún Ministerial Conference. I then turn to the NGO campaign, detailing the actors, alliances and strategies employed to prevent the launch of negotiations on a WTO investment accord at Cancún. In particular I focus on how NGOs strategically employed political opportunities to construct a campaign narrative and the ways in which they generated support for their position among relevant

NGO communities and developing countries. I then detail the way in which NGOs informed the negotiating position of developing countries in the lead-up to the Cancún ministerial. The final section inspects the events that unfolded at the Cancún ministerial and the subsequent development of the 2004 July Package that rescued the Doha Round and removed the Singapore issues (including investment) from the negotiations.

MULTILATERAL RULES FOR REGULATING FOREIGN INVESTMENT: RATIONALE AND OPPOSITION

Foreign investment is becoming an increasingly significant component of the global economy, having grown at unprecedented rates over the past decade (UNCTAD 2005). In 1998, at the time the issue gained traction in the WTO arena, foreign direct investment (FDI) inflows increased by 39 per cent globally despite adverse economic conditions such as the Asian financial crisis and declining commodity prices (UNCTAD 1999). Like international trade, foreign investment has the potential to provide the capital and technology required for the economic development of under-developed and newly industrializing nations, thereby contributing towards economic growth and technology transfer (Jenson 2003: 587). Many economists believe that investment should be considered equivalent to the international flow of goods and services through trade (Gilpin 2001: 280).

FDI and portfolio investment (PI) are the two main categories of foreign investment. PI refers to investment in holdings of foreign stocks, bonds, corporate stock or other financial assets not actively managed (that is, the investor does not have a controlling interest in the investment) (Grabel 1998). PI is likely to be short term and thus has the greatest potential to destabilize a recipient economy if it comes to rely upon it. In contrast, FDI often involves foreign ownership through corporate mergers, takeovers or inter-corporate alliances, or a completely new business venture. FDI is primarily driven by MNCs through the creation of foreign affiliates; its purpose is 'part of an international corporate strategy to establish a permanent position in another economy' (Gilpin 2001: 278). FDI has been growing at twice the rate of international trade (UNCTAD 1999, 2005), and is therefore much more significant than PI in terms of its contribution to economic growth and development. It can generate employment, technology advances and improvements in productivity, and thus has great potential to boost the economic growth of developing countries. While both PI and FDI have been under discussion for a multilateral agreement in various intergovernmental arenas, the debate at the WTO has mainly focused on FDI.

The strongest supporters of a multilateral investment agreement have included the EU, the US, Canada and Japan, as well as peak business associations such as the ICC, the Foreign Trade Association for the European Union (FTA), the European Services Forum and the Union of Industrial and Employers' Confederations of Europe (UNICE). Advocates of a multilateral foreign investment agreement offer two main reasons why such an accord is needed. First, a multilateral agreement would provide an opportunity to restructure the present investment regime: most FDI has remained highly concentrated in industrialized countries while the poorest countries receive less than 2 per cent of global FDI flows (UNDP 2007: 6). Second, a new comprehensive investment accord would reduce the complexity of the current regime, which consists of a vast number of sectoral, bilateral and regional foreign investment agreements (Dolzer and Stevens 1995) therefore providing greater stability, uniformity and predictability for both investors and host states.

In total, the existing regime governing international investment consists of more than 2,300 bilateral investment treaties (BITs), 2,500 double taxation treaties, 200 regional co-operation arrangements and 500 multilateral conventions and instruments for cross-border investment flows (UNCTAD 2005: xix). Some of these treaties are linked to private and public arbitration systems, allowing investors to take disputes directly to international arbitration. Host states also use a range of different policy instruments to regulate foreign investment, including pre- and post-admission restrictions and incentives to attract foreign investors (Kurtz 2002: 724). Investment agreement proponents therefore advocate the establishment of a comprehensive multilateral investment agreement in order to reduce the complexity in the current investment regime, promote investment flows and accelerate economic development in LDCs.

In contrast, opponents of a multilateral foreign investment regime, which include a large number of reformist and radical NGOs and larger developing nations such as India, point out that there is no automatic link between investment and economic growth. They contend that a range of factors such as political stability, market access and appropriate governance and economic management are important for facilitating economic growth. But they do concede that the current system, in which BITs dominate and states compete against each other to attract investment by offering tax incentives and other benefits is also not ideal. Competition for foreign investment, especially among developing countries, is said to result in a 'race to the bottom', whereby states lower their regulatory standards in areas such as labour standards and the environment to attract investors. But in establishing 'one size fits all' multilateral investment rules, opponents are concerned that national governments may lose control over certain sectors deemed vital for ensuring stable and sustainable economic growth, such as transport and energy. This would lead to greater volatility and instability in developing and newly industrializing countries (Kurtz 2002: 725). National interest concerns such as these saw the adoption of a range of discriminatory policies in most of the now highly industrialized nations. These include limits on foreign ownership; performance requirements for exports and local employment; the requirement of joint ventures with domestic firms; infant industry protection; corporate governance requirements (for example, compelling all members of boards of directors to be local citizens); and limits on the voting rights of non-resident foreign shareholders.

Overall, opponents of a multilateral investment agreement are sceptical about the capacity of multilateral investment rules to generate economic growth in poorer nations automatically. They question the motives of powerful states such as the US and EU in supporting such an agreement, given that these nations are primarily sources of foreign investment and developing nations are mostly recipients. Investment agreement opponents consequently viewed the push for a WTO foreign investment accord as a thinly veiled effort to maintain the dominance of rich nations in the global economy to the detriment of LDCs. While both opponents and supporters concur that the current piecemeal investment regime is far from perfect, divisions over the capacity of investment rules to contribute to economic development and the motives of wealthy nations have been the basis of a protracted international debate dating back to the 1940s.

INTERNATIONAL COOPERATION ON THE RULES FOR FOREIGN INVESTMENT

The Growth of BITS

At international discussions about the design of institutions to govern the global economy after the Second World War, the US argued for the inclusion of foreign investment rules at the proposed ITO. This sparked strong opposition from developing countries and the US was subsequently forced to weaken the proposed investment provisions (Wilcox 1949). But in turn, this outcome upset the US business community, which argued that the revised accord favoured host countries (Ostry 2000). Their objections ultimately contributed to the failure of the US Senate to ratify the ITO Charter. The GATT, agreed in place of the ITO, did not include an investment accord. In 1955, GATT member states instead adopted a resolution entitled 'International Investment for Economic Development', which urged all nations to conclude BITs in order to provide protection and security for foreign investors.

During the 1960s BITs proliferated and became the major instruments for governing foreign investment. Most of these treaties included strong investment protection and compensation provisions to discourage host state expropriation (Kurtz 2002: 720). To deal with the growth of BITS, two international agencies linked to the World Bank were created. The International Centre for Settlement of Investment Disputes (ICSID) established in 1966, provides facilities for the conciliation and arbitration of disputes between member states and investors who qualify as nationals of other member countries, though participation in this mechanism is voluntary (World Bank). Much later, in 1988, the Multilateral Investment Guarantee Agency (MIGA) was created to promote FDI in developing countries in order to stimulate economic growth (MIGA). MIGA provides political risk insurance for foreign investments in developing countries; technical assistance to developing nations to improve investment climates and promote investment opportunities; and a dispute mechanism to resolve differences between investors and host states. Through the 1990s and 2000s BITs continued to proliferate due to the limited progress towards a multilateral investment agreement.

Investment and the GATT

During the Tokyo Round of GATT negotiations (1973–79), the US continued its quest to establish foreign investment rules linked to trade but developing countries stood firm in opposition. Similarly the Uruguay Round (1986–93) saw the US propose that a comprehensive investment agreement be adopted. Though developing countries voiced their reluctance at the initial meeting in Punta del Este, Uruguay, a compromise deal was reached in the form of the Trade-Related Investment Measures (TRIMs) Agreement, which imposed performance requirements on an investor *after* entry into a host nation. TRIMs prohibits trade-related investment measures, such as local content requirements, that are inconsistent with the basic provisions of GATT 1994, though this only applies to trade in goods (WTOl). Foreign investment in relation to services was to be dealt with by GATS (currently subject to negotiation as part of the Doha Round). GATS addresses foreign investment in services as one of its four modes of supply of services: that is, the supply of services by a foreign company setting up operations in a host country. With aspects of investment rules contained in both TRIMs and GATS, the WTO was only able to deal with foreign investment in a piecemeal manner, thus reflecting the nature of the international investment regime more broadly.

NAFTA Chapter 11

Perhaps the most significant advance in international cooperation in the area of foreign investment has been the development of the North American Free Trade Agreement (NAFTA) comprising the US, Canada and Mexico, which came into force in 1991. Chapter 11 of NAFTA provides a comprehensive set of foreign investment rules pertaining to investment liberalization and investor protection. For dispute settlement it uses the ICSID and the United Nations International Convention on International Trade Law. Chapter 11 has proved controversial with a number of disputes resulting in the award of compensation to MNCs by governments. One prominent case is that of California-based group Metalclad Corporation, which attempted to open a $US 20 million hazardous waste landfill in the central Mexican state of San Luis Potosí (DePalma 2001). Before it could open, however, the state governor designated the site an ecological reserve. At a NAFTA tribunal, the Mexican government was ordered to pay Metalclad compensation comprising damages, interest and legal fees close to the sum it had invested in the project, though Mexico appealed. A subsequent tribunal upheld the ruling, approving compensation slightly lower than the original amount. Disputes such as these have attracted the attention of public interest NGOs, especially environmental groups such as CIEL, Council of Canadians, Public Citizen and the IISD, which contend that NAFTA rules threaten environmental protection. These NGOs have remained active in monitoring and publicizing the negative impacts of Chapter 11 (and NAFTA in its entirety). NAFTA supporters in contrast have held hopes that Chapter 11 would provide a blueprint for the roll-out of an investment agreement encompassing all nation-states. NAFTA already employs the MFN and non-discrimination principles that underpin WTO trade rules.

The Failure of the MAI at the OECD

Around the time of NAFTA's establishment in 1991, the US proposed that work on a multilateral investment accord begin at the OECD. Given the absence of developing countries at this institution, the US was far more optimistic about the chances for success (Smythe 2003–04: 63). In May 1995 the results of a feasibility study into a Multilateral Agreement on Investment (MAI) were presented to the OECD Council of Ministers. The OECD subsequently announced its decision to develop the MAI within two years. It was to be a free-standing treaty open to all OECD members as well as non-OECD (mostly developing) countries by accession. In content the MAI was similar to NAFTA, with its major objectives being investment liberalization, harmonized rules for FDI and the establishment of dispute settlement procedures (Kurtz 2002).

During the MAI negotiation period, a number of disagreements emerged, which had the effect of dampening the enthusiasm of MAI proponents. There was considerable discord between the US and the EU over the extraterritoriality of the US Cuban Liberty and Democratic Solidarity Act (the Helms-Burton Act), which had come into force during the MAI negotiation period in March 1996.[2] The EU was concerned that the Helms-Burton Act would discriminate against non-US investors operating in Cuba (see Jackson 1997). In an attempt to resolve this issue, the EU filed a complaint at the WTO, though it was eventually resolved in May 1998 through a mutual understanding. Another point of disagreement revolved around the inclusion of cultural industries in the MAI. Canada and France argued that host nations should retain the right to regulate investment to preserve and promote national identity and cultural and linguistic diversity. The US strongly opposed this caveat as its media and entertainment sector constitutes its second largest export industry.

Further to the disagreements among OECD member states, an NGO campaign opposing the MAI emerged in early 1997, which proved to be extremely disruptive (Goodman 2002; Deibert 2003). In February 1997 a draft text of the MAI was leaked and Public Citizen, a prominent US NGO, published the draft on its website. By October 1997 a group of 25 NGOs concerned by the content of the leaked draft (and who had previously taken part in MAI discussions at the OECD) announced their withdrawal from the process. These NGOs stated that the OECD was overly focused on the promotion of business interests at the expense of social and economic justice (Goodman 2002: 217). Their withdrawal strengthened the anti-MAI campaign, with many more NGOs ranging from environmental groups, trade unions, human rights groups, religious organizations and anti-globalization, social movements' activists lending their support. In the US, public opposition to the MAI became associated with the investment chapter of NAFTA and this consolidated support for the campaign among activists.

In May 1997 the OECD Ministerial Council agreed that the MAI negotiations be carried over to the 1998 meeting. But by this time, the disagreements among member states and the pressure generated by the NGO campaign had taken their toll on the support and goodwill of OECD members for the MAI negotiations. Furthermore the Asian financial crisis (which severely impacted the 'miracle' economies of Thailand, Korea, Indonesia, Malaysia and the Philippines) saw some of the affected nations impose conditions on capital outflows in order to stem the financial disaster. Given that the aim of the MAI was to liberalize all investment flows, this response called the wisdom of the MAI into question. The Asian financial crisis thus added to the emergent hostile political and economic atmosphere surrounding the development of the MAI at the OECD.

At the April 1998 OECD ministerial meetings, OECD member states affirmed the progress made towards the MAI, but agreed that a further period of assessment was required for the negotiating parties and their citizens in preparation for an October 1998 meeting. To address the public anxiety over the MAI generated by the NGO campaign, five OECD member nations

(Australia, Canada, France, the UK, and the US) implemented a review of the MAI. The French government's review was highly critical of the MAI both in terms of the negotiating procedures and the substantive content, particularly the inclusion of cultural industries (Lalumiere 1998). As a result, on 14 October 1998, just prior to the OECD ministerial meeting, France withdrew from the negotiations – marking the beginning of the end for the MAI. Less than two months later, the OECD announced that the MAI negotiations were effectively over (OECD).

Efforts to establish multilateral rules for foreign investors at the OECD were thus added to previously unsuccessful attempts to gain international cooperation in this important area of international economic governance. But despite this failure, investment agreement proponents returned their attention to the international trade regime and the WTO as a host arena for foreign investment rules.

FOREIGN INVESTMENT RULES AND THE WTO

The issue of a comprehensive investment agreement has been under discussion at the WTO since the 1996 Singapore meeting. It was introduced then alongside three other issues for WTO members' consideration: transparency in government procurement, trade and competition policy, and trade facilitation. These issues have become collectively known as the Singapore issues or 'new issues' for which the EU, Japan and Canada were the major proponents. For EU member states, in particular the UK and France, one of the motives for a WTO foreign investment agreement over an OECD agreement was the representational advantage of European nations at the WTO, where EU member states not only represent themselves independently, but also have the benefit of regional level representation through the European Commission. EU states also considered that a WTO investment agreement would have more immediate benefit due to the greater number of member states at the WTO over the OECD. The US in contrast was only lukewarm to a WTO investment agreement because of successive disappointments over the issue within GATT and the Uruguay Round, and their view that other international arenas were more amenable to a high standard foreign investment agreement.

Prior to the Singapore Ministerial Conference there had been little consensus about the establishment of a comprehensive investment accord at the WTO with some developing countries (especially India) voicing strong opposition. Others though, like Mexico and Brazil, were initially supportive. In mid-October 1996 (two months before the conference) the WTO secretariat released an issues paper entitled 'Trade and Foreign Direct

Investment' in order to assist WTO members evaluate how they might deal with the issue (WTO 1996h). The report examined the costs and benefits of an investment agreement, reviewed the bilateral and regional agreements currently in place, and outlined the key policy issues facing WTO members. At the Singapore conference in December 1996, a compromise was eventually reached whereby members agreed on the establishment of a working group (the WGTI) to further discuss the trade-investment relationship. It was stipulated, however, that the creation of the WGTI would 'not prejudice whether negotiations will be initiated in the future' (WTO 1996g). Even so, investment proponents viewed this development as a first step towards building consensus on the issue and beginning negotiations. Those opposed saw the WGTI as a way to stall the issue while appearing to have made a compromise.

At the inaugural WGTI meeting in June 1997, members agreed upon the focus areas of their discussions. These were: current international arrangements for foreign investment; gaps in the current regional and bilateral arrangements; the capacity for multilateral rules to provide benefits over current arrangements; the economic relationship between trade and investment; and the impact of a linkage between trade and investment on development and economic growth. Yet, after 18 months of WGTI discussions, the only real areas of consensus that emerged from the meetings related to the potential of FDI to boost economic development and the acknowledgement that international trade and foreign investment are closely linked (Smythe 2003–04: 65). Despite this, in December 1998, the WGTI recommended to the General Council that its work continue on in 1999. Those members that favoured the launch of investment negotiations held hope that some progress would be achieved by mid-1999 that could be taken to the WTO's Seattle Ministerial Conference.

Two competing draft paragraphs on the investment issue for the Seattle Ministerial Declaration emerged in the lead-up to the conference. One, endorsed by the developing countries, simply called for further study on the issue, while the draft put forward by investment proponents led by the EU called for the launch of detailed negotiations as part of the 'Millennium Round' of trade negotiations (WTO 1999f). At the Seattle conference, disagreement over the issue deepened. India was the most vocal opponent, while the US was also opposed stating that the EU was using it as a diversionary tactic to avoid committing to concessions in other areas. Although a leaked draft text states that study into the investment issue would continue with a view to further negotiations, the meeting dramatically collapsed for a host of reasons (see Chapter 4).

During 2000 and 2001, the WGTI met on five occasions and despite the lack of progress achieved, the issue was placed on the 2001 Doha Ministerial

Conference agenda where it emerged as one of the major controversies. At the conference the EU and Japan continued to push for the start of negotiations on investment (WTO 2001d). Unexpectedly, the G-77 developing nations did not staunchly oppose the launch of negotiations on investment, instead focusing on eliminating agricultural subsidies, textile negotiations, reforming anti-dumping and countervailing duties and clarifying the TRIPS safeguards (G-77 2001). Within the G-77 though, there was vocal opposition from India, Malaysia and Pakistan, which maintained their stance that further study on the matter was required before negotiations could possibly begin. In total 22 developing countries issued statements outlining their opposition to the inclusion of the Singapore issues while three developing countries, Mexico, South Korea and Venezuela, supported it (Bailey et al. 2003: 7). The US did not join the investment supporters for a range of reasons including the OECD failure; domestic disputes within US government agencies over bilateral agreements with Singapore and Chile; their preoccupation with the Free Trade Agreement of the Americas (FTAA); and the fact that PI was not included in the proposal for a WTO investment agreement (Kurtz 2002: 774).

Despite the high level of disagreement over investment at Doha, a reference to the start of investment negotiations found its way into the ministerial declaration. The Doha Declaration stated that negotiations on investment (FDI only) along with the other Singapore issues (competition policy, government procurement, and trade facilitation) would begin following the Fifth Ministerial Conference in 2003:

> Recognizing the case for a multilateral framework to secure transparent, stable and predictable conditions for long-term cross-border investment, particularly FDI, that will contribute to the expansion of trade, and the need for enhanced technical assistance and capacity-building in this area as referred to in paragraph 21, we agree that negotiations will take place after the Fifth Session of the Ministerial Conference on the basis of a decision to be taken, by explicit consensus, at that session on modalities of negotiations. (WTO 2001a)

The larger developing countries (and a range of NGOs) were furious that a reference to investment appeared in the Doha Declaration and that their opinions had been ignored. NGOs alleged that the delegations of several developing nations were pressured to accept the reference to investment and the other Singapore issues 'through a combination of stick and carrot methods of "persuasion"' (Tandon 2003: 13). LDCs were offered incentives such as technical assistance while the ACP countries were granted a waiver on the issue of the Cotonou Agreement, which led to a split among developing nations on the investment issue (Tandon 2003: 13).

In response to the investment reference in the Doha Declaration, India and a dozen other countries raised the issue with the Qatari Chairperson, requesting that the text be changed to reflect that consensus was required if investment negotiations were actually to begin. A compromise was reached whereby the declaration would remain but that the chairperson would clarify the position of India and the other members in a formal statement. The chairperson's statement read:

> Let me say that with respect to the reference to an 'explicit consensus' being needed, in these paragraphs, for a decision to be taken at the Fifth Session of the Ministerial Conference, my understanding is that, at that session, decision would indeed need to be taken by explicit consensus, before negotiations on trade and investment and trade and competition policy, transparency in government procurement, and trade facilitation could proceed. In my view, this would also give each member the right to take a position on modalities that would prevent negotiations from proceeding after the Fifth Session of the Ministerial Conference until that member is prepared to join in an explicit consensus. (WTO 2001e)

No objections or reservations from members about this clarification were raised. The WGTI continued to meet during 2002 and 2003, though with a new chairperson, a new checklist of issues to address, and the Cancún Ministerial Conference in September 2003 as the deadline.

Regardless of the Qatari Chairperson's statement, the contest surrounding the Doha mandate and broader concerns about the impact of a WTO investment agreement for developing countries led to the emergence of an international NGO campaign that opposed a WTO investment accord. The campaigners played an important role in harnessing political opportunities to publicize the disadvantages of a WTO investment agreement and mobilize support among LDCs and other NGOs concerned with trade issues. Their actions helped bolster the position of the African Group, the LDC Group and the ACP countries in strongly opposing the issue at the 2003 Cancún Ministerial Conference.

THE NGO CAMPAIGN AGAINST A WTO INVESTMENT AGREEMENT

Sparked by the controversy surrounding the Doha Declaration's reference to the beginning of investment negotiations and the ongoing efforts of pro-investment members within the WGTI, the NGO campaign against a WTO foreign investment agreement was established in late-2002 in preparation for the September 2003 Cancún Ministerial Conference. The NGOs involved were outraged that pro-investment member states had been able to keep investment and the other Singapore issues on the negotiating table in the face of strong opposition from developing nations. The NGOs also highlighted the limited progress achieved on the issues of importance to developing countries such as market access, agricultural barriers, the TRIPS flexibilities and special and differential treatment. Thus NGOs opposed a WTO investment accord because they saw it as antithetical to the development character of the Doha Round and had concerns about the effects of such an agreement on domestic policy flexibility and MNC power in the global economy. Their ultimate goal in waging this campaign was to have investment (and the other Singapore issues) removed from the Doha Development Agenda: '[w]e call on all governments in the discussions ahead to reject the start of negotiations and to remove these issues from the WTO' (TWN 2002).

Key Actors

The anti-investment campaign targeting the WTO comprised religious organizations, development NGOs, environmental groups, economic justice groups, trade unions, research institutes, and agricultural unions. Table 6.1 lists the major international and national NGOs from around the globe that supported the campaign. Among these Oxfam International, TWN, CIEL, IISD, FOEI, Public Services International (PSI), WWF and IAPT were centrally involved in the organization of international workshops and conferences as well as the development of NGO sign-on statements and other campaign documents.

As the number of national NGOs involved in the campaign attests, there was a great deal of regional and national level campaigning against a WTO investment agreement. In the UK in July 2003, WDM launched its 'Cut the corporate out of Cancún' campaign, which opposed negotiations on all of the Singapore issues on the basis that they were contrary to the wishes of EU citizens and developing countries (WDM 2003). At a regional level, European NGOs together targeted European governments and the European Commission – the chief proponent of a WTO foreign investment agreement. In Africa NGOs like the Southern and Eastern African Trade Information and Negotiations Institute (SEATINI) worked with African governments to build unity and mobilize opposition to a WTO investment agreement. At the same time, leading environmental NGOs, for example WWF and IISD, advocated that environmental conditions should be imposed on foreign investors. The anti-investment campaign was also boosted by the related NGO campaign aimed at 'derailing' the Cancún Ministerial Conference entitled 'No deal is better than a bad deal'. These national, regional and international NGOs together sought to publicize the hazards of a potential WTO investment agreement and boost the capacity of developing nations to oppose the issue at Cancún.

Table 6.1   Major international and national NGOs involved in the campaign against a WTO investment agreement

Location	NGO
International	ActionAid
	Greenpeace International
	International Centre for Trade and Sustainable Development (ICTSD)
	International Gender and Trade Network (IGTN)
	International Institute for Sustainable Development (IISD)
	Oxfam International
	Public Services International (PSI)
	Third World Network (TWN)
	World Wide Fund for Nature (WWF)
	World Forum of Fish Harvesters and Fishworkers
Europe	Berne Declaration
	Catholic Agency for Overseas Development (CAFOD)
	Corporate Europe Observatory
	Friends of the Earth, England, Wales and Northern Ireland
	Friends of the Earth, Europe
	Heinrich Böll Foundation
	Our World is Not For Sale (OWINFS)
	Seattle to Brussels – Taking Action Against Corporate Globalization (S2B Network)
	World Economy, Ecology and Development (WEED)
	World Development Movement (WDM)
North America	Alliance for Democracy
	American Lands Alliance
	California Coalition for Fair Trade and Human Rights
	Center for International Environmental Law (CIEL)
	Center of Concern
	Church World Service
	Citizens' Network on Essential Services
	Citizens' Trade Campaign
	Global Exchange
	Institute for Agriculture and Trade Policy (IAPT)
	National Environmental Trust
	Public Citizen's Global Trade Watch
	Sierra Club

Location	NGO
	Union of Needletrade, Industrial and Textile Employees (UNITE)
	United Auto Workers
	United Steelworkers of America
Asia and Oceania	Australian Fair Trade and Investment Network (AFTINET)
	Equations
	Focus on the Global South
	Global Trade Watch (GTW)
	Research Foundation for Science, Technology and Ecology
	Society for Conflict Analysis and Resolution
	Transform India Group
Central and South America	Brazilian Institute for Consumer Defense (IDEC)
	Brazilian Network for People's Integration (REBRIP)
	Caribbean Reference Group on External Relations
	Centre for Consumer Defence of El Salvador
	Centro para la Denfensa del Consumia, El Salvador
	Instituto del Tercer Mundo (ITeM)
	Social Watch, Uruguay
	Solon Foundation, Bolivia
	Third World Institute
Africa	Africa Trade Network
	Congress of South African Trade Unions (COSATU)
	EcoNews Africa, Kenya
	Institute of Economic Affairs
	Kenya National Farmers' Union
	Social Development Network (SodNet)
	Southern and Eastern African Trade, Information and Negotiations Institute (SEATINI)
	Trade Law Centre for Southern Africa (TRALAC)

Building Support: NGO Workshops and Information Dissemination

NGO campaigning on the investment issue got underway in late-2002 and intensified during 2003. The leading NGOs organized a number of conferences and workshops to discuss the investment issue and establish a campaign platform. In mid-September 2002, a group of 40 European NGOs launched their campaign against an investment agreement, issuing a declaration entitled 'Joint statement by European civil society groups against an agreement on investment in the WTO' (S2B Network 2002). It called on the European Commission to drop its proposal to begin investment negotiations at the WTO, requesting instead that the lack of enforceable rules governing the behaviour of MNCs be addressed, not at the WTO, but within the UN. In late September 2002 European NGOs finalized their campaign plans for the Cancún conference at a strategy meeting in Copenhagen, Denmark (FOE Europe 2002).

During 2003 NGOs undertook a range of activities to publicize the negative ramifications of a potential WTO investment agreement and initiate support for the campaign among civil society more generally. At the January 2003 WSF in Porto Alegre, Brazil, CIEL organized a workshop on trade and foreign investment. Through presentations from representatives of CIEL, Oxfam International and the American Lands Alliance, the workshop examined the evolution of the legal framework for FDI, current trends in bilateral and multilateral investment regimes and the challenges involved in the move towards sustainable investment (CIEL 2003a). In March 2003 TWN, Oxfam International, WWF, PSI, CIEL and IATP jointly organized a high-profile conference in Geneva specifically timed to inform the 14–15 April 2003 WGTI meeting. It included an international NGO workshop and a public seminar to which representatives of WTO members and international organizations were invited, as well as academics and other trade experts (CIEL 2003b). The NGO workshop component, 'Briefing and update on WTO negotiations on investment and new issues', dealt with possible future WTO rules on investment and the other Singapore issues. More than 50 NGOs and social movements voiced their concerns about a WTO investment agreement and its impact on development, gender rights, environmental sustainability and labour rights. The workshop consolidated the position of the NGOs on the issue and gave the opportunity to develop a common NGO position to present at the public seminar that followed (Interview, Oxfam International 2006).

In an attempt to influence the discussions at the WTO, the 20 March public seminar, 'The nature and implications of a WTO investment agreement', brought together the key WTO members engaged in the debate. It included presentations from the WTO ambassadors of India, Kenya and Uganda, diplomats representing the EU and the US, and academics and experts on foreign investment issues. At the meeting, the EU representative claimed that its proposal for a WTO investment agreement was 'very modest' and would not limit domestic policy space or prevent governments from regulating investment (TWN 2003a). Taking a different approach, the US representative reiterated the preference of the US for high standard bilateral investment arrangements and pointed out that too much national flexibility in an investment agreement can result in investors attempting to buy influence with a government.

In contrast, the presentations of the developing country ambassadors all argued against beginning negotiations at the WTO, citing the uncertainty surrounding the relationship between trade and investment and the weak capacity of most developing countries to negotiate the issues. The Kenyan Ambassador argued that the sheer enormity of the Doha work programme meant that the resources of LDCs were already strained, while the Indian Ambassador contended that it was uncertain whether a WTO investment agreement would increase investment in a manner that would be beneficial for developing countries (Permanent Mission of India, Geneva 2003). In his presentation, the director of UNCTAD's division on globalization and development strategies, Dr Yilmaz Akyuz, supported developing countries by pointing out that developed nations had employed a number of policies to restrict foreign investment in the past and that 'one size fits all' investment rules at the WTO were inappropriate given the different levels of development of WTO members.

During the meetings, NGOs supported the developing countries by recounting the ongoing difficulties faced by developing countries in implementing existing WTO agreements and pointing to the potential for a WTO investment agreement to impact negatively sustainable development and national policy flexibility. NGOs argued that a WTO investment agreement 'will tilt the balance against the host country governments just as the TRIPS agreement had done in favour of holders of IPRs [intellectual property rights]' (Raja 2003). NGOs also expressed doubts about the adequacy of WTO negotiating procedures and the enforcement of an investment accord through the WTO's DSB. At the conclusion of the meetings, NGOs called upon WTO member governments to abandon the launch of investment negotiations and the other Singapore issues in their joint declaration entitled 'No investment negotiations at the WTO: declaration of non-governmental groups and civil society movements' (CIEL 2003c). Signed by more than 50 NGOs, this statement was released at the media conference following the 21 March public seminar and was sent to all WTO members.

In the months following the March meetings, a number of NGO-organized events were held in Europe and North America. In April 2003 the German NGO, Forum on Environment and Development, organized a conference at which NGOs discussed investment and the other Singapore issues with government representatives including the European Commission's Director-General for Trade, Carlo Pettinato, and German government representatives (Bach 2003). The meeting resulted in NGOs agreeing that foreign investment should be regulated outside the WTO framework in order to harness FDI for economic development. In May 2003 CIEL, with FOE, Oxfam America, National Wildlife Federation, Heinrich Böll Foundation and the Global Development and Environment Institute of Tufts University, organized a conference entitled 'Investment, sustainable development and the WTO: allies or antagonists?' (CIEL 2003d). Held at the Carnegie Endowment for International Peace in Washington DC, a variety of speakers presented a range of views on developing an investment agreement at the WTO. The NGOs also used the WTO's 2003 Public Forum, 'Challenges ahead on the road to Cancún', as an opportunity to question the benefits of a WTO investment agreement. CIEL, TWN, IATP, WWF, PSI, Oxfam International, and the International Gender and Trade Network (IGTN) hosted a session at the forum entitled 'Investment in the WTO? Myths and realities' (WTO 2003a).

To coincide with the final WGTI meeting before Cancún, on 10 June 2003, a group of four NGOs held a media conference in Geneva to voice their concerns about proposals to begin investment negotiations at the WTO (Raja 2003). At the event, ActionAid released its new report *Unlimited Companies*, while three other NGOs, the International Union of Foodworkers, CIEL and TWN explained their opposition to a WTO investment agreement (ActionAid). In July, at a meeting in Italy of European trade ministers at which Europe's position for the WTO's Cancún conference was discussed, over 70 European NGOs demanded that the European Commission drop its push to begin WTO negotiations on the Singapore issues (WDM 2003). A joint NGO statement developed by WDM, Greenpeace, and FOE was presented to the ministers, urging them to put citizens and communities before the rights of MNCs (WDM 2003). Meanwhile in the US, despite the Bush administration's preference for BITS over an investment agreement at the WTO, an NGO sign-on letter was sent to USTR Robert Zoellick and the United States Congressional Oversight Group on Trade Policy. The August 2003 letter, entitled 'Oppose the initiation of investment negotiations within the World Trade Organization', was signed by 32 mostly US-based NGOs (CIEL 2003e).

In addition to hosting workshops and conferences and producing declarations and sign-on statements, NGOs published and disseminated a number of research papers and articles challenging the efficacy of a WTO foreign investment agreement. These included Oxfam's policy paper *The Emperor's New Clothes: Why Rich Countries Want a WTO Investment Agreement*, published in April 2003, FOEI's August 2003 position paper, *No New Rights for Big Business at the WTO* and the UK Trade Network's *Unwanted, Unproductive and Unbalanced: Six Arguments Against an Investment Agreement at the WTO* produced in May 2003. Chang and Green's 2003 paper, *The WTO and Foreign Investment: Don't Do As We Did, Do As We Say* also proved a significant resource for NGO campaigners in articulating their concerns about a WTO investment accord, as did the April special edition of the SEATINI Bulletin devoted to the investment issue. In addition, FOE England, Wales and Northern Ireland and WDM produced the report *Investment and the WTO: Busting the Myths* to counter the EU's arguments for supporting a WTO investment agreement (FOE England, Wales and Northern Ireland and WDM 2003; Lobe 2003).

Throughout the campaign, NGOs monitored and reported on developments on the issue at the WTO, which were important for LDC members and the NGO community. The IISD provided foundation funding for an electronic newsletter devoted to foreign investment issues at all levels of governance (Smythe 2003–4: 74). This was supplemented by regular newsletters and papers such as ICSTD's weekly newsletter, *Bridges*, which is not only a resource for other NGOs, but according to Smythe, is consulted by WTO member negotiators (2003–4: 73–4). TWN, Focus on the Global South, and IATP also provide information services on WTO trade negotiations as well as conduct research and analysis on trade issues. For example TWN publishes the *South–North Development Monitor*, which provides information about and analysis of the formal and informal negotiation processes at the WTO and other international arenas for the benefit of LDC negotiators and NGOs (South–North Development Monitor). These materials are consulted regularly by not only NGOs but also developing country negotiators (Interview, WTO 2006; Smythe 2003–4: 74).

To supplement their claims about the risks of a WTO investment agreement, NGOs successfully sought and used the support of prominent international institutions. They cited the August 2002 recommendation of the UN Sub-Commission on the Promotion and Protection of Human Rights that called for WTO members to ensure that all negotiations on investment respect internationally-agreed environmental, social, labour and human rights standards and promote corporate accountability (United Nations Sub-Commission on the Promotion and Protection of Human Rights 2002). UNCTAD had also been active in monitoring developments at the WTO, and the UK Trade Network drew upon UNCTAD's work as evidence that a liberalized foreign investment regime would be of dubious benefit to LDCs (Bailey et al. 2003: 2; Smythe 2003–4: 73; UNCTAD 1999, 2000a, 2000b). The UK Trade Network also pointed to the World Bank's unenthusiastic assessment of proposed global rules for foreign investment. Their report quotes from the World Bank's report *Global Economic Prospects and the Developing Countries 2003: Investing to Unlock Global Opportunities*, which stated that: 'merely creating new protections does not seem to be strongly associated with increased investment flows. For these reasons, the overall additional stimulus of multilateral rules that apply to new investment over and above unilateral reforms would probably be small – and virtually nonexistent for low-income developing countries' (World Bank 2003 in Bailey et al. 2003: 2). Similarly, Oxfam International's report, *The Emperor's New Clothes*, used World Bank research as evidence that governments require policy flexibility to respond to local conditions and that domestic investors are vitally important to an economy. And FOEI employed a UNDP report, *Making Global Trade Work for People*, which found that there is 'no clear correlation between the volume of foreign direct investment and development success' (FOEI 2003: 3). By incorporating the work of these international organizations into their own research papers, NGOs were able to boost the legitimacy of their claims about an investment agreement at the WTO.

Despite their campaign efforts, NGOs encountered little success in persuading the European Commission to abandon its push for a WTO investment agreement. The European Commission responded with an attempt to re-label its push for a WTO investment agreement as an 'investment for development' initiative. It also proposed that investment negotiations proceed on a 'plurilateral' basis whereby individual members submit a request list of commitments to other members. This offer was condemned by NGOs. NGO campaigners similarly failed to convince the US to actively oppose the negotiation of investment rules within the WTO arena. This was because the Bush administration was seeking an investment agreement with an even higher level of investment protection than was achievable at the WTO and was thus petitioning for BITs with high standards. Though NGOs failed to convince developed members, having worked to publicize the investment issue at a range of international forums and produced a body of research and analysis on the issue, they were well positioned to inform the negotiating stance of developing countries in preparation for the Cancún meeting.

In attempting to unite developing country governments in order to more aggressively and coherently challenge the issue at the WTO, NGOs including TWN, SEATINI, and the South Centre visited the individual WTO missions of a number of developing countries and organized a number of seminars to exchange views and other information on investment rules (CIEL 2003g; Smythe 2003–04: 74). For example, in April 2003 at a workshop run by SEATINI in Arusha, Tanzania, NGOs urged African policymakers and negotiators from Angola, Kenya, Lesotho, Malawi, Mozambique, Tanzania, Uganda, Zambia and Zimbabwe to oppose the launch of negotiations on the Singapore issues (SEATINI 2003). In their negotiating strategy recommendations for Cancún, these states agreed that 'African countries should take a position that the Cancún meeting decide that negotiations on the four issues should not begin. African countries should take the position that instead of starting negotiations, the process of clarification of issues (for each of the issues) should continue in the respective working groups' (SEATINI 2003). During May and June 2003, opposition to investment was further consolidated at a number of meetings of developing countries. In late May 2003 the ministers of trade from Eastern and Southern Africa met in Nairobi, Kenya, to discuss trade issues including the Singapore issues in preparation for Cancún. In June 2003 the trade ministers of the African Union meeting in Mauritius and the LDC trade ministers meeting in Bangladesh both called for the continuation of the study process on a foreign investment agreement rather than beginning negotiations (Ministers of Trade of the Member States of the African Union 2003; LDC Trade Ministers 2003).

On the sidelines of these meetings, NGOs actively supported developing countries. At the Bangladesh meeting for example, 150 NGO participants from 13 countries attended the 'International Civil Society Forum' organized by NGOs including the Centre for Policy Dialogue Bangladesh, Consumers International (Malaysia), EU-LDC Network (the Netherlands), Oxfam International, South Asia Watch on Trade, Economics and Environment (SAWTEE, Nepal) and SEATINI. In their declaration the NGO participants called upon LDC ministers 'to insist for a decision to be taken in Cancún that negotiations on investment will not be launched. There is no evidence that an investment agreement would lead to more and better quality FDI, while it would effectively limit governments' flexibility to regulate foreign investment' (Centre for Policy Dialogue 2003a: 28). NGOs additionally sent a letter of support to the LDCs (Centre for Policy Dialogue 2003b).

THE 2003 CANCÚN MINISTERIAL CONFERENCE

In the run-up to the Cancún conference, developing countries stepped up their opposition to a WTO investment agreement and the other Singapore issues at a number of WTO meetings. At the WTO's Trade Negotiations Committee on 2–3 April 2003, both the African Group and the LDCs Group reaffirmed their opposition to the launch of negotiations on these issues (Bailey et al. 2003: 7). The Bangladeshi ambassador stated that the WTO should focus on addressing the problems facing LDCs rather than obsessing over a WTO investment agreement (Bach 2003). In June 2003 developing countries asserted that there were still areas that needed clarification such as the obligations of investors to host countries, issues surrounding technology transfer and the lack of capacity of LDCs. But proponents argued that following the detailed discussions at WGTI, as mandated by the Doha Declaration, the time was approaching to begin negotiations. Costa Rica and South Korea joined Canada in defending the work of the WGTI and urged all WTO members to negotiate on investment (WTO 2003c).

At the July 2003 meeting of the WTO's General Council, a group of 12 developing countries submitted a statement reiterating their argument that the Doha Declaration did not authorize the start of investment negotiations. Despite this, a draft ministerial (with an annex) was released in late August 2003 that contained a bracketed section assuming that investment negotiations would take place post-Cancún. The annex laid out the modalities, which closely reflected those outlined in the position papers of the EU and Japan, which had been fiercely debated at the WGTI. Although another bracketed section reflected the developing countries' position that negotiations would not begin following Cancún, it did not elaborate in equal detail the reasons why many developing countries opposed the issue (Focus on the Global South 2003).

In late August 2003 resentment among developing country governments over the text helped promote the creation of the Group of 20 (G-20), a bloc of developing nations based on promoting agricultural exporting developing countries' interests, headed by Brazil, India, South Africa and China (see Table 2.2). The G-20 raised the issue of the draft text annex at the August meeting of the General Council. In response, the chairperson agreed to prepare a cover letter that acknowledged the extent of the disagreement about the text, though the text itself was not altered (WTO 2003d). Throughout this period, most developed WTO members, notably Canada, the European Commission, Japan and Chinese Taipei, continued to claim that the Doha Declaration provided a mandate to begin investment negotiations. Divisions became so bitter that it got to the point where India, followed by Brazil, Malaysia, and other Asian and African countries questioned the need for a WTO investment agreement at all.

The Cancún Ministerial Conference began on 10 September 2003 and ran for four days before deep divides between the developed and developing nations over the Singapore issues, agriculture, non-agricultural market access, and special and differential treatment resulted in the abandonment of the meeting. For the first three days, the conference focused on reducing barriers to agricultural trade, with the main protagonists being the EU and US on one side, and the G-20 on the other. A grouping of 33 other developing countries also emerged as the Alliance for Special Products and Special Safeguard Mechanism, which championed stronger special and differential elements for developing countries (Khor 2003b). The Group of 90 (G-90) essentially a coalition of the ACP countries, the African Group and LDCs Group (together comprising 64 WTO members) also emerged at the conference to oppose the launch of investment negotiations.[3]

Just as the meetings of OECD ministers in Paris became important strategic and symbolic sites for NGO counter-summits during the anti-MAI campaign, the NGOs accredited to observe the Cancún conference used the opportunity to actively campaign against the launch of investment negotiations. At the conference CIEL distributed a research paper entitled *International Law on Investment: The Minimum Standard of Treatment*, the Heinrich Böll Foundation organized a debate entitled 'Money makes the world go round – the Singapore issues: a WTO agreement for development spurring investments or a 2nd MAI?'. IISD sponsored a seminar entitled 'Investment as if sustainable development really mattered'. The Our World Is Not For Sale (OWINFS) network organized a workshop on BITs and CIEL hosted a workshop entitled 'Impacts of trade and investment liberalization on local communities' (CIELg). NGOs also issued statements supporting the positions of developing countries including the newly formed G-20 and G-90 (Hurrell and Narlikar 2006).

Furthermore NGO resources and expertise resulted in developing WTO members granting NGOs places on their official governmental delegations to the WTO's Cancún Ministerial Conference. The delegations of Bangladesh, India, Nepal, and several African nations included NGO representatives who provided technical and negotiating advice to government delegates (Suleri 2003). The coordinator of SEATINI for instance was granted an official place on Uganda's delegation to the Cancún conference (Rowden 2003). At the conference itself, the presence of NGOs on government delegations gave NGOs a privileged insider status enabling them to further influence national positions, negotiating strategies and gain access to the normally secretive WTO negotiations. The decision of these nations to allow NGOs to form part of their delegations reflected the complementary nature of NGO objectives on trade issues of key concern to developing nations, as well as the technical and strategic assistance that NGOs had provided to developing nations prior to the conference.

The WTO negotiations on the Singapore issues began on the first day of the Cancún conference within the smaller, issue-specific 'green room' meetings from which facilitators reported back to the plenary session. Despite arguments that members with significant interests in certain issues should not facilitate negotiations on those issues (as this may influence the outcome of the negotiations) the Singapore issues group was led by the Canadian international trade minister, a strong supporter of launching the negotiations in these areas. At the meetings, pro- and anti-investment members hardened their positions. During a break in the discussions, for example, the G-90 members agreed that they would stick to their mandate that negotiations on all four Singapore issues should not begin until the EU and the US removed preferential domestic subsidies to allow greater market access for G-90 products (Khor 2003b).

On the second day of the Singapore issues green room meetings, a total of 60 developing members (comprising 30 developing nations plus Bangladesh representing 30 LDCs) sent a letter to the Canadian facilitator and the Mexican chairperson comprehensively outlining their reasons for opposing an investment agreement and the other Singapore issues (Khor 2003b). The letter complained about the process, the lack of 'explicit consensus', raised concerns about the limited negotiating capacity of some developing nations and potential implementation difficulties. They demanded the four Singapore issues be dealt with separately, stating that the investment issue in particular required further clarification. They also offered an alternative wording for the draft ministerial text. According to the South Centre, NGO activities also served to highlight the position of the developing countries:

> [o]utside of the meeting rooms, some of the G-90 ministers called a press briefing in the Convention Centre's press briefing area to reiterate their opposition to the launch of negotiations on Singapore issues. It was at this press briefing that NGOs, led by WDM and Friends of the Earth International (FOEI), distributed t-shirts and badge cords that stated the dictionary meaning of 'explicit consensus' to the press and delegates in order to show support for the G-90's negotiating position on Singapore issues. (2003: 5)

Meanwhile the Canadian facilitator continued to hold intensive consultations within the green room meeting, submitting his draft text to the conference chairperson on day three of the conference.

On day four (13 September), despite the objections of a large number of developing members, a revised draft declaration appeared. This became known as the 'Derbez text' named after the Mexican chairperson Luis Ernesto Derbez (WTO 2003e). The Derbez text maintained the stance that investment negotiations should begin, as supported by the European Commission, Canada and several other developed WTO members. Specifically it stated that a special session of the WGTI be convened to decide the procedural and substantive modalities for negotiations. The Derbez text provided little evidence of compromise on the part of developed nations in regard to agriculture: requests from the G-20 that the US eliminate cotton subsidies, for example, were not met. The frustration and anger of developing country delegates was evident when countless developing country delegates stood to condemn the draft text and the process by which it had been developed (WTO 2003f). An Indian delegate was reported as stating that the revised text had 'arbitrarily disregarded views and concerns expressed by us the developing countries. We wonder now whether development here refers to only further development of the developed countries' (Alpert 2003).

In response to the intense criticism directed at the Derbez text by the G-90 and G-20, chairperson Derbez met with ministers from the US, Europe, Mexico, Brazil, China, India, Malaysia, Kenya and South Africa in an attempt to overcome the impasses before the end of the conference (WTO 2003f). At this point the European Commission displayed some willingness to drop the negotiations on investment as well as competition policy but maintained its support for the other two issues of trade facilitation and government procurement programmes (European Commission 2004). But this concession came too late and the G-90 decided to maintain its opposition to all four issues. At this juncture, Derbez stated that without consensus on the Singapore issues, the ministerial conference was effectively over (WTO 2003g).

During the first half of 2004, developing country ministers from the G-20 and G-90 agreed to set the July General Council meeting as the deadline for getting the entire WTO negotiations back on track. Meanwhile they continued to call for the Singapore issues to be dropped from the Doha agenda. In July 2004 (prior to the WTO General Council meeting) the G-90 held a ministerial meeting in Mauritius for a strategy session on global trade negotiations. Their negotiating platform document stated:

> [w]ith regard to the Singapore issues, the G-90 agrees that the three issues (Trade and Competition Policy; Trade and Investment and Transparency in Government Procurement) should be dropped from the Work Programme. The Alliance also indicates its willingness to favourably consider Trade Facilitation provided that its concerns in this area are substantively addressed and there is a satisfactory balance in the overall framework. (ACP and G-90 2004)

Though Europe had offered a concession on investment and competition policy in the closing hours of the Cancún conference, in 2004, the European Commission reverted to its previous position that the Singapore issues were part of the single undertaking adopted in Doha (European Commission 2004; Khor 2003c). In the meantime the Cairns Group of agriculture exporting nations led by Australia became active in efforts to re-engage the G-20 developing countries by seeking common ground in the area of agricultural reform (DFAT 2004). The resumption of negotiations gave rise to the establishment of the 'Five Interested Parties' consisting of Australia, Brazil, the US, India and the EU (WTOb). In an attempt to clarify and resolve as many differences as possible before the WTO's July meeting, the Five Interested Parties met a number of times at ministerial level, including on the sidelines of the April 2004 OECD Ministerial Council meeting in Paris (DFAT 2004). The APEC nations also lent their strong support to the conclusion of a WTO package in their declaration from Pucon, Chile, in June (APEC 2004).

Throughout the entire period, NGOs continued to campaign for and lobby WTO members to drop the Singapore issues from the Doha agenda. In November 2003 CIEL, Focus on the Global South, IGTN, IATP, PSI, TWN, Oxfam International and WWF wrote to the WTO's General Council chairperson reiterating their opposition to the negotiation of these issues and offering alternative recommendations (CIEL 2003f). In May 2004 a joint NGO meeting was co-organized by TWN, World Council of Churches, Oxfam International, PSI, ICFTU, IAPT and WWF at which NGOs discussed strategies for removing the Singapore issues from the Doha agenda altogether (Trade For People Campaign 2004).

Eventually at the WTO's General Council meeting on 1 August 2004, members approved a revised Doha Development Agenda work programme (WTO 2004). This rescue package, which became known as the 'July package', not only blocked but removed investment and two other Singapore issues (competition policy and transparency in government procurement) from the Doha Round:

> the Council agrees that these issues, mentioned in the Doha Ministerial Declaration in paragraphs 20–22, 23–5 and 26 respectively, will not form part of the Work Program set out in that Declaration and therefore no work towards negotiations on any of these issues will take place within the WTO during the Doha Round. (WTO 2004)

The other Singapore issue of trade facilitation remained on the negotiating table in line with the concession made by the G-90. The removal of three out of four of these issues from the Doha Round, including investment, is seen as a victory not only for developing countries, but the NGOs that campaigned to prevent the WTO from creating a foreign investment accord since late-2002.

CONCLUSION

While NGOs were not entirely pleased with the 2004 July package (they argued that the provisions for liberalization in agriculture and other areas important to developing countries were weak) this does not subtract from their input into the international debate over the launch of a WTO investment agreement both in the lead-up to, and during, the Cancún conference. In waging an intense campaign to generate support for their position on foreign investment rules, the NGOs drew parallels with the previous attempt to enact multilateral foreign investment rules at the OECD. The activities of the NGOs worked to inform and support a large number of developing WTO member states, including both those strongly opposed to the investment issue, such as Brazil and India, and LDCs that were initially uncertain about the potential consequences of such an agreement. By meeting with developing country negotiators at NGO-organized conferences, visiting individual WTO missions, producing numerous reports and analyses into the issue and monitoring developments at the WTO, NGOs helped build consensus among developing countries about the risks of an investment agreement.

At the Cancún conference, NGOs continued to support the position of developing countries by reporting on and denouncing the procedures that led to the development of the draft ministerial declaration text and conducting seminars and workshops on the issue for other NGO observers. Some member governments even invited NGO representatives onto their delegations to the WTO's Cancún Ministerial Conference, an arena in which NGOs are normally excluded. Having united together in the form of the G-90, developing countries were able to put enough pressure on pro-investment states to either make some concessions in other areas important to developing countries (particularly agriculture) or allow the negotiations to collapse. Essentially the developing countries were able to take advantage of the WTO's consensus rules to block the negotiations until they achieved progress on their objectives. Throughout the conference, NGOs monitored and reported on the proceedings lending moral support to the G-90 and G-20. This chapter thus reveals that in addition to their external campaign activities, a crucial aspect of NGO activity in international trade governance is the provision of policy and negotiating advice to LDCs, which can boost their leverage in the WTO arena. This is explored in further detail in the following chapter in which I compare and contrast the three cases of NGO campaigns in order to improve understanding about the roles of NGOs in the international trade regime.

NOTES

1. The 'July package' was the WTO General Council's decision, agreed to on 1 August 2004. It contains frameworks and other agreements designed to advance the negotiations.
2. Title III of the Helms-Burton Act allows US citizens and corporations whose property was expropriated by the Cuban government (dating back to 1 January 1959) to sue for damages against anyone who traffics in their former property after 1 November 1996.
3. There is a cross-membership among these groups. The African Group comprises all 41 African WTO members, the ACP countries comprise 56 WTO members and the LDC group comprises 32 members. See Table 2.2.

7. Understanding the agenda-setting roles of NGOs at the WTO

INTRODUCTION

Each of the preceding case studies – the campaign for WTO labour standards, the access to medicines campaign, and the campaign against a WTO invest-ment agreement – suggest that NGOs play a number of important roles in the agenda-setting phase of the international trade policy process. This chapter draws together these threads in a way that permits NGO campaigns to be assessed in the context of governance-based neoliberal approaches to concep-tualizing the role of NGOs in international trade politics. In doing so I explain that the campaign activities of reformer NGOs on international trade issues more often facilitated, rather than impeded, international trade governance. Through their campaigns, NGOs promote issues often neglected by WTO member states; boost the resources of LDCs; publicize normative dimensions of trade issues; and lend moral support to the negotiating positions of member states. The chapter shows that despite their exclusion from the decision-making floor of the WTO, NGOs are nonetheless important actors in the inter-national trade regime.

The first part of the chapter contends that NGOs publicize issues over-looked (sometimes deliberately) by WTO member states. NGOs instigate debates about the potential consequences of WTO agreements; identify aspects of WTO agreements that require review and refinement; pinpoint implementation problems at the national level; and even identify new policy areas that might be better dealt with by WTO rules. In demonstrating this I focus on the ways in which each set of NGO campaigners used political oppor-tunities to instigate international debate. Opportunities included policy crises; the self-serving activities of industrialized nations and MNCs; national elec-tions; past campaigns; and deficiencies in existing international agreements. These types of opportunities were important first steps for NGOs in lobbying for issues to be placed on the WTO's agenda.

I then go on to examine the major campaign tactics used by NGOs in attempting to mobilize support for their positions among nation-states. These are: promoting consensus among relevant NGOs to project a unified position among civil society; working through the negotiating arenas offered by intergovernmental institutions other than the WTO; enhancing the resources of LDC members; and using ties to influential member states. Where NGO goals resonated with developing countries, they tended to favour the first three tactics. In contrast, the labour campaigners primarily used their links to influential WTO member states and thus placed less emphasis on mobilizing support among NGOs and at international institutions other than the WTO.

While NGO activity supported select groups of nation-states at the WTO (depending upon the issue), it is important to note that they appear to have little input into the ways in which issues are dealt with once on the WTO decision-making table. This reflects the nature of the agenda-setting phase: while decision-making can only take place within the WTO arena, agenda-setting may occur external to formal centres of authority. Moreover agendas can be modified and reshaped to fit national interests or even abandoned altogether during the negotiation phase. Nevertheless there is some evidence emerging that a small number of NGOs are beginning to play insider roles through their participation in official government delegations to WTO ministerial conferences.

The third part of the chapter argues that by publicizing normative aspects of trade issues on human rights, equity and other social issues, NGO activity often complements the instrumental objectives of various member states, thereby having the effect of boosting their negotiating positions. In contrast to the constructivist literature on NGOs in international politics, which focuses on how norms can transform interests, I examine junctions of norms and interests. Indeed, the complementary nature of NGO and state objectives in regard to each campaign issue saw NGOs serve as 'legitimacy enhancers' for particular member states. I find that while NGOs fulfilled this role in all three cases under review in this book, they were constrained to varying degrees by campaign opponents (including other NGOs, states, and business actors), who attempted to mount competing normative rationales on each issue. For the access to medicines and investment cases, these counter-campaigns did little to undermine the claims of NGOs. But in the labour standards case, the arguments of developing countries and NGOs opposing the social clause negatively impacted the human rights rationale put forward by the ICFTU and other labour standards advocates.

In the concluding section of the chapter I contend that the relationships between NGOs and states and the type of policy changes advocated by NGOs are crucial for understanding the agenda-setting roles of reformer NGOs at the WTO. Specifically, the ways in which campaign tactics differed across the cases depended upon the influence and power of WTO members with whom NGOs shared complementary objectives, and whether the campaign goal concerned issues already covered by the WTO (TRIPS and investment) or new issues they wanted to see addressed by the organization (labour standards). I also find that the US domestic political arena was important for the labour standards and medicines campaigners in publicizing their issues. Finally, I explain that even though NGO activity may have the effect of boosting the negotiating positions of WTO member states, NGOs are transnational in character and their activities are substantially independent from states. They should not therefore be merely considered state instruments.

PUBLICIZING 'NEGLECTED' ISSUES: HARNESSING POLITICAL OPPORTUNITIES

The cases reveal that in order to provide impetus for change at the WTO, NGOs strategically employ available political opportunities to construct the campaign 'narrative' in a manner that boosts the international profile of the campaign issue and generates controversy. The most potent opportunities for NGOs include health policy crises; the self-serving activities of industrialized nations and non-state actors (particularly MNCs); the US presidential elections; past NGO campaigns; and the deficiencies of existing international agreements including those administered by institutions other than the WTO. The ways in which NGOs harnessed these opportunities is outlined in detail below. I argue that while the medicines and anti-investment NGOs were able to create, and use these types of opportunities as leverage to project their campaign issues as pressing problems, the labour standards campaigners had fewer opportunities. This reflects the greater difficulties involved in persuading WTO members to take on a new issue rather than modifying or removing an existing agreement.

Policy Crises

For the medicines campaigners, a significant political opportunity was the HIV epidemic that emerged in the 1980s. Essentially a health policy crisis, the HIV epidemic provided campaigners with an illustration of the consequences of stringent IP rights in the face of national health emergencies. NGOs argued that the TRIPS agreement was exacerbating the suffering of those affected by the disease who could not afford patented anti-retroviral medication. The existence of the HIV crisis thus contributed to the sense of urgency generated by the NGO campaigners, enabling the NGOs to portray the clarification of the TRIPS safeguards as a matter of 'life and death', an effectual strategy for NGOs (see Keck and Sikkink 1998). Additionally, the focus on the HIV epidemic had the impact of drawing a number of additional organizations into the campaign network. These included groups fighting for the rights of people with HIV, such as the international group ACT UP and local NGOs in developing nations such as the Thai Coalition on HIV/AIDS. The focus on HIV thereby served not only as an opportunity to highlight the urgency of the issue, but to encourage a broader range of NGOs not normally engaged with trade issues to become involved.

Self-serving Activities of Industrialized Nations and MNCs

The pharmaceutical companies' legal action against the South African government over its patent law amendment served not only as a catalyst for the access to medicines campaign, but provided a ready illustration of how the WTO's TRIPS agreement, without clearly defined safeguards, permits pharmaceutical patent owners to seek limits on the production of affordable generic medicines in developing countries. The initiation of legal action allowed NGOs to argue that research-based pharmaceutical companies (backed by the governments of wealthy nations in which many of their headquarters are based) were using the legal ambiguity surrounding the TRIPS safeguards for their own economic benefit. NGOs argued that this behaviour was resulting in countless deaths from diseases such as HIV. Thus the medicines campaigners were able to turn the case into a public relations disaster for the MNC plaintiffs, which culminated in the withdrawal of their case against the South African government in 2000.

The subsequent initiation of dispute proceedings by the US government against Brazil at the WTO in early 2001 provided the medicines campaigners an opportunity to directly pinpoint the role of the US in pressuring developing countries and its allegiances to the research-based pharmaceutical companies. A sustained campaign against the US government's WTO action against Brazil and the eventual decision of the US government to withdraw these proceedings added weight to the NGOs' claims. In a similar fashion, the letter from Europe's Trade Commissioner to then South African Vice-President Mbeki in which the EU requested that South Africa repeal its amendment because it disadvantaged European firms was also publicized by the NGOs. Furthermore, the events of 9/11 and the subsequent bio-terror threats against the US undermined their hard line stance on TRIPS compliance and bolstered NGO claims that the US had long employed compulsory licensing as a tool to lower the price of medicines and other goods. Put simply, the legal proceedings and pressure tactics mounted against developed countries, giving the NGOs an advantage in contending that the TRIPS agreement reduced equitable access to medicines with 'life and death' consequences and therefore required review and modification.

For the investment campaigners, the manner in which most industrialized nations had previously dealt with foreign investment represented a political opportunity to highlight the potential unfairness of a multilateral investment agreement for developing nations. Most developed nations had in the past imposed a range of conditions on investors to generate economic growth and development. As Chang and Green state,

> [h]istory also shows that a strategic and flexible approach is essential if countries are to use foreign investment to pursue long-term national interests. Rather than sticking to one rigid recipe, most successful economies have changed their policies towards foreign investment according to changes in their stages of development, national priorities, and the world economic environment. (2003: 36)

The historical use of conservative policies towards foreign investment gave NGO campaigners leverage to accuse pro-investment WTO members of adopting double standards and 'historical amnesia' towards developing countries over investment liberalization and economic development (Bailey et al. 2003).

As the access to medicines NGOs did in relation to research-based pharmaceutical companies, the anti-investment campaigners drew upon existing concerns among NGOs and the general public about unrestrained corporate globalization and its adverse effects on local communities and developing nations. They pinpointed MNCs as the major beneficiaries of an investment agreement, proclaiming that MNCs would exploit developing nations and, instead of boosting developing country economies, redirect profits back to their home countries. They also contended that a multilateral investment regime might promote financial instability in developing countries like that witnessed during the 1994 crisis in Mexico and the Asian economic meltdown in 1997.

In highlighting these issues, NGOs drew upon fears about unaccountable global corporations, arguing that a multilateral investment accord would grant MNCs too much power in the global economy at the expense of developing states. In their joint statement announcing the campaign, for example, the leading NGOs proclaimed that a WTO investment agreement 'will create a corporate bill of rights that will fundamentally favour multinational corporations while at the same time eviscerating the ability of governments to regulate foreign investment' (Oxfam International 2003). NGOs also argued that discussions on foreign investment among WTO members failed to mention the obligations of MNCs to host nations. They rejected the notion that MNCs will operate in a socially and environmentally responsible manner in the absence of government regulation (Bailey et al. 2003: 5).

US Presidential Elections

America's presidential elections in 2000 provided an important opportunity for both the medicines and labour standards campaigners to employ shaming tactics against the US government to publicize their issues. As Thomas Risse explains, shaming tactics remind 'national governments of their own standards of appropriateness and collective identities and demand that they live up to these norms' (2002: 268; see also Keck and Sikkink 1998: 23–4). But as this study demonstrates, shaming tactics must not only resonate with the supposed ideals of target actors but involve real costs, such as the US presidential elections or threats to reputation (and thus future profits) for MNCs. Given the intense media scrutiny of presidential candidates in the US, NGOs were well placed to have their complaints about the Clinton administration's actions on international trade issues acted upon.

In the lead-up to the 2000 presidential elections, the medicines campaigners highlighted the support of the US government for the MNCs that took legal action against South Africa, and the direct role of the US in challenging developing states through the WTO's dispute process. As Vice President and the Democratic Party's presidential candidate in the 2000 elections, Al Gore was vulnerable to the accusations of HIV protesters and other access to medicines campaigners who hijacked several of his presidential campaign rallies. Gore was particularly susceptible to NGO pressure due to his close links with prominent figures in the pharmaceutical industry such as Tony Podesta, a top Gore advisor and PhRMA lobbyist, his acceptance of campaign funds from this industry, and his role in authorizing trade sanctions against South Africa and other developing WTO members employing TRIPS safeguard measures (see ACT UP New York 1999). NGO pressure threatened to compromise Gore's bid for the presidency by putting key allies offside, including the Congressional Black Caucus. In their defence, Gore and the Clinton administration reiterated economic arguments stating that IP rights are necessary to encourage innovation in medical technology. But this argument was ineffective against NGO claims of millions of deaths in developing nations from a range of treatable diseases. Having been implicated in the court action in South Africa, Clinton was forced to make a statement and issue an Executive Order declaring that the US would not penalize sub-Saharan African nations for using the TRIPS safeguards in order to retain key Democratic supporters to boost Gore's bid for the presidency (see Clinton 2000).

For the labour standards campaigners, the 2000 presidential elections were important in providing the AFL-CIO (an ICFTU affiliate) leverage over the Clinton administration's position on labour standards for the Seattle Ministerial Conference. From the start of his presidency, Clinton had a troubled relationship with US labour unions. Although NAFTA had been instigated by President George H.W. Bush, on assuming the presidency Clinton endorsed the NAFTA treaty, which proved an unpopular move with labour unions, (Stigliani 2000: 177–94; O'Brien et al. 2000). Clinton attempted to pacify the labour unions by implementing a NAFTA side agreement on labour standards but this was viewed as insufficient due to its weak sanctions. With the establishment of the WTO in 1995, Clinton was careful not to put the rela-tionship with trade unions at further risk: the AFL-CIO was granted opportu-nities to provide input into the US negotiating position. By the late 1990s, the looming presidential election motivated Clinton to further engage the support of labour, historically one the Democratic Party's strongest supporting groups, in order to keep his party in power at the White House (Haworth and Hughes 2004: 132). This meant that the AFL-CIO was well placed to inform the US position on a WTO social clause at the Seattle Ministerial Conference. Held less than 12 months prior to the elections, press accounts claimed that the AFL-CIO played an influential role at this meeting (Nyhan 1999a; Nyhan 1999b; Stigliani 2000: 190). In the *Seattle Post-Intelligencer* for instance, Nyhan wrote that 'the events represented one of the labor movement's most successful efforts to help shape the Clinton administration's trade agenda' (Nyhan 1999b).

Past NGO Campaigns

While the medicines campaigners had a number of unfolding political oppor-tunities available to them, the NGOs contesting the establishment of a WTO investment agreement drew upon prior NGO campaign events to illustrate the potentially adverse effects of a WTO investment accord, notably the mid-1990s campaign against the MAI at the OECD. The anti-MAI campaign was a prominent, 'watershed' NGO campaign, being one of the first to employ the internet as a tool to mobilize domestic opposition to pressure individual OECD governments (Lalumiere 1998; Deibert 2003). Drawing upon the success of this campaign, NGOs argued that the EU and other pro-investment agreement states were simply attempting to resurrect the failed MAI at the WTO. NGOs were able to revive opposition to a multilateral investment agreement within civil society and draw upon the research and analysis already conducted and apply it to the newest attempt for an investment agree-ment at the WTO. The previous anti-MAI campaign thus created conditions conducive for a concerted push at the WTO. It enabled key NGOs to reinvig-orate support among a wider group of NGOs for what is a complex economic policy issue. This in turn allowed NGOs to present a unified opposing position on the issue. The NGO campaign against the OECD's MAI was thus a major opportunity for the NGOs in opposing a similar investment agreement at the WTO.

Deficiencies in Existing International Agreements

Deficiencies in existing international WTO agreements and those adminis-tered by other intergovernmental organizations presented campaigning opportunities for NGOs. For the anti-investment NGOs, the WTO's over-crowded agenda, the associated ongoing implementation difficulties faced by developing members, the Doha 'mandate' to begin investment negotiations, and the long-running controversy surrounding the investment chapter of NAFTA were significant in this respect. They served the NGOs to demonstrate the potential costs of instituting an international investment agreement at the WTO in regard to investor-state dispute resolution. The investment chapter of NAFTA, for instance, has attracted a great deal of attention from North American NGOs, especially the system of arbitration whereby the award of compensation from host countries to MNCs has been said to pose financial burden for governments, particularly Mexico. The NGOs drew parallels with the WTO's DSB arguing that developing countries would come off 'second best' in investor-state dispute hearings, forcing them to compensate MNCs and/or other investors from wealthy nations. The NAFTA example thus allowed NGOs to emphasize that developing countries would lose some of their domestic policy autonomy to an international body said to be weighted towards the interests of wealthy countries and their MNCs. As stated in Oxfam International's report, '[r]ich countries will continue to use their power in this institution [the WTO] to promote the rights of investors, at the expense of developing countries' interests' (Oxfam 2003: 3). In publicizing the most contentious issues surrounding NAFTA, NGOs had a strong basis upon which to contest the issue at the WTO.

The ambitious nature of the Doha agenda and its characterization as a 'development' round of trade negotiations formed an important component of the NGOs' narrative about a potential WTO investment accord. NGOs drew attention to the fact that the number of issues to be dealt with in the Doha round was overwhelming for developing countries in terms of the resources required to negotiate effectively. In fact, many were already struggling to implement commitments made during the Uruguay Round, such as those relating to IP, textiles and agriculture. Though some attempts were made to increase the negotiating capacity of LDCs at the WTO through the provision of technical assistance, many events and programmes were not simply aimed at improving outcomes for developing countries, but directed at getting these nations to agree to begin negotiations on investment and the other Singapore issues. Critics such as SEATINI for example, point to the biases of WTO assistance programmes in seeking to ensure that developing countries comply with WTO accords. In response to hesitation on the part of LDCs to support a WTO investment accord, pro-investment states embarked upon an 'aggressive program of technical assistance and capacity building largely designed to overcome this reluctance' (Smythe 2003–04: 62).

NGOs used the controversy surrounding the 'mandate' in the text of the Doha Declaration (to launch investment negotiations) as a point of leverage. It

provided further ammunition in attacking the proponents of a WTO investment framework on the basis of the undemocratic process that had allowed
events to unfold in this manner. NGOs also pointed out that several of the
previous commitments made by wealthy nations to reduce barriers to trade in
agriculture and manufacturing, which would boost the trade balance of developing countries, were yet to be implemented. To add insult to injury, developed nations were continuing to use agriculture as a bargaining chip to extract
an increasing number of commitments from developing nations.

As well as using the US presidential elections, the ICFTU and its campaign
supporters attempted to use the enforcement deficiencies of an existing international institution – the ILO – as an opportunity to incorporate labour standards into the WTO framework. In making their case, the ICFTU and
supporters depicted a social clause at the newly established WTO as the solution to the relative weaknesses of the ILO in enforcing its conventions. Having
lobbied for a labour clause linked to international trade for several decades, the
WTO presented the ICFTU in 1995 with a new, permanent international institution with the potential to enforce core labour standards.

But rather than being received as a logical solution for upholding workers'
rights internationally, the ICFTU's push for the WTO to enforce labour standards created discord within the international community. It spearheaded a
debate about the appropriate institutional home for labour standards, which led
social clause opponents to argue that labour standards issues should remain the
exclusive domain of the ILO. While the ICFTU attempted to portray the ILO's
lack of enforcement capacity as a policy failure (and the WTO's new arena as
a new enforcement opportunity) there was an insufficient sense of urgency
surrounding this issue. It instead sparked a debate about the appropriate international arena for labour issues, thereby questioning the very basis of the
campaign push for the WTO to become involved in policing the issue.

Assessing NGO Political Opportunism in the WTO Context

The above section has showed that NGO campaigns that target the WTO
employ a number of different types of political opportunities to promote their
causes and provoke debate among WTO member states. Of particular importance is the way in which NGOs seek to depict certain activities of wealthy
WTO member states and MNCs as purely self-interested and concomitantly
detrimental to LDCs and their citizens. This type of political opportunity was
significant for both the investment and medicines campaigners, who alleged
that powerful nations and MNCs sought to implement WTO rules for their
own economic advantage with little regard for the weak and poor. Two other
types of opportunities proved especially valuable for NGOs in illustrating their
arguments about real and potential consequences of WTO accords. These were

policy crises and previous NGOs campaigns. For the NGO medicines campaigners, the HIV epidemic, an acute health policy crisis, was helpful in broadcasting the urgency of the TRIPS safeguards issues. Likewise the previous campaign against an investment accord at the OECD assisted the anti-investment NGOs in illustrating the risks of a WTO investment accord.

The cases also show that deficiencies in existing international agreements can aid NGO campaigners but that this can be a complicated message to propagate. For the anti-investment campaigners, NAFTA and the over-stretched Doha agenda served as a useful illustrative tool. In contrast the emphasis of the labour campaigners on the appropriate institutional setting for the development and enforcement of labour standards only led to a protracted debate that added to the difficulties, and deflated the urgency of addressing this regulatory issue at the WTO.

A political opportunity that was relevant to both the labour and medicines campaigners was the 2000 US presidential elections. These cases revealed that the 2000 presidential elections provided NGOs with some leverage over the US position on trade issues, mainly due to the need for presidential candidates to avoid negative publicity. The Clinton administration's decision to review its policy in relation to the TRIPS safeguards, brought about by activists' pressure, had an impact on the TRIPS and public health issue at the international level. And the Democratic Party's efforts to re-engage the support of labour unions to maintain power in the White House allowed the AFL-CIO an opportunity to influence the US position on a social clause. By working through domestic political arenas in powerful states like the US, NGOs are afforded an opportunity to influence negotiations at the WTO.

While it is important to note that NGOs cannot affect the types of political conditions that exist at the outset of their campaigns, all three sets of NGO campaigners attempted to strategically use a range of available political opportunities to publicize the controversial aspects of each issue and legitimize their campaign goals. Political opportunities that involved shaming powerful actors were most significant while efforts to highlight deficiencies in existing international agreements were shown to be problematic. All three NGO campaigns nevertheless managed to instigate international debate among WTO member states about their cause and thus create momentum for the WTO to address their issues at ministerial conferences.

MOBILIZING SUPPORT: NGO CAMPAIGN TACTICS

Having stimulated controversy and international debate about their campaign issues through strategic use of political opportunities, I now examine NGO efforts to generate support for their campaign goals and engage WTO member states on key issues. Their strategies included hosting international meetings and workshops; issuing public statements to attract media attention; monitoring developments at the WTO; producing research and analysis; and promoting campaign issues at policy-relevant international institutions other than the WTO. In employing such tactics, the medicines and anti-investment campaigners were able to de-legitimize opposition to their goals while the labour standards campaigners encountered difficulties. The ICFTU alienated many NGOs in developing countries (including several of its own affiliates), not to mention a majority of developing country governments. Below I explain how each of the NGO campaigns built upon their use of political opportunities to mobilize support for their issues among the NGO community and WTO members, beginning with the medicines case. In doing so I show that NGOs play roles in the agenda-setting phase of WTO policy processes via their support for the negotiating positions of member states.

The Medicines Campaign

From 1999 through to 2001, numerous NGO-sponsored meetings and press releases helped spearhead the international campaign on TRIPS and public health, stimulating a wider debate among states about the need to clarify the safeguard measures at the WTO. For example, in March 1999, MSF, CPTech and HAI sponsored a series of international meetings to discuss the use of compulsory licensing as a policy instrument for increasing access to essential medicines in developing nations. These high-profile meetings involved not only NGOs but also representatives of a range of governments, research-based and generic pharmaceutical companies, and the WTO and WHO. A November 1999 Amsterdam NGO statement went on to propose a WTO working group on TRIPS and public health issues and offered other solutions for dealing with the ambiguity surrounding the use of TRIPS safeguards. Throughout the course of the campaign NGOs held a number of these conferences, which provided alternative arenas for the key actors to debate the TRIPS and public health issue. NGO-organized meetings and press statements also allowed NGOs to demonstrate their support for developing WTO members and inform the discussions among WTO member states.

NGOs sought to generate further support for the TRIPS safeguards issue to be dealt with at the WTO by working through international institutions such as the WHO, and several other UN organizations where they enjoy a higher status than at the WTO. At the WHO, NGOs used the WHA session on revising the WHO's drug strategy to publicize the access to medicines issue. In seeking to expand the list of essential medicines, NGOs drew attention to the needs of those in developing nations and their struggle to access medicines and treatment in the face of WTO IP rules. NGO input at the WHO spurred the organization to become involved in the TRIPS safeguards issue; it subsequently provided legal and technical advice to developing nations on maintaining affordable access to medicines in the face of TRIPS obligations (WHO 2001). As a result, the actions of the WHO put pressure on wealthy WTO members to discuss the clarification of the TRIPS safeguards and the WHO became an observer on the WTO's TRIPS Council. This was an important step in increasing the profile of health issues at the WTO.

The debate subsequently spread to other international institutions, with the UN General Assembly, UNCHR, UNAIDS, and the World Bank weighing in on the issue. This in turn generated more publicity. UNGASS addressed the link between HIV, TRIPS, and access to medicines at their June 2001 meeting on HIV in New York. The UNCHR issued resolutions in 2000 and 2001 warning about the impact of TRIPS on human rights; UNAIDS discussed the link between health crises such as HIV and TRIPS implementation; and the World Bank stated its support for the use of compulsory licensing and parallel importing to maintain access to affordable medicines in developing countries. Overall the increasing number of international organizations that contributed to the debate not only strengthened the claims made by NGOs, but heightened the immediacy of the crisis and put pressure on the WTO to openly address the issue in 2001.

In seeking to have the TRIPS safeguards issue favourably addressed at the Doha Ministerial Conference, NGOs played a role in informing the negotiation strategy adopted by the African Group of nations. By providing information services, finances and technical advice, the NGOs helped developing WTO members to unify and consolidate their negotiating positions, boosting their standing inside the WTO. Specifically, NGOs assisted developing countries to frame their demands in terms of what they considered realistically achievable at the WTO. NGOs helped reshape the broad debate about the inequality of access to medicines to a more narrow focus upon the appropriate legal interpretation of the TRIPS safeguard provisions. With NGO assistance, the developing countries 'articulated concerns that were specific, and sought remedial measures. This was not a request for the initiation of a vaguely chartered "work program"' (Abbott 2002: 482). NGOs also encouraged developing countries to insist upon a WTO ministerial declaration to clarify the use of TRIPS safeguards at the TRIPS Council meetings (Shadlen 2004: 94). Their demands resulted in the Doha Declaration on TRIPS and Public Health.

One of the most significant aspects of the NGO role in informing the negotiating positions of developing states was their contribution to papers for the TRIPS Council meetings and the draft ministerial declaration text proposed by developing countries. For example, the lead paper submitted by 71 developing nations at the first TRIPS Council Special Session entitled, 'TRIPS and Public Health', reiterated the concerns raised by NGOs at the WHO, UN General

Assembly and the UNCHR (Abbott 2002: 482). Alongside TRIPS Council meetings, NGOs issued their own public statements that supported the position of the developing countries. On top of this, NGOs helped devise portions of what became the WTO's Declaration on TRIPS and Public Health (Sell 2002: 512). According to one NGO website, '[m]eetings at Quaker House Geneva have allowed developing countries to consolidate their positions and draft portions of the so-called Doha declaration' (Quakers in Britain). As a WTO representative contended, NGOs made a significant contribution in the agenda-setting phase leading up to the development of the Doha Declaration on TRIPS and Public Health, which ultimately incorporated a great many of their demands (Interview, WTO 2006).

The Investment Campaign

In preparation for the Cancún Ministerial Conference, the high-profile NGO workshops and conferences dedicated to investment brought a range of different NGOs together to discuss campaign strategies and generated opposition to a WTO investment agreement among member states. A number of NGO sign-on statements, letters and declarations, such as 'No investment negotiations at the WTO: declaration of non-governmental groups and civil society movements', were produced and disseminated around the world encouraging an increasing number of NGOs to lend their support. A number of research papers on the matter were also produced such as the UK Trade Network's May 2003 report *Unwanted, Unproductive and Unbalanced: Six Arguments Against an Investment Agreement at the WTO*. Distributed among NGOs and WTO member governments, these reports combined with the NGOs' conferences, workshops and other public statements to highlight the issues surrounding a potential WTO investment agreement and support developing country governments in opposing the issue at the WTO.

Among the international conferences organized by NGOs on the investment issue, the March 2003 seminar series was especially important for NGOs in supplementing the negotiating resources of developing countries. These seminars, which brought together the major voices in the debate including representatives of the US, EU, developing countries and international organizations, were important for informing and consolidating the positions of developing and under-developed nations. With strong arguments being made by NGOs, international organizations such as UNCTAD and the UNCHR and larger developing countries, many LDCs were persuaded to support the idea that a WTO investment agreement would adversely affect their interests. As a representative of Oxfam International explained, some developing WTO members were initially uncertain about the pitfalls of an investment agreement, but the Geneva meetings and numerous NGO research papers persuaded many of them to oppose the issue and present a unified position at Cancún (Interview, Oxfam International 2006).

In mobilizing support for their interpretation of the negative aspects of a WTO investment agreement, the NGOs used the work of prominent international organizations. The UNDP, UNCTAD, UNCHR and World Bank had already conducted their own research into the matter and had found that a WTO investment agreement would likely not deliver any substantial benefits to developing countries. NGOs drew upon this research and expertise to boost the credibility of their arguments about the potential risks for developing countries of liberalized international investment rules. NGOs received further support from UNCTAD's Dr Yilmaz Akyuz (director of the division on globalization and development strategies and chief economist) and Bhagirath Lal Das (UNCTAD's former director of international trade programmes). Drawing upon all of these sources in their campaign pitch, NGOs informed the position of developing countries, which subsequently declared their strong opposition to a WTO investment agreement. Prior to Cancún, trade ministers from Eastern and Southern African nations, the African Union and the LDC Group all declared their opposition to launching a WTO investment agreement and called for the study process to continue instead.

Having publicized their opposition to instituting an investment accord at the WTO and encouraged many LDCs to oppose it on the grounds that it would run counter to their national interests, the NGOs played an important role in enhancing the resources of developing states to contest the issue at the WTO. The major way in which they did so was as information providers. NGOs reported developments at the WTO in their regular newsletters and online material. IISD, ICTSD, TWN, IAPT and Focus on the Global South were most prolific in this regard. In the run-up to the Cancún conference, NGOs made a number of visits to individual WTO missions (including Brazil and South Africa) to exchange views and other information on the investment issue (CIEL). Groups such as TWN, SEATINI and the South Centre helped facilitate meetings between developing WTO members to generate consensus and build unity. These meetings allowed NGOs to contribute to the negotiating strategy for opposing the launch of investment negotiations at the Cancún conference (Symthe 2003–04: 74). This occurred at the April 2003 SEATINI workshop where NGOs urged African negotiators to oppose the launch of negotiations on all of the Singapore issues. NGO lobbying and information provision resulted in the participating nations developing a declaration of recommendations outlining their opposition to the investment issue and a clear negotiating strategy to take to the Cancún ministerial (SEATINI 2003).

NGO expertise also resulted in developing WTO members granting NGOs an official place on their government delegations to the Cancún conference. The official delegations of Bangladesh, India, Nepal, and several African nations included NGO representatives, which provided technical and negotiating advice to government delegates (Suleri 2003). The coordinator of SEATINI for example was granted an official place on Uganda's delegation to the Cancún conference (Rowden 2003). At the conference itself, the presence of NGOs on official government delegations gave NGOs a privileged insider status, enabling them to further influence national positions, negotiating strategies and gain access to the normally secretive WTO negotiations. The decision of these nations to allow NGOs to form part of their delegations reflected the complementary nature of NGO objectives on trade issues of key concern to developing nations, as well as the level of technical and strategic assistance that NGOs provided to developing nations prior to the conference.

At the Cancún meeting in September 2003, NGOs boosted the position of developing countries both inside and outside the conference. The almost unanimous denunciations of the draft text by NGOs and activists that organized street demonstrations gave psychological support to LDC government officials (Rowden 2003). Inside the conference venue, NGOs that had been accredited to observe the Cancún meeting distributed research papers, organized debates, seminars and workshops, and issued statements supporting the positions of developing countries including the newly formed G-20 and G-90. The NGOs that were part of official government delegations provided LDC negotiators with technical support and advice.

A number of participants and commentators have pointed to the evolution in relations between NGOs and developing countries at Cancún. The Brazilian minister of external relations, Celso Amorim, for example, stated that developing nations were able to hold firm to their positions due to the NGOs' work in assisting government delegations (Amorim in Delgado and Soares 2005: 21). Similarly, a representative of the Australian Bureau of Agricultural and Resource Economics (an Australian government economic research agency) compared the increasing involvement of NGOs in the negotiations and the evolving 'style of interaction' between NGOs and WTO members to that in place at UN agencies (Fisher in The Parliament of the Commonwealth of Australia 2004, 11–12). Moreover, European Commission negotiator Franz Fischler *blamed* NGOs for encouraging developing nations to 'thwart progress' on the negotiations. Fischler told the press that the failure of the meeting 'was led partly by NGOs, they conveyed the message to developing countries that no deal was better than a bad deal' (Smith 2003). David Hartridge, a trade law consultant and former acting WTO director-general contended that 'the ACP countries were very badly advised to be so intransigent over the Singapore issues … Some NGOs, including some of those who celebrated the breakdown, were very close to this negotiation, much closer than I have ever seen before' (2003). In response to such comments, CAFOD stated that if NGOs (both Northern and Southern) had influenced the Cancún breakdown, 'officials and politicians would do well to reflect why, despite their limited political clout and research budgets, NGO arguments have resonated so strongly with developing countries' own experience' (2003).

NGOs thus played a significant role in supporting developing WTO members at the Cancún meeting. NGO input informed the decision of LDCs to stake progress at Cancún on preventing the launch of investment negotiations. They eventually achieved their objectives in overseeing the removal of investment from the Doha agenda in July 2004. Had the NGOs not got involved in campaigning on the investment issue, only India and other large developing nations would have challenged the draft ministerial texts that kept the Singapore issues on the negotiating table. But because the vast majority of developing nations, comprising the G-90 and G-20, refused to agree to launch investment negotiations, it was much more difficult for pro-investment member states to dismiss their concerns.

The Labour Standards Campaign

In contrast to the strategy adopted by the medicines and anti-investment campaigners that revolved around promoting consensus among NGOs to generate a unified NGO voice on the issues, the ICFTU focused more heavily upon its links with influential WTO member states. This was due to the level of disagreement among the international NGO community on the issue of incorporating labour standards into WTO rules. The ICFTU, one of the largest international non-governmental federations, even failed to ensure the whole-hearted support of its affiliates in developing countries. This stemmed not only from the commanding top-down nature of the ICFTU's campaign, but a more fundamental divide over the merits of a WTO social clause. This was a particular problem in the lead-up to the Singapore Ministerial Conference in 1996 during which there was little discussion among ICFTU affiliates about the campaign and its goals (Anner 2001: 48).

Despite the fact that several prominent international NGOs, including Solidar, Christian Aid and Oxfam supported the cause, the ICFTU held few joint activities with other NGOs. For example, Oxfam International and Christian Aid essentially ran their own labour standards campaigns. The ICFTU's reluctance to cooperate is also illustrated by the haphazard establishment of the Workers' Rights Caucus for the Singapore conference. Not only was the invitation of NGOs to the ICFTU's pre-ministerial workshop an afterthought, but the Workers' Rights Caucus was a 'last minute' decision spearheaded by the other NGOs rather than the ICFTU (O'Brien et al. 2000: 86). Following the Singapore meeting, the Workers' Rights Caucus disintegrated. By failing to take advantage of its formal links with developing country affiliates and the potential for a greater level of joint activity with other international NGOs, the ICFTU missed an opportunity to generate momentum for the message that a social clause was essential for the international NGO community's support for trade liberalization. One major result was that the ICFTU left itself open to accusations that a WTO social clause would only benefit trade unionists in wealthy WTO member states.

Following the Singapore conference, where the ICFTU encountered unyielding opposition from the TWN-led coalition of developing country intellectuals, trade unions and NGOs, the ICFTU was forced to reassess its low level of engagement with affiliates and other NGOs. The ICFTU subsequently hosted meetings in developing countries with affiliates and disseminated campaign information material. Yet for the Geneva and Seattle ministerial meetings, the campaign remained a top-down affair. As Shankar Gopal contends, 'Western NGOs and unions made minimal efforts to coordinate or understand the needs and demands of Third World actors in formulating their agendas or strategies' (Gopal 2001 in Kolben 2006: 253). Perhaps a key part of the problem was that the issue of labour standards was of secondary interest to labour unions in developing countries. Southern unionists and NGOs were far more concerned with debt relief, fair market access for agricultural and other goods, poverty alleviation, technology transfer, development and women's rights (Anner 2001). In other words, developing country groups argued that greater market access would do more than a social clause to provide the economic conditions conducive to higher labour standards. While the campaigns to influence the Geneva and Seattle conferences were far better organized, affiliates in developing countries still had little input into the campaign. One plausible explanation for this is that the ICFTU's policies and goals were heavily influenced by the largest due paying members based in Western Europe and North America (O'Brien et al. 2000: 85).

Despite the ICFTU's inability to gain a broad consensus for its position, due to a number of campaign missteps, the labour standards issue did generate a high level of international controversy involving large developing states and pro-labour governments, as well as opposing NGOs. In combination with the support of influential WTO member states, the controversy meant that the ICFTU was still able to play an agenda-setting role. Specifically, ICFTU was able to get around these difficulties by using its relationships with the US and European states, which strongly supported the trade-labour linkage. The ICFTU received financial support from pro-labour states such as Norway; direct invitations to contribute to national trade policy positions, including those of South Africa and the UK; and to participate in national delegations to WTO ministerial conferences for states as diverse as Egypt, Canada, Denmark and Kenya. NGOs were therefore not as reliant on mobilizing consensus among the NGO community as they already had a more direct route to influencing the WTO via influential WTO member states, including the US, which shared their goal for a WTO social clause.

ASSESSING NGO CAMPAIGN TACTICS AT THE AGENDA-SETTING PHASE

Together the three cases reveal that NGOs' use of certain tactics and strategies to mobilize support for their causes has made them important actors at the agenda-setting stages of international trade policymaking. I find that NGO campaign tactics in targeting the WTO fall into four categories: hosting international workshops and issuing declarations; working through alternative intergovernmental institutions; enhancing the resources of LDCs; and using ties to influential WTO member states. But the cases vary with NGOs placing more or less emphasis on different tactics according to whether their objectives aligned with developed or developing countries. While the access to medicines and anti-investment campaigners adopted a multi-pronged approach by engaging in joint activities, boosting the resources of LDCs, and drawing upon the support of alternative intergovernmental institutions, labour standards campaigners placed more emphasis on their links with influential WTO member states.

The medicines and investment campaigners benefited from a high level of support among a broad range of NGOs active on international trade issues. To establish their campaign platforms, NGOs held meetings to discuss the key issues and coordinate their tactics. They went on to host international conferences and workshops bringing a variety of actors to the table including representatives of governments, MNCs and intergovernmental institutions. Furthermore they intensively publicized their causes within alternative international arenas to support WTO member states in contesting the campaign issues within the WTO. NGO campaign activities resulted in the production of valuable information resources for developing countries with which they shared complementary views on the issues at stake. NGO information resources informed the negotiating strategies of developing countries at WTO ministerial conferences, which was especially beneficial for the many LDCs that had limited resources to represent themselves adequately in Geneva. In this regard, Ostry has described the monitoring role of NGOs as a 'virtual secretariat launched by the internet' (2006: 146; see also Smythe 2003–4: 73–4). As the commentary from several different sources reveals – including representatives of LDCs, the WTO, NGOs and the European Commission – NGO campaigners played a significant role in assisting developing countries at WTO ministerial conferences.

Conversely, the ICFTU campaigners placed the most emphasis on their ties with influential WTO member states in their campaigning strategy. Having held the goal of institutionalizing the link between international trade and international labour standards for several decades, the ICFTU did not establish their campaign platform and goals in negotiation with a broad range of NGOs active on trade issues. The ICFTU failed to take into account the needs or campaigning suggestions of affiliates in developing countries and they did not engage adequately with other international NGOs that supported the cause. The ICFTU placed little emphasis on 'drumming up' support at alternative international institutions, which might have persuaded some LDCs to be less hostile to their goals. But despite all of these flaws, the ICFTU's links with various influential governments were sufficient to get the issue of core labour standards addressed at the WTO's Singapore, Geneva and Seattle ministerial conferences.

Although their tactics varied according to the status of the WTO member states their campaigns supported, all three sets of NGO campaigners ultimately played agenda-setting roles at the WTO. The medicines case shows that NGOs play a role in identifying areas where WTO decision-making has encountered implementation problems and requires review; the labour standards case illustrates that NGOs help highlight potential new areas that might be dealt with through WTO rules; and the investment case demonstrates that NGOs publicize potential consequences of agreements in the process of negotiation. As this discussion of the key strategies of NGO campaigners attests, while they play a variety of important roles in the agenda-setting stage of international trade policymaking, NGOs appear to have little input into the ways in which issues are dealt with once on the WTO decision-making table.

To further illustrate the relationships between NGOs and WTO member states, I now examine the role of NGOs in legitimizing the negotiating positions of WTO member states (and other private actors) whose interests align with the normative objectives of NGOs.

COINCIDING NORMS AND INTERESTS: NGOs AS 'LEGITIMACY ENHANCERS'

Though NGOs are widely understood as agents of moral or normative values in international politics, there exists only a small literature on how the normative values held by NGOs intersect with the instrumental objectives of other actors, and what the consequences are for international policy processes and outcomes (but see Boehmer-Christiansen and Kellow 2002; DeMars 2005; Ronit 2007). One problematic feature of the constructivist literature on NGOs in international politics is its relegation of interests and power to the role of norms disseminated by NGOs. To assess the role of NGOs in relation to international trade governance, however, it is necessary to examine the *convergence* of norms and interests rather than the dominance of norms over interests or *vice-versa* (Shue 1995; Sell and Prakash 2004). According to Bruce Yandle's 'Baptists and bootleggers' theory of regulation (1983), coalitions comprising organizations or individuals that support policies on ethical grounds (the 'Baptists') and those that support policies for self-interested reasons (the 'bootleggers') will come together to sponsor policies from which they both gain, albeit, for their own reasons. Combined, normative and instrumental motivations for particular policy positions can be persuasive within domestic policy processes and at the international level.

By publicizing the social and equity dimensions of international trade issues through their campaigns, NGO arguments for policy change at the WTO often complement the instrumental goals of states in relation to a given issue. NGOs can thus serve as 'legitimacy enhancers' for particular WTO member states in international trade policy debates, thereby strengthening a member's negotiating position within the WTO arena. This NGO role is apparent in regard to the labour standards campaign where pro-labour states, through their close relationships with the ICFTU and its affiliates, sought to project the human rights rationale for a WTO social clause ahead of their instrumental motivations. For the medicines and investment campaigns, NGOs highlighted human rights, equity and sovereignty norms, which served the interests of developing states in seeking to limit WTO authority over their domestic policy decisions. In all three cases, however, opposing NGOs, various states and/or business actors sought to dent the normative rationales provided by NGO campaigners with alternative normative rationales for the status quo position. TWN for instance, was adept in questioning the motives underlying the ICFTU and pro-labour states in pushing for a WTO social clause. While competing normative perspectives significantly overshadowed the claims of labour standards advocates, they had limited bearing upon the legitimacy enhancing role of the medicines and investment NGOs for developing states' interests.

The Labour Standards Campaign

The ICFTU and pro-labour WTO member states played highly complementary roles in promoting a WTO social clause. In publicizing the human rights arguments for enforcing core labour standards at the WTO over the economic aspects, the ICFTU was viewed by critics as attempting to camouflage its own self-interested motivations in supporting the clause. It should be noted that the relationship between the ICFTU, other NGO supporters and pro-labour states was not quite as simple as a 'Baptist and bootlegger' coalition whereby one party masks its instrumental objectives with a normative rationale supplied by another group (Yandle 1983). Both the ICFTU and pro-labour states shared a normative commitment to achieving greater international compliance with the core ILO conventions. And both sets of actors stood to gain from a WTO social clause, albeit in different respects: the ICFTU was attempting to prevent the erosion of working conditions of union members (particularly those in wealthy states), while pro-labour WTO member states sought to maintain domestic employment and wages, reduce trade deficits, and gain political capital from supporting local firms using labour as a key input. As a speech by Alan Larson, acting under secretary for economic, business and agricultural affairs at the US State Department reveals, Congressional budget restrictions on UN agencies and the State Department were also behind the push to shift new items such as labour onto the WTO agenda (Donald 1999). Another key motivation for supporting a labour clause at the WTO was Clinton's desire to engage the support of labour unions to help win the 2000 US elections for the Democratic Party.

In promoting a WTO social clause, *both* the ICFTU and pro-labour states deferred to human rights and fairness arguments ahead of their instrumental objectives. As acting USTR Barshefsky stated at the WTO's Singapore conference, for example, '[w]e believe strongly that increased trade and the economic growth that it brings should also engender greater respect for the basic human rights which are the focus of our core labour standards proposal' (WTO 1996). But ultimately it was the ICFTU as a high-profile, representative non-governmental group, best placed to project human rights arguments, that underpinned the push for the social clause at the WTO.

The labour standards campaign shows that NGO relationships with powerful WTO member states can be a very fine balancing act – one that in this case the ICFTU failed to manage. By working alongside powerful states to achieve a common goal, the ICFTU failed to enhance the legitimacy of their motives. In so closely aligning with the US and European states over the issue, the ICFTU traded in some of its own legitimacy, which left the organization and its goals open to accusations of selfish elitism from developing states and NGOs (including some of their own affiliates). The promotion of the moral aspects of the issue by the ICFTU failed to cloak the protectionist and other instrumental motives underlying the cause. Instead, economic interests led to the polarization of actors into developed/developing country groups. This divide meant that pro-labour states were unable to gain the support of the majority of WTO members to support the issue at the WTO.

Underpinning the ICFTU's difficulties in promoting their cause was the regulatory nature of labour standards, which threatened to impose severe costs on developing countries. The complexity of the potential allocation of costs and benefits significantly hampered the efforts of the ICFTU to project the issue as one of fundamental human rights. It also affected their capacity to frame and disseminate a simple, unambiguous rationale for a WTO social clause. The issue was not amenable to simplification because of the difficulties instituting international regulatory standards of this type. This was further exacerbated by the fact that the ICFTU campaigners wished to see punitive measures enacted to enforce labour standards through the WTO's DSB. In other words, unlike other international NGO campaigns that have successfully framed issues as inalienable human rights, this strategy was ineffective for the ICFTU due to the costs at stake for developing countries. Despite softening their stance on trade sanctions prior to the Seattle conference, opponents were left suspicious of the ICFTU's ultimate goals. As affiliate organization COSATU noted, the ICFTU 'could have done a better job' in explaining that that the campaign was not based upon protection for the global North (Anner 2001: 56). US President Clinton's comments to the press during the Seattle conference concerning the use of trade sanctions to uphold labour standards did little to help.

As a result, developing countries and NGOs (led by TWN) were able to hijack the labour standards campaign. In moving the focus away from human rights, opponents claimed that protectionist motives belied the campaign and that the entire issue was emblematic of the raw deal that developing countries were receiving at the WTO. They characterized the labour standards push as part of the bullying tactics of developed nations attempting to retain their economic power over the global South. The TWN statements succeeded in framing the issue as another North/South debate, which neutralized the ICFTU's claims about international workers' solidarity. Even though TWN and its supporters had questionable links to those they claimed to speak for, the message that the ICFTU only represented privileged Northern-based unions reinforced the accusations of protectionism. Developing countries and vocal NGOs like TWN therefore deflated the potency of the human rights rationale for a WTO social clause. They provided a competing normative rationale based on national sovereignty and economic development.

The Investment Campaign

The activities of NGO campaigners opposing the launch of investment negotiations at the WTO helped legitimize the goals of a section of WTO member states, especially India, which had opposed the investment issue from the beginning. In drawing attention to the potential consequences of an 'indiscriminate' WTO investment agreement, NGOs promoted the sovereign right of developing countries to pursue their own policy objectives, contending that the development needs of LDCs must be taken into consideration (Singh 2003: 6). At the Cancún conference those NGOs and other activists protesting under the slogan 'No deal is better than a bad deal' reinforced this position. In an ultimately unsuccessful attempt to counter NGO claims about the accord's impact on developing countries, the EU characterized the proposed accord as 'an investment for development framework' (Oxfam International 2003: 24; see also Bailey et al. 2003: 1). This alternative rationale failed to resonate as NGOs and developing nations simply discredited it by pointing to the lack of progress on the trade issues said to be of greatest benefit to developing countries.

The campaign activities of NGOs elevated the significance of the investment issue (along with the three other Singapore issues) as a key point of debate among WTO members. In doing so, NGOs provided developing countries with an important bargaining chip for the negotiations at the Cancún conference. Until the launch of the NGO campaign, the investment issue had not been on the radar of many developing countries other than India (Interview, Oxfam International 2006). Developing countries were able to point to the investment issue as yet another key area, in addition to agriculture, where developing countries' interests were being compromised by more powerful industrialized member states. With this additional bargaining chip, developing countries were well positioned to demonstrate that they were receiving little benefit from the Doha Round, despite the development ideals supposedly underpinning it. Through the G-90 and the G-20 bargaining coalitions, developing countries were able to take advantage of WTO negotiating procedures, especially the single undertaking, by making their support for an investment agreement conditional upon their receipt of concessions in the area of agriculture.

The Medicines Campaign

In lobbying for a more relaxed interpretation of the TRIPS safeguard measures, the medicines campaigners had the effect of camouflaging the interests of developing countries and generic pharmaceutical manufacturers. Most developing countries faced not only the costs of supplying patented medicines instead of cheaper generic versions, but the administrative and enforcement costs of enacting patent regimes to become TRIPS compliant. Developed nations did not face these same costs because IP rights regimes had long been in operation, in some cases for as long as two centuries. The US Congress for instance, adopted its first patent law in 1790. The larger developing nations also stood to lose out in industrial terms. Brazil and India have their own generic medicines manufacturers, thus giving them a major interest in a clarification of the TRIPS safeguards to allow compulsory licensing and parallel importing on a wider basis. For example, since abolishing patent protection for medicines in 1972 (Baker 2005), India has become the world's leading supplier of generic medicines, and exports to other developing nations where medicines have not been patented (Barton 2004; Oxfam, Make Trade Fair). Brazil also has an important domestic industry and has been exporting generic medicines to LDCs for over a decade ('t Hoen 2002).

An appreciation of the interests at stake in relation to the TRIPS safeguards helps explain the role of India and Brazil in spearheading attempts to clarify the issue at the WTO and the attempts of the African Group to present a united front at Doha. It also makes clear why generic pharmaceutical companies like Cipla and organizations representing the generic medicines industry such as the European Generics medicines Association (EGA) worked alongside public interest NGOs in contesting this issue. In emphasizing the human rights and sovereignty aspects of the TRIPS and public health issue, the NGO campaign helped mask the interests of developing countries and generic medicine manufacturers firms seeking to maintain their market shares. In their efforts to boost medicine access, MSF even exported a limited volume of generic medicines to LDCs (MSF and Cipla 2001). In doing so, they actively supported Brazil in its fight to continue exporting generic medicines produced under compulsory license to other developing countries in the face of US pressure. NGO activity thus lent support to the generic medicines manufacturing industry and the market share of generics manufacturers more generally.

In eventually withdrawing support for MNCs in their legal proceedings against South Africa and agreeing to the Doha Declaration on TRIPS and Public Health, the US did not simply capitulate to NGO demands and 'see the light' on the public health needs of developing country citizens. The US was instead motivated not only by the need to dampen criticism of presidential candidate Al Gore brought about by NGO campaigners, but also by the need later to use compulsory licensing as a bargaining chip to reduce prices for anthrax drugs in preparation for potential bio-terror threats following 9/11. It was not until after the US government recognized that it may need to issue compulsory licenses of its own for national emergencies resulting from terrorist acts that its position softened. NGOs played an important role here in publicizing US hypocrisy on compulsory licensing. The US did not simply accept the norm of equal access to medicines but responded to its shifting priorities and interests. The NGO campaign nevertheless played a significant role in highlighting offending US activities along the way.

Among the international organizations supporting the clarification of the TRIPS agreement at the WTO, the World Bank did so mostly for its own budgetary reasons. The World Bank provides funds for the supply of essential medicines to developing nations, spending approximately $US800 million on pharmaceuticals annually. The World Bank was also a co-sponsor of UNAIDS. As such the World Bank, despite its neoliberal agenda, supported the use of policy measures such as compulsory licensing and parallel importing of pharmaceuticals in developing countries which would significantly reduce the Bank's costs (Vick 1999). But like many other actors supportive of the clarification of the issue at the WTO, the World Bank wished to be seen to back the issue for social justice reasons. At a MSF meeting, for instance, a

World Bank official asserted that the pricing situation 'shows an increasing disconnect with the needs of the majority of the people in the world' (Vick 1999).

In attempting to dent the claims and arguments put forward by the medicines campaigners, generics manufacturers and developing countries, the research-based pharmaceutical industry published and disseminated the Attaran and Gillespie-White study to support the case that upholding patents is vital for the development of new medicines (Attaran and Gillespie-White 2001). This argument failed to gain traction, however, as it was a far less appealing narrative than the NGOs' emotive claims about the life and death implications of strictly upholding patents and the profiteering of unaccountable global pharmaceutical companies. Had the Attaran and Gillespie-White study more explicitly pinpointed the economic benefits and other instrumental interests at stake in the debate, it may have been better received.

Though the human rights motivations of developing countries were tied up with their instrumental reasons for promoting a broader interpretation of the TRIPS safeguards, one interesting point of departure from this position that undermined NGO claims was South African President Thabo Mbeki's publically stated scepticism about the link between HIV and AIDS (CNN 2000). Shortly after becoming South Africa's President in 1999, Thabo Mbeki created a great deal of controversy when he invited several outspoken HIV 'deniers' – people who rejected the link between HIV and AIDS – to join his Presidential AIDS Advisory Panel. In response, the international scientific community challenged President Mbeki's views through the publication of a document affirming that HIV causes AIDS (the Durban Declaration), signed by over 5000 scientists and physicians. This declaration appeared in the journal *Nature* shortly before the thirteenth AIDS conference, held in Durban, South Africa, in July 2000 (Anonymous 2000). But for two years, President Mbeki and his government continued to vacillate over the causes of AIDS and how the disease should be dealt with (van Rijn 2006: 522). These actions were seen as a distraction from the NGO campaign that sought to impress the urgency of the HIV crisis and the need to provide affordable access to treatment.

In all three case studies of NGO campaigns, NGOs played a role in legitimizing the interests of WTO member states by highlighting moral arguments for policy change at the WTO. These arguments complemented the instrumental objectives of member states. The ICFTU highlighted the human rights dimensions of labour standards over the economic benefits for industrialized states, the investment campaigns provided LDCs with an additional bargaining chip for the Cancún conference, and the medicines campaigners helped promote the interests of developing countries with generic medicines industries, as well as the generics manufacturers themselves. In response, various campaign critics seeking to protect their own interests (including opposing

NGOs, states and MNCs) attempted to mount competing normative rationales, albeit, with differing levels of success.

The analysis here shows that the relationships between NGOs and states with complementary objectives cannot simply be described as 'Baptist-bootlegger' coalitions whereby NGOs mask the interests of states. States also possess normative goals in relation to international trade issues, though they are not always well placed to project such arguments. In examining the role of NGOs in packaging and publicizing normative rationales for trade policy positions, I find that NGOs play roles at the agenda-setting stages of the international trade policy process that (depending upon the issue) have the effect of supporting or undermining the capacity of various nation-states to achieve their goals at the WTO.

CONCLUSION

While NGO activities can pose a challenge to intergovernmental organizations, they also play important roles that supplement the policymaking work of these organizations and the negotiating resources of member states within these arenas. In comparing and contrasting the findings of the three case studies of NGO campaigns directed at the WTO, I have found that NGOs play roles at the agenda-setting stage of policymaking. In their publicist role, NGOs seek to strategically use political opportunities (such as policy crises; the self-serving activities of industrialized nations and MNCs; elections; past campaigns; and deficiencies in existing international agreements) to provoke international debate about their issues. In attempting to mobilize support among relevant NGOs and amenable WTO member states for their goals, NGO campaigners host international conferences; release joint declarations and press statements; work through alternative intergovernmental arenas; enhance the resources of LDCs; and use their ties with powerful WTO member states. In highlighting normative rationales for policy change, NGO campaign activity has the effect of boosting the legitimacy of negotiating positions adopted by WTO member states.

This study has revealed that in the WTO context, NGOs have different relationships with WTO member states according to their development status and this shapes the roles they play in international trade policymaking. NGOs are most active in the policy process when their normative objectives align with LDCs rather than with influential WTO member states. NGO campaigners produce valuable information materials that enhance the negotiating resources of capacity-constrained LDCs. They facilitate the WTO decision-making process by producing reports, updates and commentary on WTO issues and the progress of negotiations. NGOs also host international conferences that bring together the key players in trade policy debates. By contributing to the information and analysis available and airing alternative perspectives on trade policy matters, NGO activity has the effect of putting developing countries in a more equal negotiating position in the WTO arena thereby increasing their potential to realize gains from trade negotiations. For the medicines campaign, NGOs contributed to the negotiating strategy of the African Group and for the investment case NGOs informed the position of the G-90. Given that WTO decision-making procedures are premised upon the equality of member states in the negotiating arena (one member, one vote), the role of NGOs as resource enhancers for LDCs is an important role indeed.

Further to their resource-enhancing activities, NGOs publicize normative rationales for policy change at the WTO thereby serving to enhance the legitimacy of WTO member states that possess complementary instrumental objectives. This role is especially visible for wealthy states and the larger developing states, such as India and Brazil, which (unlike LDCs) already have the capacity to raise issues of concern at the WTO. For the investment and medicines cases where NGOs supported developing countries, NGOs promoted the sovereign right of states to pursue national objectives rather than adhere to international trade rules. For the medicines case, NGOs lent moral support to the economic interests of developing states and their generics manufacturers (as well as generics firms located in wealthy regions of the world). For the investment case, NGOs provided developing member states with an additional bargaining chip in their attempts to negotiate a better deal on agriculture. And, in relation to labour standards, NGOs served to legitimize (albeit less successfully) the goals of already influential WTO member states by emphasizing the human rights dimensions of labour standards. Though these issues were dealt with at the WTO in ways that did not necessarily align with NGO objectives, their role in promoting these issues at the agenda-setting stage was nevertheless significant.

Another factor that shaped the role played by NGOs in the international trade regime at the WTO was the *type* of policy change advocated. As Paul Nelson contends, in contesting international economic policy, attempts by NGOs to defend and strengthen national authority against international rule-making are more likely to be successful than attempts to invoke international authority to shape or override national authority (2002: 389). This certainly appears to be the case at the WTO where a proposed policy change involving a contraction of the WTO's mandate seems more likely to be acted upon than policy changes involving an expansion of the WTO's jurisdiction. This relates to the WTO's institutional characteristics such as consensus decision-making and the single undertaking approach to negotiations which mean that progress on any issue can only be achieved with the agreement of all members on every aspect of every agreement. In other words, removing issues or modifying existing issues is an easier task than adding a whole new issue to the WTO agenda. This is evidenced by the WTO arena's amenability to the medicines and investment campaigns and its hostility to the 'new' issue of labour standards. This factor helps to explain why power-based outcomes do not always prevail at the WTO. With a unified position and carefully constructed arguments informed by NGOs, less powerful developing countries seeking to modify or remove issues from the agenda can boost their leverage at the WTO by taking advantage of the consensus-based decision-making rules.

Two of the cases of NGO campaigns (medicines and labour standards) reveal that the US domestic political arena can be strategically important for NGOs campaigning on international trade issues. For the medicines campaign, the US presidential elections provided the NGOs with leverage to pressure the Clinton administration over its role in attempting to limit the access of developing countries to generic medicines. Publicizing the role of presidential candidate Al Gore and his links to the research-based pharmaceutical industry, NGOs were able to extract a commitment from the Clinton administration in the form of an Executive Order, which stated that sub-Saharan African nations would not be targeted. But it should be noted that this did not prevent the US (the Bush administration) from subsequently pressuring Brazil over its IP laws. For the labour standards campaigners, the US presidential elections saw President Clinton attempt to reinvigorate the support of the US labour movement providing the AFL-CIO (an ICFTU affiliate) an important avenue through which to influence the US position on labour standards.

Though James Rosenau accurately describes NGO activity at the international level as 'sovereignty-free' (1990), this book has found that their transnational character does not preclude NGOs from supplementing the resources and legitimacy of nation-states in international trade politics at the WTO. But the cases reveal that NGOs should not simply be seen as state instruments. Their campaign activities are sufficiently independent from states to warrant this detailed study into how their activities affect the international trade policy process. In illustrating this, I have found that WTO institutional settings and processes, as well as NGO relationships with states outside formal WTO bargaining, are significant contributors to the agendas, instruments, and postures of state participants in the WTO arena.

8. Conclusion

Taking into account the empirical reality of the increasing number of NGOs actively engaged with international trade policy issues and the WTO, this book has sought to shed light on the roles undertaken by reformer NGOs in the international trade regime. I found that while NGOs do not 'restructure' states' interests as suggested by constructivist scholars, neither are they 'servants of state policy' (Haufler 1995: 108). NGOs undertake important roles, independently of states, at the agenda-setting phase of the international trade policy process, though their campaign activities inevitably assist various member states that possess complementary objectives. Specifically, through their international campaigns, NGOs publicize neglected trade-related issues; persuade other relevant actors to support their positions; boost the resources of developing member states; and highlight normative rationales for policy positions. NGOs achieve all of this despite their exclusion from the WTO decision-making arena. This study has thus found that NGOs certainly do matter in international trade politics, as they do in international politics more generally.

In examining the literature on NGOs and the WTO, as well as scholarship on NGOs in international politics more generally (see Chapter 2), I found that the major concerns revolve around the potential of NGOs to rectify the WTO's democratic and legitimacy deficits and the role of NGOs in creating and disseminating normative ideas and values. For example, sympathy for the causes of many NGOs, especially in the areas of human rights and environmental protection, has led constructivist scholars to focus on demonstrating that normative ideas and values can shame states (and other actors such as MNCs) into vanquishing their less noble instrumental objectives. Meanwhile global social movement theorists investigate the constraints and opportunities for sustaining social movement activity internationally and the interrelationships between different types of transnational activists. But both the constructivist and social movement approaches do not provide a significant enough role for power and interests, and fail to clearly specify how norms disseminated by NGOs affect international policy processes. Consequently constructivist and social movement perspectives can only be considered partial accounts of NGOs in international politics that do not take account of the full breadth and influence of NGO activity and their impacts on governance at the international level.

Given this book's focus on the international trade policy process and the economic interests and domestic political consequences at stake for WTO member states in the negotiation of international trade rules, this book took a different approach. Based on Keohane and Nye's notion of complex interdependence (1977), the governance-centred approach adopted in this study provided scope to examine not only the normative values and ideas disseminated by NGOs, but the role of states' interests, the interconnections between normative values and interests, and the WTO's institutional characteristics. In highlighting structural and interest-based factors alongside normative values and institutional practices, a governance-centred approach allowed for an understanding of how NGOs work strategically to affect international decision-making in the area of trade liberalization. It therefore provided a more balanced framework upon which to understand the role of NGOs in international trade politics than either the constructivist or global social movement approaches.

Having examined the WTO-NGO literature and the more general transnational advocacy literature, I employed a comparative case study method to set up the methodological framework for the study. Three cases studies of NGO campaigns in the areas of labour standards, IP rights and foreign investment rules were selected to examine the tactics and strategies used by NGOs to contest WTO decision-making and to assess their role in the international trade regime. The key differences across the cases included the type of policy change advocated by NGOs for the WTO arena, and the development status and international influence of the WTO member states with which NGO objectives aligned. Given their limited formal status within the WTO decision-making arena, NGO influence was conceptualized in terms of 'agenda-setting' and 'mobilizing support'. In the detailed examination of NGO campaigns in the case study chapters (Chapters 4, 5 and 6), I analysed the core conflicts and previous international cooperation in the issue areas, the key actors involved and NGO campaign tactics and strategies. The way in which each campaign issue was eventually dealt with at the WTO was investigated.

Chapter 7 of the book compared and contrasted the insights generated by each of the cases to examine the agenda-setting roles played by NGOs in the international trade policy process. It was found that NGOs undertake what can be broadly described as publicist roles: they highlight neglected trade-related issues by harnessing political opportunities to construct plausible narratives that contain particular interpretations of alleged policy problems, which privilege the policy solutions favoured by NGOs. The major types of political opportunities that NGOs used to promote their campaign issues included policy crises, especially those concerned with the implementation of international trade rules; political events such as US presidential elections; the offending activities of particular MNCs and nation-states; and deficiencies in existing international agreements.

Having developed a rationale for change at the WTO and instigated international debate about their campaign issues, NGOs attempted to mobilize support for their campaign goals. They did so by: hosting international conferences that bring together representatives of NGOs, nation-states and international institutions; conducting and publishing their own research and analysis; monitoring the WTO negotiations; lobbying at relevant international institutions other than the WTO; and staging publicity events and demonstrations to capture the attention and support of the general public. These external campaign tactics put pressure on nation-states to address the issues at the WTO. In addition, where NGO objectives aligned with those of developing WTO members, NGOs enhanced the resources of these states by providing technical and legal advice; monitoring services; negotiating strategies; and assisting with texts for consideration at WTO meetings. In these cases, NGO activity served to boost the capacity of developing countries to contest these issues inside the WTO.

The case studies reveal that in addition to their role in publicizing neglected issues through political opportunism and mobilizing support, NGO campaign activity may serve to enhance the legitimacy of states' self-interested motivations for policy changes at the WTO. For the access to medicines and investment campaigns, the intersection of NGOs' normative goals (in regard to human rights and domestic policy flexibility) with the developing nations' strategic, economic and domestic political interests boosted the negotiating positions of these states at the WTO. NGOs and developing states were able to fend off attempts by campaign opponents (the European Commission in the investment case and research-based pharmaceutical companies in the medicines case) to undermine their objectives with alternative normative rationales. The labour standards campaigners were less successful in highlighting the human rights aspects of a potential WTO social clause. Despite the level of cooperation between the ICFTU and the US and Norwegian governments, the normative aspirations underpinning the push for a labour standards clause, as promoted by the ICFTU, were overshadowed by the competing claims of developing country governments and NGOs such as TWN. Their economic arguments for the negative impacts of a WTO social clause on developing countries had the effect of undermining the ICFTU's campaign and heightening opposition among developing countries to the social clause.

The three cases of NGO campaigns together illustrate that the roles of NGOs in international trade politics differ according to whether their campaign objectives resonate with developing or developed nations. Where NGO campaign objectives align with those of LDCs, NGOs are enabled to play a greater role. By providing information and analysis on key issues and monitoring progress at the WTO, NGOs can persuade LDCs to contest issues at the WTO and in doing so, may inform their negotiating positions. In this respect NGOs may facilitate the international trade regime by bolstering the political clout of LDCs at the WTO, putting them on a more equal footing with their industrialized counterparts. Based on the insights of the labour standards case, where NGO campaign goals resonate with already influential states at the WTO, NGOs appear to play a greater role in highlighting the moral dimensions of the proposed policy change thus strengthening the negotiating position of the member states involved. This explains why the Norwegian and US governments provided campaign finances and liaised so closely with ICFTU affiliates in the lead-up to WTO ministerial conferences.

In explaining the treatment of each campaign issue within the WTO arena, the *type* of policy change advocated by NGOs and WTO member states was significant and reflects the importance of the WTO's unique institutional characteristics. In all three campaign issues, the WTO's decision-making processes prevented power-based outcomes from prevailing. Unlike the World Bank and IMF, where powerful donor states can achieve their objectives as a result of their larger voting share, decision-making at the WTO occurs on a single undertaking, consensus basis. These decision-making practices heavily conditioned the outcome of NGO campaign issues once on the WTO agenda. Specifically, proposed policy changes that involve the WTO removing an issue from its jurisdiction or modifying an existing issue appear more likely to be acted upon than policy changes involving an expansion of the WTO's powers. This helps explain why the push for a WTO social clause was unsuccessful, despite backing from influential states, while the attempts to remove investment negotiations and resolve the TRIPS safeguard issues were achieved by developing members.

While it is unlikely that NGOs will be granted participation status at the WTO in the foreseeable future, an examination of recent NGO activity on international trade nonetheless contributes to our understanding of the important roles of NGOs in international politics. Overall the cases demonstrate that NGOs are significant actors in international trade politics at the WTO, which represents a hard test case for examining the influence of nonprofit advocacy organizations in international politics given that they lack formal status at the institution and expectations that business actors enjoy privileged access. Contrary to much of the existing WTO-NGO literature, this book demonstrates that understandings of NGOs should not be confined to their untapped potential to improve the democratic accountability of the WTO. NGOs are highly active on international trade policy matters and make important contributions at the agenda-setting stages of the international trade policy process. The institutional characteristics of the WTO arena and the compatibility of NGOs' normative objectives with states' interests are key factors that shape interactions between states and NGOs in this context.

AVENUES FOR FURTHER RESEARCH

The findings of this study reveal a number of avenues for future research into NGOs at the WTO. More case studies of NGO campaigns that target the organization are required to further appreciate the relationship dynamics between NGOs and WTO member states according to the policy change advocated. Based on the cases selected for this study, it was found that NGOs played more active agenda-setting roles when their objectives aligned with developing countries in having an existing WTO accord modified or a potential new issue removed from the agenda, while they played more of a legitimacy-enhancing role when they supported influential members to add a new issue to the WTO's agenda. To further test these factors, additional case studies might examine NGO campaigns that align with the goals of developing member states and which seek to expand the WTO's authority. This would not only allow for a more thorough examination of the policy change variable, but how the power status of the states involved affects the agenda-setting roles of NGOs. Other focus areas might include the extent to which NGOs can move beyond their 'legitimacy-enhancing' role where their campaign goals align with influential developed states. More research is also needed to examine the circumstances surrounding NGO campaigns that fail to achieve an agenda-setting role at the WTO.

A comprehensive analysis of the increasing trend for NGO representatives to obtain places on the official delegations of member states to WTO ministerial conferences is required. Very little has been written about NGO participation via government delegations at the WTO: there appears to be no comprehensive list of states that have extended this privilege to NGOs and it is difficult to find any detailed analysis or authoritative source on this issue. While this study touched upon this phenomenon to provide evidence about the increasing activity of NGOs relating to the WTO, and Coulby and Ndrangu (2001) discuss it from an NGO practitioner's perspective, a more thorough investigation is necessary to determine which particular NGOs are gaining access, and the advantages and disadvantages for both NGOs and states. For example, what impact does the insider status have on the capacity of NGOs to realize their objectives? To what extent are NGOs hamstrung by their close associations with governments at ministerial conferences? For member states, there are likely to be differing motivations behind the decision to include NGO representatives on government delegations to WTO ministerial conferences. LDCs may seek to use NGO input simply as an additional source of technical advice, while for wealthy states, the presence of NGOs may simply indicate the consultation processes that governments undertake with a range of interest groups at the national level. This may explain the strong presence of business and trade union representatives for other issues on government delegations to WTO ministerial conferences.

Given the growth of the NGO sector internationally and the trend towards global governance, improving understanding of the nature and implications of NGO activity in policymaking at this level is imperative.

Select bibliography

Abbott, F.M. (2002), 'The Doha declaration on the TRIPS agreement and public health: lighting a dark corner at the WTO', *Journal of International Economic Law*, **5**(2): 469–505.

ACP and G-90 (2004), 'Ministerial meetings in Mauritius: for a common strategy at the WTO', accessed 28 July 2008 at www.acp.int/en/archives/G90_en.html.

ActionAid (2003), accessed 8 June 2006 at www.actionaid.org.uk/591/press_release.html.

ACT UP Philadelphia (1999), 'Al Gore's "Apartheid 2000" campaign comes to Philadelphia: people with AIDS, people of color demand AIDS drugs for Africa', ACT UP press release, 23 June 1999, accessed 6 July 2007 at www.healthgap.org/press_releases/99/062899_AU_PR_GORE_PHILLY.html.

ACT UP New York (1999), 'Gore's patented money moves' accessed 1 November 2008 at www.actupny.org/actions/gorezaps.html.

Ahnlid, A. (2002), 'The consultative process with civil society in the formulation of Sweden's positions on trade policy within the EU', working paper prepared for the Inter-American Development Bank Regional Policy Dialogue Trade and Integration Network, Washington DC, 17–18 September 2002, accessed 13 February 2008 at <http://idbdocs.iadb.org/wsdocs/getdocument.aspx?docnum=600787.

Alben, E. (2001), 'GATT and the fair wage: a historical perspective on the labor-trade link', *Columbia Law Review*, **101**(6): 1410–47.

Alger, C.F. (1997), 'Transnational social movements, world politics and global governance', in J. Smith, C. Chatfield, and R. Pagnucco (eds), *Transnational Social Movements and Global Politics*, New York: Syracuse University Press.

Alpert, A. (2003), 'Cancún "collapse": victory for global justice movement', report from the WTO meeting, American Friends Service Committee, accessed 6 November 2008 at www.afsc.org/TradeMatters/ht/d/Content Details/i/2394.

Anheier, H., M. Glasius, and M. Kaldor (2001), *Global Civil Society 2001*, Oxford: Oxford University Press.

Anner, M. (2001), 'The international trade union campaign for core labor standards in the WTO', *WorkingUSA*, **5**(1): 43–63.

Anonymous (2000), 'The Durban declaration', *Nature*, **406**(6791): 15.

APEC (2004), 'Ministerial statement on Doha development Agenda (DDA) negotiations', accessed 28 June at www.apec.org/apec/ministerial_statements/sectoral_ministerial/trade/2004_trade/dda_negotiations.html.

Arts, B. (1998), *The Political Influence of Global NGOs. Case Studies on the Climate and Biodiversity Conventions*, Utrecht, Netherlands: International Books.

ASEAN (1994), 'Joint communiqué of the 10th ASEAN labour ministers meeting', Singapore, 16–17 May 1994, accessed 4 February 2008 at www.aseansec.org/2194.htm.

Atik, J. (2001), 'Democratizing the WTO', *The George Washington International Law Review*, **33**(3–4): 451–72.

Attaran A. and L. Gillespie-White (2001), 'Do patents for antiretroviral drugs constrain access to AIDS treatment in Africa?', *Journal of the American Medical Association*, **286**(15): 1886–92.

Ayres J.M. (1998), *Defying Conventional Wisdom: Political Movements and Popular Contention Against North American Free Trade*, Toronto, ON, Buffalo, NY, and London: University of Toronto Press.

Bach, A. (2003), 'The controversy about a new investment agreement in the WTO in the run-up to Cancún', *WIDE – News* 6: 4–5, accessed 6 July 2007 at www.saunalahti.fi/finnwid/News%20N6_2003%20June1.pdf.

Bailey, M., D. Green, P. Hardstaff, J. Hilary, and C. Melamed (2003), 'Unwanted, unproductive and unbalanced: six arguments against an investment agreement at the WTO', report from the World Development Movement, accessed 6 July 2007 at www.wdm.org.uk/resources/reports/trade/unwantedunproductiveunbalanced01052003.pdf.

Baker, B.K. (2005), 'India's 2005 Patent Act: death by patent or universal access to second- and future-generation ARVs?', HealthGAP background paper, 19 September 2005 accessed 1 November 2008 at www.healthgap.org/press_releases/05/091905_HGAP_BP_India_patent_baker.html.

Bandy, J. and J. Smith (2005), *Coalitions Across Borders: Transnational Protest and the Neoliberal Order*, Lanham, MD: Rowman and Littlefield.

Banta, D. (2001), 'Public health triumphs at WTO conference', *Journal of the American Medical Association*, **286**(21): 2655–6.

Barber, S. (1998), 'US withholds benefits over Zuma's bill', *Business Day*, 15 July 1998 accessed 1 November 2008 at www.essentialdrugs.org/edrug/archive/199807/msg00039.php.

Barfield, C. (2001), *Free Trade, Sovereignty, Democracy: The Future of the World Trade Organization*, Washington, DC: American Enterprise Institute Press.

Barton, J.H. (2004), 'TRIPS and the global pharmaceutical market', *Health Affairs*, **23**(3): 146–55.

Basu, K., H. Horn, L. Román and J. Shapiro (2003), *International Labor Standards: History, Theory, and Policy Options*, Oxford: Blackwell Publishing.

Baumgartner, F.R. and B.D. Jones (1993), *Agendas and Instability in American Politics*, Chicago, IL: University of Chicago Press.

Bellmann, C. and R. Gerster (1996), 'Accountability in the World Trade Organization', *Journal of World Trade*, **30**(6): 31–74.

Bennett, L.W. (2005), 'Social movements beyond borders: understanding two eras of transnational activism', in D. della Porta and S. Tarrow (eds), *Transnational Protest and Global Activism: People, Passions and Power*, Lanham, MD, and Oxford: Rowman and Littlefield.

Bermudez, J. and M. Oliveira (2004), *Intellectual Property in the Context of the WTO TRIPS Agreement: Challenges for Public Health*, Rio de Janeiro: WHO/PAHO Collaborating Center for Pharmaceutical Policies, National School of Public Health Sergio Arouca, Oswaldo Cruz Foundation.

Betsill, M. and E. Corell (2001), 'NGO influence in international environmental negotiations: a framework for analysis', *Global Environmental Politics*, **1**(4): 65–85.

Bhagwati, J. (2002), 'Afterword: the question of linkage', *American Journal of International Law*, **96**(1): 126–34.

Bob, C. (2005), *The Marketing of Rebellion: Insurgents, Media and International Activism*, New York: Cambridge University Press.

Boehmer-Christiansen, S. and A. Kellow (2002), *International Environmental Policy: Interests and the Failure of the Kyoto Process*, Cheltenham, UK and Northampton, MA, USA: Edward Elgar.

Boli, J. and G.M. Thomas (1997), 'World culture in the world polity: a century of non-governmental organization', *American Sociological Review*, **62**(2): 179–90.

Boli, J. and G.M. Thomas (1999), *Constructing World Culture: International Nongovernmental Organizations Since 1875*, Stanford, CA: Stanford University Press.

Boulet, P., C. Garrison and E. 't Hoen (2004), *Drug Patents under the Spotlight: Sharing Practical Knowledge about Pharmaceutical Patents*, 3rd edn, Médecins Sans Frontières.

Buchanan, R. (2003), 'Perpetual peace or perpetual process: global civil society and cosmopolitan legality at the World Trade Organization', *Leiden Journal of International Law*, **16**(4): 673–99.

Burgess, J. (1999), 'AFL-CIO backs agenda for WTO', *The Washington Post*, 29 October.

Blackett, A. (1999), 'Whither social clause? Human rights, trade theory and treaty interpretation', *Columbia Human Rights Review*, **31**(1): 1–80.

Bradsher, K. (2001), 'Bayer halves price for Cipro, but rivals offer drugs free', *New York Times*, 26 October 2001, accessed 1 November 2008 at <http://query.nytimes.com/gst/fullpage.html?res=9C03EEDB1031F935A1 5753C1A9679C8B63.

Braithwaite, J. and P. Drahos (2000), *Global Business Regulation*, New York: Cambridge University Press.

CAFOD (2003), 'The Cancún WTO ministerial meeting, September 2003: what happened? What does it mean for development?', Fifth informal consultation between the OECD trade committee and civil society organizations (CSOs), CAFOD submission, OECD Trade Directorate, accessed 1 November 2008 at www.oecd.org/dataoecd/13/54/ 16686227.pdf.

Campaign for Labor Rights accessed 27 January 2007 at www.campaignfor laborrights.org.

Capling, A. (2005), 'Can the democratic deficit in treaty-making be overcome? Parliament and the Australia–US free trade agreement', in Charlesworth, H., M. Chiam, D. Hovell and G. Williams (eds), *The Fluid State: International Law and National Legal Systems*, Sydney, NSW: The Federation Press.

Capling, A. and K.R. Nossal (2003), 'Parliament and the democratization of foreign policy: the case of Australia's joint standing committee on treaties', *Canadian Journal of Political Science*, **36**(4): 835–55.

Cappella, J.N. and K.H. Jamieson (1997), *Spiral of Cynicism: The Press and the Public Good*, New York: Oxford University Press.

Carroll, J. and R. Winslow (2001), 'Bayer to slash by nearly half price: US pays for anthrax drug', *Wall Street Journal*, 25 October 2001, accessed 1 November 2008 at www.essentialdrugs.org/edrug/archive/200110/ msg00105.php.

Centre for Policy Dialogue (2003a), 'LDC priorities and Dhaka Declaration – International civil society forum: advancing LDC interests in the fifth WTO ministerial', report from the Centre for Policy Dialogue, accessed 5 November 2008 at www.cpd-bangladesh.org/ldc2.html.

Centre for Policy Dialogue (2003b), letter to LDC trade ministers, accessed 5 November 2008 at www.cpd-bangladesh.org/ldc_let.jpg.

Chakravarthi, R. (1999), 'EC labour standards move trashed', Third World Network news story, accessed 7 February 2008 at www.twnside.org.sg/ title/trashed-cn.htm.

Chang, H-J. (2002), *Kicking Away the Ladder: Development Strategy in Historical Perspective*, London: Anthem Press.

Chang, H-J., and D. Green (2003), *The WTO and Foreign Investment: Don't Do As We Did, Do As We Say*, London and Geneva: Catholic Agency for Overseas Development and South Centre.

Charnovitz, S. (1987), 'The influence of international labour standards on the world trading regime: a historical overview', *International Labour Review*, **126**(5): 565–84.

Charnovitz, S. (2000), 'Opening the WTO to non-governmental interests', *Fordham International Law Journal*, **18**(2): 173–216.

Charnovitz, S. (2002), 'WTO cosmopolitics', *Journal of International Law and Politics*, **34**(2): 299–354.

Charnovitz, S. (2004), 'The WTO and cosmopolitics', *Journal of International Economic Law*, **7**(3): 675–82.

Cho, S. (2004), 'A bridge too far: the fall of the Fifth WTO Ministerial Conference in Cancún and the future of trade constitution', *Journal of International Economic Law*, **7**(2): 219–44.

Cho, S. (2005), 'Linkage of free trade and social regulation: moving beyond the entropic dilemma', *Chicago Journal of International Law*, **5**: 625–40.

CIEL 'Conferences and other fora in which CIEL has addressed investment issues', accessed 1 November 2008 at www.ciel.org/Tae/Trade_Investment_Fora.html#WTO.

CIEL (2003a), report from trade and investment workshop held at World Social Forum in 2003, accessed 6 July 2007 at www.ciel.org/Tae/WSF_Trade_26Jan03.html.

CIEL (2003b), Seminar on the nature and implications of an international investment agreement: sample invitation accessed 6 July 2007 at www.ciel.org/Publications/Investment_Invite_20Mar03.pdf.

CIEL (2003c), 'No investment negotiations at the World Trade Organization: declaration of non governmental groups and civil society movements', accessed 4 August 2008 at www.ciel.org/Tae/WTO_NoInvestNeg_6May03.html.

CIEL (2003d), 'Investment, sustainable development and the WTO: allies or antagonists?', accessed 6 July 2007 at www.ciel.org/Tae/Carnegie_WTO_22May03.html.

CIEL (2003e), 'Sign on to letter to USTR's Ambassador Zoellick to oppose the initiation of investment negotiations within the World Trade Organization', accessed 6 July 2007 at www.ciel.org/Tae/Zoellick_7Aug03.html.

CIEL (2003f), letter to Ambassador Carlos Perez del Castillo, Chairman, General Council World Trade Organization, 28 November 2003, accessed 6 July 2007 at www.ciel.org/Publications/singapore_issues_Dec03.pdf.

CIEL (2003g), 'CIEL hosts meetings on the nature of implications to a WTO investment agreement', accessed 6 July 2007 at www.ciel.org/Tae/WTO_InvestAgree_27Mar03.html.

CIEL (2008), 'Learn About CIEL', webpage accessed 1 November 2008 at www.ciel.org/contents.html.

Clean Clothes Campaign, accessed 9 December 2005 at www.clean clothes.org/codes/ccccode/htm.

Clinton, W.J. (1999), 'Remarks at a World Trade Organization luncheon in Seattle', *Weekly Compilation of Presidential Documents* **35**: 2494–7.

Clinton, W.J. (2000), 'Access to HIV/AIDS pharmaceuticals and medical technologies', Executive Order No. 13 155, 10 May 2000, *Federal Register* **65**: 30 521.

Clinton, W.J. (2004), *State of the Union Addresses*, Kessinger Publishing Company.

CNN (2000), Hundreds walk out on Mbeki at AIDS conference, 10 July 2000, accessed 1 November 2008 at http://edition.cnn.com/2000/HEALTH/AIDS/07/10/aids.economics/index.html.

Cobb, R.W. and C.D. Elder (1983), *Participation in American Politics: The Dynamics of Agenda-Building*, second edition, Baltimore and London: The Johns Hopkins University Press.

Cohen, R. and S.M. Rai (2000), 'Global social movements: towards a cosmopolitan politics', in Cohen, R. and S.M. Rai (eds), *Global Social Movements*, London, Athlone, Ireland and Piscataway, NJ: Transaction Publishers.

Commission on Trade and Investment Policy (2003), 'ICC's expectations regarding a WTO investment agreement', policy statement, 7 March 2003, accessed 5 June 2007 at www.iccwbo.org/home/statements_rules/statements/2003/wto_investment_agreement.asp.

Coulby, H. and G. Ndrangu (2001), 'Going to Qatar: how to get an NGO representative on your government delegation: two case studies from the WTO ministerial in Seattle' breiefing paper from UK NGO Trade Network, accessed 13 February 2008 at www.wto.org/english/forums_e/ngo_e/ukngo1.doc.

Cox, S. (2007), 'EU "wasting" cash on lobby groups', Radio 4's The Investigation, BBC News, accessed 10 December 2007 at http://news.bbc.co.uk/1/hi/world/europe/7127182.stm.

CPTech (1999a), 'Compulsory licenses and access to essential medicines', NGO-sponsored meeting held in Geneva on 26 March 1999, accessed 6 July 2007 at www.cptech.org/march99-cl/pr1.html.

CPTech (1999b), sample invitation to 26 March meeting on compulsory licensing accessed 6 July 2007 at www.cptech.org/march99-cl/invite.html.

CPTech (2000a), 'Bilateral trade disputes involving the United States, over intellectual property and health care', accessed 1 November 2008 at www.cptech.org/ip/health/country/allcountries.html.

CPTech (2000b), letter from Sir Leon Brittan, Vice-President of the European Commission, to Thabo Mbeki, Vice-President of South Africa (23 March 1998), accessed 6 July 2007 at www.cptech.org/ip/health/eu/brittan.html.

CPTech (2000c), 27 September 2000 letter from six NGOs to Commissioner Lamy and Commissioner Nielson, accessed 6 July 2007 at www.cptech.org/ip/health/eu/lamynielson27092000.html.

CPTech, HAI, MSF, Oxfam International and TAG (2001), 'Joint statement of Consumer Project on Technology (CPT), Health Action International (HAI), Médecins sans Frontières (MSF), Oxfam and Treatment Action Group (TAG) on the WTO/WHO on differential pricing & financing of essential drugs', 11 April 2001 accessed 1 November 2008 at www.cptech.org/ip/wto/norwaystatement.html.

Croome, J. (1995), *Reshaping the World Trading System: A History of the Uruguay Round*, Geneva: World Trade Organization.

Crossette, B. (2001), 'Brazil's AIDS chief denounces Bush position on drug patents', *New York Times*, 3 May 2001 accessed 1 November 2008 at http://query.nytimes.com/gst/fullpage.html?res=980CE5D81538F930A35 756C0A9679C8B63.

Cutler, C., V. Haufler and T. Porter (1999), *Private Authority and International Affairs*, Albany, NY: SUNY Press.

CUTS International (2000), 'Labor standards in the WTO: protecting workers' rights or protecting privileges in the North?', excerpts of debate between Deepmala Mahla of CUTS and James Howard of ICFTU in 5th International Business Forum, Hanover, Germany, October 2000, accessed 1 November 2008 at www.cuts-international.org/linkages-debat.htm.

Ddamilura, D. and N.A. Halima (2003), *Civil Society and the WTO: Participation in National Trade Policy Design in Uganda and Kenya*, London: CAFOD Trade Justice Campaign.

Deibert, R. (2003), 'Deep probe: the evolution of network intelligence', *Intelligence and National Security*, **18**(4): 175–93.

Delechat, C. and OECD (1996), *Trade, Employment, and Labour Standards: A Study of Core Workers' Rights and International Trade*, Paris and Washington DC: Organisation for Economic Co-operation and Development and OECD Washington Center.

Delgado, N. and A. Soares (2005), 'The G-20: its origin, evolution, meaning and prospects', accessed 9 April 2008 at www.ecofair-trade.org/pics/en/ GIP25-G20-en.pdf.

DeMars, W.E. (2005), *NGOs and Transnational Networks: Wild Cards in World Politics*, London: Pluto Press.

DePalma, A. (2001), 'NAFTA dispute is in court once again', *New York Times*, 19 October 2001, accessed 1 November 2008 at http://query.nytimes.com/ gst/fullpage.html?res=9B01E6DD123EF93AA25753C1A9679C8B63.

Department of Foreign Affairs and Trade, Australian Government (2004), 'WTO Doha Round framework package – July 2004', accessed 30 July 2008 at www.dfat.gov.au/trade/negotiations/doha_framework_package. html.

Dery, D. (2000), 'Agenda setting and problem definition', *Policy Studies*, **21**(1): 37–47.

Dessing, M. (2001), 'The social clause and sustainable development', International Centre for Trade and Sustainable Development resource paper no. 1, accessed 1 May 2008 at www.icstd.org/pubs/series.htm.

Dolzer, R. and M. Stevens (1995), *Bilateral Investment Treaties*, Leiden, Netherlands: Brill Academic Press.

Donald, B. (1999), 'The World Trade Organization (WTO) Seattle Ministerial Conference, December 1999: issues and prospects', current issues brief 12, Foreign Affairs, Defence and Trade Group [Australian Government], accessed 8 June 2008 at www.aph.gov.au/Library/Pubs/CIB/1999-2000/2000cib12.htm.

Drahos, P. (1995), 'Global property rights in information: the story of TRIPs at the GATT', *Prometheus*, **13**(1): 6–19.

Dunoff, J.L. (1998), 'The misguided debate over NGO participation at the WTO', *Journal of International Economic Law*, **1**(3): 433–56.

Esty, D. (1998), '*Why the World Trade Organization needs environmental NGOs*', International Centre for Trade and Sustainable Development, accessed 6 July 2007 at www.ictsd.org/English/esty.pdf.

Esty, D. (2002), 'The World Trade Organization's legitimacy crisis', *World Trade Review*, **1**(1): 7–22.

Edwards, M. and D. Hulme (1996), 'Introduction: NGO performance and accountability', in M. Edwards and D. Hulme (eds), *Beyond the Magic Bullet: NGO Performance and Accountability in the Post-Cold War World*, West Hartford, CT: Kumarian Press.

Elliot, K.A. and R. Freeman (2003), *Can Labor Standards Improve Under Globalization?*, Washington, DC: Institute for International Economics.

Essential Action, accessed 26 June 2006 at www.essentialaction.org/access/.

European Commission (1998), Note on the WHO's revised drug strategy, document no 1/D/3/BW D 98, 5 October 1998, accessed 8 October 2007 at www.cptech.org/ip/health/who/eurds98.html.

European Commission (2001a), 'Communication from the Commission to the Council and the European Parliament Programme for Action: accelerated action on HIV/AIDS, malaria and tuberculosis in the context of poverty reduction', accessed 1 November 2008 at http://trade.ec.europa.eu/doclib/docs/2006/september/tradoc_130243.pdf.

European Commission (2001b), 'Assessment by the Chairman of the Health Issue Group/Access to Medicines, 16 January', accessed 1 November 2008 at http://trade.ec.europa.eu/doclib/docs/2005/april/tradoc_122202.pdf.

European Commission (2001c), 'Issue papers', accessed 1 November 2008 at http://trade.ec.europa.eu/doclib/docs/2005/march/tradoc_122030.pdf.

European Commission (2004), 'Singapore issues: clarification of the EU position (a line to take for Member States and the Commission', accessed 31 July 2008 at http://trade.ec.europa.eu/doclib/docs/2004/april/tradoc_116808.pdf.

European Parliament (2001), 'Resolution on access to drugs for HIV/AIDS victims in the Third World', accessed 1 June 2007 at http://www.europarl.europa.eu/omk/omnsapir.so/pv2?PRG=CALDOC&FILE=010315&LANGUE=EN&TPV=PROV&SDOCTA=13&TXTLST=1&Type_Doc=FIRST&POS=1.

Fairwear (2007), website accessed 6 February 2007 at www.fairwear.org.au/engine.php.

Falk, R. (1995), *On Humane Governance: Toward a New Global Politics*, University Park, PA: Pennsylvania State University Press.

Falk, R. (1999), *Predatory Globalization: A Critique*, Cambridge: Polity Press.

Florini, A.M. (2000), *The Third Force: The Rise of Transnational Civil Society*, Tokyo and Washington, DC: Japan Centre for International Exchange and Carnegie Endowment for International Peace.

Focus on the Global South (2003), 'Comments on Cancún draft ministerial text, 25 August 2003', accessed 6 November 2008 at www.nadir.org/nadir/initiativ/agp/free/wto/news/0825comments_cancún_draft.htm.

Focus on the Global South (2008a), 'Who we are', accessed 23 October 2008 at www.focusweb.org/who-we-are.html.

Focus on the Global South (2008b), 'Trade campaigns', accessed 23 October 2008 at www.focusweb.org/trade-campaign/2.html.

FOE [Friends of the Earth] England, Wales and Northern Ireland and WDM (2003), 'Investment and the WTO: busting the myths', accessed 6 July 2007 at www.foeeurope.org/trade/Investment_and_the_WTO.pdf.

FOE Europe [Friends of the Earth] (2002), 'From Brussels to Cancún: European civil society groups launch campaign on global trade and investment talks', press release 13 Sep 2002, www.foeeurope.org/press/AW_13_09_02_trade_and%20_investment.htm.

FOEI (2003), 'No new rights for big business at the WTO', FOEI position paper, accessed 6 July 2007 at www.foei.org/en/publications/pdfs/investment-english-final_letter.pdf.

FOEI (2008a), 'Who we are', accessed 5 November at www.foei.org/en/who-we-are.

FOEI (2008b), 'Campaigns', accessed 5 November at www.foei.org/en/campaigns.

Ford, L.H. (2003), 'Challenging global environmental governance: social movement agency and global civil society', *Global Environmental Politics*, **3**(2): 120–34.

Ford, N. (2004), 'Patents, access to medicines and the role of non-governmental organizations', *Journal of Generic Medicines*, **1**(2): 137–45.

Fields, G. (1994), 'Changing labor market conditions and economic development in Hong Kong, the Republic of Korea, Singapore, and Taiwan, China', *World Bank Economic Review*, **8**(3): 395–414.

Fox, J.A. and D.L. Brown (1998), *The Struggle for Accountability: The World Bank, NGOs, and Grassroots Movements*, Cambridge, MA: MIT Press.

Frutiger, D. (2002), 'AFL-CIO China policy: labor's new step forward or the Cold War revisited?', *Labor Studies Journal*, **27**(3): 67–80.

G-15 [Group of 15] (1995), 'Joint communiqué, V summit of the heads of state and governments of the Group of Fifteen', Buenos Aires, Argentina, 5–7 November 1995, accessed 4 February 2008 at www.g15.org/communiques5.pdf.

G-20 'G-20 – History', accessed 13 August 2007 at www.g-20.mre.gov.br/history.asp.

G-77 (2001), 'Declaration by the Group of 77 and China on the Fourth WTO Ministerial Conference at Doha, Qatar', accessed 1 February 2008 at www.org?Docs/Doha.htm.

George, A.L. (1979), 'Case studies and theory development: the method of structured, focused comparison', in P.G. Lauren (ed.), *Diplomacy: New Approaches in History, Theory, and Policy*, New York: Free Press.

Gilpin, R. (2001), *Global Political Economy: Understanding the International Economic Order*, Princeton, NJ: Princeton University Press.

Goodman, J. (2002), *Protest and Globalization: Prospects for Transnational Solidarity*, Annandale, VA: Pluto Press.

Grabel, I. (1998), 'Portfolio investment', *Foreign Policy in Focus*, **3**(13), accessed 25 June 2008 at www.fpif.org/briefs/vol3/v3n13inv.html.

Greenhouse, S. and J. Kahn (1999), 'Talks and turmoil: workers' rights; US effort to add labor standards to agenda fails', *New York Times*, 3 December 1999, accessed 7 February 2008 at http://query.nytimes.com/gst/fullpage.html?res=9905E7D6173EF930A35751C1A96F958260.

Greenpeace International (2007), 'Questions about Greenpeace in general', accessed 3 September at www.greenpeace.org/international/about/faq/questions-about-greenpeace-in.

Griffin, G., C. Nyland and A. O'Rourke (2003), 'Trade unions and the trade-labour rights link: a North–South union divide?', *The International Journal of Comparative Labour Law and Industrial Relations*, **19**(4): 469–94.

Guidry, J.A., M.D. Kennedy and M.N. Zald (2001), *Globalizations and Social Movements Culture, Power, and the Transnational Public Sphere*, Ann Arbor, MI: University of Michigan Press.

Guzman, A.T. (2003), 'Trade, labor, legitimacy', *California Law Review*, **91**(3): 885–902.

Haas, P. (1990), 'Obtaining international environmental protection through epistemic consensus', *Millennium: Journal of International Studies*, **19**(3): 347–63.

Haas, P. (1992), 'Banning chlorofluorocarbons: epistemic community efforts to protect stratospheric ozone', *International Organization*, **46**(1): 187–224.

HAI (2006a), website accessed 10 June at www.haiweb.org.

HAI (2006b), website accessed 10 June at www.haiweb.org/campaign/access/wemos22feb2001.html.

Harmon, A. and R. Pear (2001), 'Canada overrides patent for Cipro to treat anthrax', *New York Times*, 19 October, accessed 1 November 2008 at http://query.nytimes.com/gst/fullpage.html?res=9B0DEEDE133EF93AA2 5753C1A9679C8B63.

Hartridge, D. (2003), speech at SITPRO World Trade Post-Cancún Conference, Westminster, London, 21 October 2003.

Haufler, V. (1993), 'Crossing the boundary between public and private: international regimes and non-state actors', in V. Rittberger (ed.), *Regime Theory and International Relations*, Oxford: Clarendon Press.

Haworth, N. (2002), 'International labour and its emerging role in global governance: regime fusion, social protection, regional integration and production volatility', in S. Hughes and R. Wilkinson (eds), *Global Governance: Critical Perspectives*, London and New York: Routledge.

Haworth N. and S. Hughes (2004), 'From Marrakesh to Doha and beyond: the tortuous progress of the contemporary trade and labour standards debate', in D. Kelly and W. Grant (eds), *The Politics of International Trade*, London: Palgrave.

He, B. (2004), 'Transnational civil society and the national identity question in East Asia', *Global Governance*, **10**(2): 227–46.

Health GAP (2001a), 'Activists protest US-based plaintiffs in South Africa "medical apartheid" lawsuit; kick-off month of action against big pharma during industry-induced trial delay', accessed 1 November 2008 at www.healthgap.org/press_releases/01/030801_AU_PA_SA_DCdemo.htm.

Health GAP (2001b) 'Health GAP timeline direct actions, advocacy, and response January 2001–December 2001', accessed 1 November 2008 at www.healthgap.org/hgap/Timeline_of_HGAP_2001.html.

Health GAP (2001c), 'TRIPS: will the majority prevail?', WTO/TRIPS: NGO statement on Doha Declaration, 11 November 2001, accessed 6 July 2007 at www.healthgap.org/press_releases/01/111101_JOINT_PS_Doha_decl.html.

Hensman, R. (2001), 'World trade and workers' rights: in search of an internationalist position', *Antipode*, **33**(3): 427–50.

Hernández, S. (1998), 'The dynamics of WTO, NGOs and trade unions, and the co-option of civil society', edited version of speech given at the founding convention of the Joint Action Forum of Indian People against WTO and Anti-People Policies, Hyderabad, 29–30 April and 1 May 1998, accessed 1 June 2006 at www.savanne.ch/cooption.sh.

Hirst, P. and G. Thompson (1999), *Globalization in Question: The International Economy and the Possibilities of Governance*, 2nd edn, Cambridge: Polity Press.

't Hoen, E.F.M. (2002), 'TRIPS, pharmaceutical patents and access to essential medicines: a long way from Seattle to Doha', *Chicago Journal of International Law*, **3**(1): 27–46.

't Hoen, E.F.M. (2003), 'TRIPS, pharmaceutical patents and access to essential medicines: Seattle, Doha and beyond', in J.P. Moatti, B. Coriat, Y. Souteyrand, B. Barnett, J. Dumoulin, and Y.A. Flori (eds), *Economics of AIDS and Access to HIV/AIDS Care in Developing Countries: Issues and Challenges*, Paris: Agence Nationale de Recherches sur le Sida.

Hormeku, T. (2004), 'G90 softens on trade facilitation, hardens on NAMA and cotton', *SEATINI Bulletin*, **7**(10), accessed 22 June 2007 at www.seatini.org/bulletins/7.10.php.

Howse, R. (1999), 'The World Trade Organization and the protection of workers' rights', *Journal of Small and Emerging Business Law*, **3**(1): 131–72.

Howse, R. (2003), 'How to begin to think about the "democratic deficit" at the WTO', in S. Griller (ed.), *International Economic Governance and Non-Economic Concerns: New Challenges for the International Legal Order*, Vienna and New York: Springer.

Howse, R., B. Langille and J. Burda (2006), 'The World Trade Organization and labour rights: man bites dog', in V.A. Leary and D. Warner (eds), *Social Issues, Globalization and International Institutions: Labour Rights and the EU, ILO, OECD and WTO*, Leiden, Netherlands: Brill Academic Press.

Hughes, S. and N. Haworth (1997), 'Trade and international labour standards: issues and debates over a social clause', *Journal of Industrial Relations*, **39**(2): 179–195.

Hughes, S. and R. Wilkinson (1998), 'International labour standards and world trade: no role for the World Trade Organization?', *New Political Economy*, **3**(3): 375–89.

Hulme, D. and M. Edwards (1997), *NGOs, States and Donors: Too Close for Comfort*, New York: St Martin's Press.

Humphreys, D. (2004), 'Redefining the issues: NGO influence on international forest negotiations', *Global Environmental Politics*, **4**(2): 51–74.

Huntington, S.P. (1973), Transnational organizations in world politics, *World Politics*, **25**(2): 333–68.

Hurrell, A. and A. Narlikar (2006), 'A new politics of confrontation? Developing countries at *Cancún* and beyond', *Global Society*, **20**(4): 415–33.

ICTSD (1999), 'Coverage of the Seattle ministerial', *BRIDGES Weekly Trade News Digest*, **3**(46), accessed 8 June 2006 at www.ictsd.org/ministerial/seattle/story24-11-99.htm.

ICTSD (2003), 'NGOs launch campaign against investment agreement', accessed 6 July 2007 at www.ictsd.org/weekly/03-03-26/story3.htm.

ICTSD (2007), 'Welcome to ICTSD', accessed 24 May 2008 at www.ictsd.org/about/index.htm.

ICFTU (1996), 'International labour standards and trade: an anti-protectionist mechanism for promoting basic workers' rights in the global market', ICFTU discussion paper for the first ministerial meeting of the World Trade Organization, Singapore 9–13 December 1996, accessed 21 February 2008 at www.old.itcilo.org/actrav/actravenglish/telearn/global/ilo/standard/trade.htm.

ICFTU (1998), 'Fighting for workers' human rights in the global economy: defending fundamental trade union rights', accessed 25 January 2008 at www.icftu.org/displaydocument.asp?Index=990916201&Language=EN.

ICFTU (1999), 'Development, environment and trade: statement to the high-level symposia of the World Trade Organization (WTO) on "trade and environment" and "trade and development"', accessed 21 February 2008 at www.icftu.org/displaydocument.asp?Index=990916238&Language=EN.

ICFTU (1999a), 'Building workers' human rights into the global trading system', accessed 21 February 2008 at www.icftu.org/www/english/els/escl99BWRGTS.pdf.

ICFTU (1999b), 'Enough exploitation is enough: a response to the Third World intellectuals and NGO's statement against linkage (TWIN-SAL)', accessed 7 February 2008 at www.icftu.org/displaydocument.asp?Index+990916168&Language+EN.

ICFTU (2003), 'Trade union statement on the agenda for the 5th Ministerial Conference of the World Trade Organization', accessed 1 February 2008 at www.icftu.org/displaydocument.asp?Index=991217396&Language=EN.

ICFTU (2004), 'A trade union guide to globalization', (second edition), accessed 6 February 2008 at www.icftu.org/pubs/globalisation/EN/report.pdf.

ICFTU (2007a), 'ICFTU: what it is, what it does', accessed 21 November at www.icftu.org/displaydocument.asp?DocType=Overview&Index=990916422&Language=EN.

ICFTU (2007b), 'Country reports: WTO & labour standards in order of date', accessed 6 February 2008 at www.icftu.org/list.asp?Language=EN&Order=Date&Type=WTOReports&Subject=ILS&start=0&finish=19.

ICFTU-AFRO [International Confederation of Free Trade Unions African Regional Organization] (2001), 'Report on activities, XIII regional congress', Nairobi, Kenya, 23–25 May 2001, accessed 6 February 2008 at

http://209.85.175.104/search?q=cache:rmIh5c4z6osJ:www.icftuafro.org/
public/CONGRESS-Final%2520Report%2520on%2520Activities%
25201997-2000-open.doc+ICFTU+lobby+governments+WTO+
delegation&hl=en&ct=clnk&cd=16&gl=au.

IISD (2006), 'Investment and developing countries', accessed 8 July at www.iisd.org/investment/dci.

ILO (1919), 'Text of the constitution, preamble', accessed 18 February 2008 at www.ilo.org/ilolex/english/constq.htm.

ILO (1998), 'ILO declaration on fundamental principles and rights at work', 86th session, Geneva, June 1998, accessed 6 February 2008 at www.ilo.org/public/english/employment/skills/hrdr/instr/decla.htm.

ILO (2007), 'Introduction to international labour standards', accessed 24 March 2007 at www.ilo.org/global/What_we_do/InternationalLabour Standards/Introduction/lang—en/index.htm.

IMF (2007), 'About the IMF – IMF members' quotas and voting power, and IMF board of governors', accessed 10 May at www.imf.org/external/np/sec/memdir/members.htm.

Imig, D. and S. Tarrow (2001), *Contentious Europeans: Protest and Politics in an Emerging Polity*, Lanham, MD: Rowman and Littlefield.

IP Australia (2008), 'What is Intellectual Property?', accessed 23 October 2008 at www.ipaustralia.gov.au/ip/index.shtml.

Jackson, J.H. (1997), 'Helms-Burton, the US, and the WTO', The American Society of International Law Insights, accessed 1 November 2008 at www.asil.org/insight7.cfm.

Jacobson, H.K. (2000), 'International institutions and system transformation', *Annual Review of Political Science*, **3**: 149–66.

Jenson, N.M. (2003), 'Democratic governance and multinational corporations: political regimes and inflows of foreign direct investment', *International Organization*, **57**(3): 587–616.

Jordan, L. and P. van Tuijl (2000), 'Political responsibility in transnational NGO advocacy', *World Development*, **28**(12): 2051–65.

Joachim, J. (2003), 'Framing issues and seizing opportunities: the UN, NGOs, and women's rights', *International Studies Quarterly*, **47**(2): 247–74.

Joachim, J. (2007), *Agenda Setting, the UN, and NGOs: Gender Violence and Reproductive Rights*, Washington, DC: Georgetown University Press.

Katz, H. (2008), 'Data programme: indicator suites of global civil society', in M. Albrow, H. Anheier, M. Glasius, M.E. Price and M. Kaldor (eds), *Global Civil Society 2007–08: Communicative Power and Democracy*, London: Sage Publications.

Keane, J. (2003), *Global Civil Society?*, Cambridge: Cambridge University Press.

Keck, M.E. and K. Sikkink (1998), *Activists Beyond Borders: Advocacy Networks in International Politics*, Ithaca, NY: Cornell University Press.

Kellow, A. (2000), 'Norms, interests and environmental NGOs: the limits of cosmopolitanism', *Environmental Politics*, **9**(3): 1–22.

Kellow, A. (2001), 'The constitution of international civil society', in C. Sampford and T. Round (eds), *Beyond the Republic: Meeting the Global Challenges to Constitutionalism*, Annandale, VA: Federation Press.

Kellow, A. (2002), 'Comparing business and public interest associability at the international level', *International Political Science Review*, **23**(2): 175–86.

Keohane, R.O. and J.S. Nye (1972), *Transnational Relations and World Politics*, Cambridge, MA: Harvard University Press.

Keohane, R.O. and J.S. Nye (1977), *Power and Interdependence: World Politics in Transition*, Boston, MA: Little, Brown and Company.

Keohane, R.O. and J.S. Nye (2001a), 'The club model of multilateral cooperation and problems of democratic legitimacy', in R. Porter, P. Sauve, A. Subramanian, and A.B. Zampetti (eds), *Efficiency, Equity and Legitimacy: The Multilateral Trading System at the Millennium*, Washington DC: Brookings Institution Press.

Keohane, R.O. and J.S. Nye (2001b), *Power and Interdependence: World Politics in Transition* (3rd edn), Boston: Little, Brown and Company.

Kerbel, M.R. (1995), *Remote and Controlled: Media Politics in a Cynical Age*, Boulder, CO: Westview Press.

Khagram, S., J.V. Riker, and K Sikkink (2002), *Restructuring World Politics: Transnational Social Movements, Networks, and Norms*, Minneapolis, MN: University of Minnesota Press.

Khor, M. (1996), 'After Singapore, the battle of interpretations begin: labour standards', accessed 1 November 2008 at www.twnside.org.sg/title/bat-cn.htm.

Khor, M. (2003a), 'Fate of ministerial hangs on a thread – as developing countries express frustration with text', TWN info service on WTO Issues, 15 September, accessed 5 July 2007 at www.twnside.org.sg/title/twninfo75.htm.

Khor, M. (2003b), 'Analysis of the collapse of the WTO Cancún ministerial', TWN info service on WTO issues, 16 September, accessed 6 December 2005 at www.twnside.org.sg/title/twninfo76.htm.

Khor, M. (2003c), 'Lamy still insists that Singapore issues are part of Doha single undertaking: report of panel discussion at the UN on WTO and Cancún', TWN info service on WTO issues, 7 November, accessed 1 November 2008 at www.twnside.org.sg/title/twninfo91.htm.

Kingdon, J.W. (1984), *Agendas, Alternatives and Public Policy*, Boston, MA: Little, Brown and Company.

Kitschelt, H.P. (1986) 'Political opportunity structures and political protest: anti-nuclear movements in four democracies', *British Journal of Political Science*, **16**(1): 57–86.

Klotz, A. (1995), 'Norms reconstituting interests: global racial equality and US sanctions against South Africa', *International Organization*, **49**(3): 451–78.

Kolben, K. (2006), 'The new politics of linkage: India's opposition to the workers' rights clause', *Indiana Journal of Global Legal Studies*, **13**(1): 225–59.

Knowlton, B. (1999), 'US Is upbeat, but poorer nations refuse to relent on labor standards: in a quiet Seattle, WTO starts its work', *International Herald Tribune*, 3 December, accessed 1 February 2008 at www.iht.com/articles/1999/12/03/a1_2.php.

Khor, M. (1997), 'The WTO and the battle over labor standards', Third World Network Features, 13 January, accessed 31 January 2008 at www.globalpolicy.org/socecon/labor/wtolabor.htm.

Krasner, S.D. (1982), 'Structural causes and regime consequences: regimes as intervening variables', *International Organization*, **36**(2): 185–205.

Kratochwil, F.V. (1989), *Rules, Norms, and Decisions: On the Conditions of Practical and Legal Reasoning in International Relations and Domestic Affairs*, Cambridge: Cambridge University Press.

Kucera, D. (2004), 'Core labor standards and economic development', *Labor History*, **45**(4): 516–22.

Kurtz, J. (2002), 'A general investment agreement at the WTO? Lessons from Chapter 11 of NAFTA and the OECD Multilateral Agreement on Investment', *University of Pennsylvania Journal of International Economic Law*, **23**(4): 713–89.

Labour Behind the Label (2007), website accessed 22 May 2007 at www.labourbehindthelabel.org/.

Lacarte, J.A. (2004), 'Transparency, public debate and participation by NGOs in the WTO: a WTO perspective', *Journal of International Economic Law*, **7**(3): 683–6.

Lalumiere, C. (1998), 'Report on the Multilateral Agreement on Investment – intermediary report, September 1998', translated by C. Dumonteil, accessed 1 September 2007 at www.geocities.com/w_trouble_o/lumier.htm.

LDC Trade Ministers (2003), 'Dhaka Declaration', second LDC trade ministers' meeting, Dhaka, Bangladesh, 31 May–2 June, document number LDC-II/2003/L.1/Rev.1, accessed 1 November 2008 at www.mincom.gov.bd/images/additional_images/Dhaka%20Declaration.doc.

Lethbridge, J. (2004), 'Combining worker and user interests in the health sector: trade unions and NGOs', *Development in Practice*, **14** (1–2): 234–47.

Leebron. D.W. (2002), 'Linkages', *American Journal of International Law*, **96**(5): 5–27.

Lipschutz, R. (1996), *Global Civil Society and Global Environmental Governance*, Albany, NY: SUNY Press.

Lisowski, M. (2005), 'How NGOs use their facilitative negotiating power and bargaining assets to affect international environmental negotiations', *Diplomacy and Statecraft*, **16**(2): 361–83.

Loy, F. (2001), 'Public participation in the World Trade Organization', in G.P. Sampson (ed.), *The Role of the WTO in Global Governance*, Tokyo: United Nations University Press.

Lobe, J. (2003), 'NGOs organize against proposed WTO investment agreement', OneWorld.net, 23 June, accessed 22 May 2008 at www.commondreams.org/headlines03/0623-02.htm.

Mackie, T. and D. Marsh (1995), 'The comparative method', in D. Marsh and S. Stoker (eds), *Theory and Methods in Political Science*, London: Macmillan.

Marceau, G. and P.N. Pedersen (1999), 'Is the WTO open and transparent? A discussion of the relationship of the WTO with non-governmental organizations and civil society's claims for more transparency and public participation', *Journal of World Trade*, **33**(1): 5–49.

Mason, M. (2004), 'Representing transnational environmental interests: new opportunities for non-governmental organization access within the World Trade Organization?', *Environmental Politics*, **13**(3): 566–89.

Mavroidis, P.C. (2003), 'Commentary 4.2: the need to micro-manage regulatory diversity', in K. Basu, H. Horn, L. Román and J. Shapiro (eds), *International Labor Standards: History, Theory, and Policy Options*, Oxford: Blackwell Publishing.

McAdam, D., J.D. McCarthy and M.N. Zald (1996), *Comparative Perspectives on Social Movements: Political Opportunities, Mobilizing Structures, and Cultural Framings*, Cambridge: Cambridge University Press.

McCombs, M. and D.L. Shaw (1972), 'The agenda setting function of mass media', *Public Opinion Quarterly*, **36**(2): 176–87.

McCombs, M., D.L. Shaw and D. Weaver (1997), *Communication and Democracy: Exploring the Intellectual Frontiers in Agenda Setting Theory*, London: Lawrence Erlbaum Associates.

McMichael, P. (2000), 'Sleepless since Seattle: what is the WTO about?', *Review of International Political Economy*, **7**(3): 466–74.

McNeil, D.G. (2001), 'Yale pressed to help cut drug costs in Africa', *New York Times*, 12 March, accessed 1 November 2008 at http://query.nytimes.com/gst/fullpage.html?sec=health&res=9C05E1DB133AF931A25750C0A967 9C8B63&n=Top%2fReference%2fTimes%20Topics%2fOrganizations%2f Y%2fYale%20University%20.

Mendelson, S.E. and J.K. Glenn (2002), *The Power and Limits of NGOs: A Critical Look at Building Democracy in Eastern Europe and Eurasia*, New York: Columbia University Press.

MIGA (Multilateral Investment Guarantee Agency) (2008), website, accessed 25 June at www.miga.org/sitelevel2/level2.cfm?id=1069.

Ministers of Trade of the Member States of the African Union (2003), 'Grand Baie ministerial declaration on the fifth ministerial conference of the WTO', Grand Baie, Mauritius, 19–20 June 2003, accessed 1 November 2008 at www.union-network.org/UNIsite/In_Depth/Interna_Relations/GATS/2003PDF/*Cancún*%20-%20African%20Trade%20Ministers%20Decl%20June.pdf.

Morrison, S.J. (2001), 'The African pandemic hits Washington', *The Washington Quarterly*, **24**(1): 197–209.

MSF (Médecins Sans Frontières) (2007), 'The campaign: frequently asked questions', accessed 6 July 2007 at www.accessmed-msf.org/campaign/faq.shtm.

MSF (2006), 'Neither expeditious nor a solution: the WTO Aug. 30th decision is unworkable', paper presented at the 16th International AIDS Conference, Toronto, 13–18 August, accessed 22 May 2007 at www.accessmedmsf.org/prod/publications.asp?scntid=10820061618476&contenttype=PARA&.

MSF and Cipla (2001), 'Joint statement Médecins Sans Frontières and Cipla: progress reported on implementation of offer for more affordable anti-AIDS drugs', 23 February, accessed 1 November at www.essentialdrugs.org/edrug/archive/200102/msg00096.php.

Nanz, P. and J. Steffek (2004), 'Global governance, participation and the public sphere', *Government and Opposition*, **39**(2): 314–35.

Narlikar, A. and D. Tussie (2004), 'The G20 at the *Cancún* ministerial: developing countries and their evolving coalitions in the WTO', *The World Economy*, **27**(7): 947–66.

Narlikar, A. (2003), *International Trade and Developing Countries: Bargaining Coalitions in the GATT and WTO*, London: Routledge.

Nelson, P. (2002), 'New agendas and new patterns of international NGO political action', *Voluntas: International Journal of Voluntary and Nonprofit Organizations*, **13**(4): 377–92.

Newell, P. (2000), *Climate for Change: Non-State Actors and the Global Politics of the Greenhouse*, Cambridge: Cambridge University Press.

Non-Aligned and other Developing Countries (1995), 'Fifth conference of labour ministers of non-aligned and other developing countries, draft Delhi declaration', New Delhi, 19–23 January.

Nyhan, P. (1999a), 'Clinton's proposals praised by labor groups', *Seattle Post-Intelligencer*, 2 December, accessed 22 May 2008 at http://seattlepi.nwsource.com/business/labr02.shtml.

Nyhan, P. (1999b), 'Labor's claim of WTO victory is validated', *Seattle Post-Intelligencer*, 8 December, accessed 22 May 2008 at http://seattlepi.nwsource.com/business/labr08.shtml.

O'Brien, R.J., A.M. Goetz, J.A. Scholte and M.A. Williams (2000), *Contesting Global Governance: Multilateral Economic Institutions and Global Social Movements*, Cambridge: Cambridge University Press.

OECD (2008), 'Multilateral Agreement on Investment: documentation from the negotiations: introduction', accessed 1 November at www1.oecd.org/daf/mai/intro.htm.

Ostry, S. (2000), 'Looking back to look forward: the multilateral trading system after 50 years', in *From GATT To The WTO: The Multilateral Trading System in the New Millennium*, Geneva: WTO Secretariat.

Ostry, S. (2006), 'The world trading system: in the fog of uncertainty', *Review of International Organizations*, **1**(2): 139–52.

Oxfam International (2001), 'Cut the cost', accessed 6 July 2007 at www.maketradefair.com/en/index.php?file=26032002170734.htm.

Oxfam International (2003), 'The emperor's new clothes: why rich countries want a WTO investment agreement', Oxfam briefing paper 46, accessed 6 July 2007 at www.oxfam.org.uk/what_we_do/issues/trade/bp46_wto.htm.

Oxfam (2006), 'Make Trade Fair', accessed 5 December at www.maketradefair.com/en/index.php?file=a2m_india.htm&cat=2&subcat=4&select=4.

Panagariya, A. (2000), 'Trade-labour link: a post-Seattle analysis', in Z. Drabek (ed.), *Globalization Under Threat: The Stability of Trade Policy and International Agreements*, Cheltenham, UK and Northampton, MA, USA: Edward Elgar.

Parliament of the Commonwealth of Australia (2004), 'The Fifth WTO Ministerial Conference at Cancún', in 'Australia's engagement with the World Trade Organisation: a report on the proceedings of the 2003 Annual Public Hearing Joint Standing Committee on Foreign Affairs Defence and Trade Sub-committee', accessed 12 April 2008 at www.aph.gov.au/house/committee/jfadt/worldtrade/report/chapter2.pdf.

Paulson, M. (1999), 'Clinton says he will support trade sanctions for worker abuse', *Seattle Post-Intelligencer*, 1 December, accessed 22 May 2008 at http://seattlepi.nwsource.com/national/clin012.shtml.

Payne, R.A. and Samhat, N.H. (2004), 'The democratization of the World Trade Organization', in R.A. Payne and N.H. Samhat (eds), *Democratizing Global Politics: Discourse Norms, International Regimes, and Political Community*, Albany, NY: SUNY Press.

Permanent Mission of India, Geneva (2003), 'Trade and investment: some issues', presentation by Indian ambassador to WTO, seminar on WTO investment agreement, Geneva, 20 March, *TWN info service on WTO issues*, 11 May, accessed 8 March 2008 at www.twnside.org.sg/title/twninfo16.htm.

Petersmann, E-U. (2001), 'European and international constitutional law: time for promoting "cosmopolitan democracy" in the WTO', in G. de Búrca and J. Scott (eds), *The EU and the WTO: Legal and Constitutional Issues*, Oxford: Oxford University Press.

PhRMA (2005), 'What Goes into the Cost of Prescription Drugs?', accessed 28 October 2008 at www.phrma.org/files/Cost_of_Prescription_Drugs.pdf.

Pianta, M. (2001), 'Parallel summits of global civil society', in H. Anheier, M. Glasius and M. Kaldor (eds), *Global Civil Society 2001*, Oxford: Oxford University Press.

Pianta, M. and F. Silva (2003), 'Parallel summits of global civil society: an update', in M. Kaldor, H. Anheier and M. Glasius (eds), *Global Civil Society Yearbook 2003*, Oxford: Oxford University Press.

della Porta, D., H. Kriesi and D. Rucht (1999), *Social Movements in a Globalizing World*, London: Macmillan.

della Porta, D. and S. Tarrow (2005), *Transnational Protest and Global Activism: People, Passions and Power*, Lanham, MD and Oxford: Rowman and Littlefield.

Price, R. (1998), 'Reversing the gun sights: transnational civil society targets land mines', *International Organization*, **52**(3): 613–44.

Princen, T. and M. Finger (1994), *Environmental NGOs in World Politics: Linking the Local and the Global*, London and New York: Routledge.

Putnam, R.D. (1988), 'Diplomacy and domestic politics: the logic of two-level games', *International Organization*, **42**(3): 427–60.

Quakers in Britain (2007), 'Finance, trade and development – factsheet', accessed 31 January at www.quaker.org.uk/Templates/Internal.asp?NodeID=90143.

Raghavan, C. (1999), 'Seattle WTO ministerial ends in failure', *South–North Development Monitor* 4567, accessed 8 June 2007 at www.twnside.org.sg/title/deb2-cn.htm.

Ragin, C. (1991), *Issues and Alternatives in Comparative Social Research*, Leiden, Netherlands and New York: Brill.

Reinicke, W.H. (1998), *Global Public Policy: Governing Without Government?*, Washington, DC: Brookings Institution Press.

Reinicke, W.H. (1999–2000), 'The other world wide web: global public policy networks', *Foreign Policy*, **117**: 44–57.

Richwine, L. (1999), 'Groups say US hurts world access to AIDS drugs', *Reuters*, 11 April, accessed 1 November 2008 at http://lists.essential.org/pharm-policy/msg00051.html.

van Rijn, K. (2006), 'The politics of uncertainty: the AIDS debate, Thabo Mbeki and the South African government response', *Social History of Medicine*, **19**(3): 521–38.

Risse, T. (2000), 'Let's argue! Communicative action in world politics.' *International Organization*, **54**(1): 1–39.

Risse, T. (2002), 'Transnational actors and world politics', in W. Carlsnaes, T. Risse and B.A. Simmons (eds), *Handbook of International Relations*, London: Sage Publications.

Risse-Kappen, T. (1995), *Bringing Transnational Relations Back In: Non-State Actors, Domestic Structures and International Institutions*, Cambridge: Cambridge University Press.

Risse, T., S.C. Ropp and K. Sikkink (1999), *The Power of Human Rights: International Norms and Domestic Change*, Cambridge: Cambridge University Press.

Robertson, D. (2000a), 'Setting the record straight free trade and the WTO', Issue analysis, 4 September, St. Leonards, NSW: Centre for Independent Studies.

Robertson, D. (2000b), 'Civil society and the WTO', *The World Economy*, **23**(9): 1119–34.

Ronit, K. (2007), *Global Public Policy: Business and the Countervailing Powers of Civil Society*, London: Routledge.

Rosenau, J.N. (1980), *The Study of Global Interdependence: Essays on the Transnationalization of World Affairs*, London: Pinter.

Rosenau, J.N. (1990), *Turbulence in World Politics: A Theory of Change and Continuity*, Princeton, NJ: Princeton University Press.

Rosenau, J.N. and E.-O. Czempiel (1992), *Governance Without Government: Order and Change in World Politics*, Cambridge: Cambridge University Press.

van Roozendaal, G. (2002), *Trade Unions and Global Governance: The Debate on a Social Clause*, London: Routledge.

Ragin C. and H. Becker (1992), *What is a Case? Exploring the Foundations of Social Inquiry*, Cambridge: Cambridge University Press.

Raja, K. (2003), 'NGOs voice opposition to WTO investment negotiations', TWN info service on WTO issues, 13 June, accessed 1 November 2008 at www.twnside.org.sg/title/twninfo25.htm.

Ricupero, R. (1998), *Integration of Developing Countries into the Multilateral Trading System*, Ann Arbor, MI: University of Michigan Press.

S2B Network [Seattle to Brussels Network] (2002), 'Invitation to sign joint statement by European civil society groups against an agreement on investment in the WTO', accessed 22 June 2007 at http://62.149.193.10/s2bnetwork/download/S2B%20Investment%20statement.pdf?id=36.

Salazar-Xirinachs, J.M. and J.M. Martínez-Piva (2003), 'Trade, labour standards and global governance: a perspective from the Americas', in S. Griller (ed.), *International Economic Governance and Non-Economic Concerns: New Challenges for the International Legal Order*, Vienna and New York: Springer.

Salazar-Xirinachs, J.M. (2000), 'The trade–labor nexus: developing countries' perspectives', *Journal of International Economic Law*, **32**(2): 377–80.

Sampson, G.P. (2001), *The Role of the WTO in Global Governance*, Tokyo: United Nations University Press.

Scholte, J.A., R. O'Brien and M. Williams (1999), 'The WTO and civil society', *Journal of World Trade*, **33**: 107–23.

SEATINI (2003), 'Recommendations from the sixth SEATINI workshop held in Arusha from 2–5 April, 2003', *SEATINI Bulletin* **6**(6), accessed 22 June 2007 at www.seatini.org/bulletins/6.06.php.

Seidman, G.W. (2004), 'Deflated citizenship: labor rights in a global era', in A. Brysk and G. Shafir (eds), *People Out of Place: Globalization, Human Rights and the Citizenship Gap*, New York: Routledge.

Sell, S. (1998), *Power and Ideas: North–South Politics of Intellectual Property and Antitrust*, Albany, NY: SUNY Press.

Sell, S. (2002), 'TRIPS and the Access to Medicines Campaign', *Wisconsin International Law Journal*, **20**(3): 481–522.

Sell. S. (2003), *Private Power, Public Law: The Globalization of Intellectual Property Rights*, Cambridge: Cambridge University Press.

Sell, S. and C. May (2005), *Intellectual Property Rights: A Critical History*, Boulder, CO: Lynne Rienner.

Sell, S. and A. Prakash (2004), 'Using ideas strategically: the contest between business and NGO networks in intellectual property rights', *International Studies Quarterly*, **48**(1): 143–75.

Shadlen, K.C. (2004), 'Patents and pills, power and procedure: the north–south politics of public health in the WTO', *Studies in Comparative International Development*, **39**(3): 76–108.

Shue, H. (1995), 'Ethics, the environment and the changing international order', *International Affairs*, **71**(3): 453–61.

Sikkink, K. (1993), 'Human rights, principled issue-networks and sovereignty in Latin America', *International Organization*, **47**(3): 411–41.

Sikkink, K. (2002), 'Restructuring world politics: the limits and asymmetries of soft power', in S. Khagram, J.V. Riker and K. Sikkink (eds), *Restructuring World Politics. Transnational Social Movements, Networks, and Norms*, Minneapolis, MN: University of Minnesota Press.

Singh A. and A. Zammit (2000), *The Global Labour Standards Controversy: Critical Issues for Developing Countries*. Geneva: South Centre, accessed 8 March 2008 at www.southcentre.org/index.php?option=com_content&task=view&id=401&Itemid=67.

Singh, K. (2003), 'Multilateral Investment Agreement in the WTO: issues and illusions', Asia-Pacific Research Network Paper, accessed 1 November 2008 at www.wto.int/english/forums_e/ngo_e/multi_invest_agree_july03_e.pdf.

Smith, J. (2002), 'Globalizing resistance: the battle of Seattle and the future of social movements', in J. Smith and H. Johnston (eds), *Globalization and Resistance: Transnational Dimensions of Social Movements*, Lanham, MD: Rowman and Littlefield.

Smith, J. (2003), 'WTO mood At Cancun worsened by NGOs: EU's Fischler', accessed 12 April 2008 at www.globalpolicy.org/ngos/int/wto/2003/0919cancun.htm.

Smith, J. (2004), 'The World Social Forum and the challenges of global democracy', *Global Networks*, **4**(4): 413–21.

Smith, J. and J. Bandy (2005), *Coalitions Across Borders: Transnational Protest and the Neoliberal Order*, Lanham, MD: Rowman and Littlefield.

Smith, J., C. Chatfield and R. Pagnucco (1997), *Transnational Social Movements and Global Politics*, New York: Syracuse University Press.

Smith, J. and T. Fetner (2007), 'Structural approaches in the sociology of social movements', in B. Klandermans and C. Roggeband (eds), *Handbook of Social Movements Across Disciplines*, New York: Springer.

Smith, J. and H. Johnston (2002), *Globalization and Resistance: Transnational Dimensions of Social Movements*, Lanham, MD: Rowman and Littlefield.

Smith, P.J. and E. Smythe (2003), 'This is what democracy looks like: globalization, new information technology and the trade policy process: some comparative observations', *Perspectives on Global Development and Technology*, **2**(2): 179–214.

Smythe, E. (2003–4), 'Just say no!: The negotiation of investment rules at the WTO', *International Journal of Political Economy*, **33**(4): 60–83.

South Centre (2003), 'Chronology of events in the Cancún Ministerial Conference 10–14 September 2003', South Centre analytical note, September, accessed 1 August 2008 at www.southcentre.org/index.php?option=com_docman&task=doc_download&gid=226&Itemid=.

South–North Development Monitor (2008), 'SUNS – about', accessed 22 May at www.sunsonline.org/about.html.

Staiger, R.W. (2003), 'A role for the WTO', in K. Basu, H. Horn, L. Román and J. Shapiro (eds), *International Labor Standards: History, Theory, and Policy Options*, Oxford: Blackwell Publishing.

Starr, A. (2005), *Global Revolt: A Guide to the Movements Against Globalization*, London: Zed Books.

Steinberg, R.H. (2002), 'In the shadow of law or power? Consensus-based bargaining and outcomes in the GATT/WTO', *International Organization*, **56**(2): 339–74.

Stigliani, N.A. (2000), 'Labor diplomacy: a revitalized aspect of US foreign policy in the era of globalization', *International Studies Perspectives*, **1**(2): 177–94.

Stiles, K.W. (2000), *Global Institutions and Local Empowerment: Competing Theoretical Perspectives*, New York: St. Martins Press.

Summers, C. (2001), 'The battle in Seattle: free trade, labor rights, and societal values', *University of Pennsylvania Journal of International Economic Law*, **22**: 61–90.

TAC (2006a), accessed 27 June at www.tac.org.za/about.html.

TAC (2006b), 'Treatment Action Campaign: an overview', accessed 1 November 2008 at www.tac.org.za/Documents/Other/tachist.pdf.

Tandon, Y. (2003), 'Editorial: negotiations on the Singapore issues should not begin', *SEATINI Bulletin*, **6**(7): 11–16, accessed 1 November 2008 at www.seatini.org/bulletins/6.07.php.

Tarrow, S. (1996), 'Social movements in contentious politics: a review article', *American Political Science Review*, **90**(4): 872–8.

Tarrow, S. (2001), 'Transnational politics: contention and institutions in international politics', *Annual Review of Political Science*, **4**: 1–20.

Tellez, V.M. 'The global campaign on access to medicines: re-shaping intellectual property rules at the World Trade Organization', accessed 6 July 2007 at www.ipngos.org/NGO%20Briefings/Access%20to%20medicines %20campaign.pdf.

Thirkell-White, B. (2004), 'The International Monetary Fund and Civil Society', *New Political Economy*, **9**(2): 251–70.

Thomas, D.C. (2001), *The Helsinki Effect: International Norms, Human Rights, and the Demise of Communism*, Princeton, NJ: Princeton University Press.

Thomas, C. (2002a), 'Trade policy and the politics of access to drugs', *Third World Quarterly*, **23**(2): 251–64.

Thomas, C. (2002b), 'Trade-related labor and environmental agreements?', *Journal of International Economic Law*, **5**(4): 791–819.

Trades Union Congress (2000), 'International', General Council Report, accessed 27 July 2008 at www.tuc.org.uk/congress/chapter10.pdf.

Trebilcock, M. (2003), 'International trade and international labour standards: choosing objectives, instruments, and institutions', in S. Griller (ed.), *International Economic Governance and Non-Economic Concerns: New Challenges for the International Legal Order*, Vienna and New York: Springer.

Tuerk, E. (2003), 'The role of NGOs in international governance. NGOs and developing country WTO members: is there potential for an alliance?', in S. Griller (ed.), *International Economic Governance and Non-Economic Concerns: New Challenges for the International Legal Order*, Vienna and New York: Springer.

van Tuijl, P. (1999), 'NGOs and human rights: sources of justice and democracy', *Journal of International Affairs*, **52**(2): 493–512.

TWN (Third World Network) (1996), 'Joint NGO statement on issues and proposals for the WTO ministerial conference', accessed 30 January 2008 at www.twnside.org.sg/title/issue-cn.htm.

TWN (1999), 'Enough is enough: Third World intellectuals and NGOs' statement against linkage (TWIN-SAL)', 15 September, accessed 7 February 2008 at www.cuts.org/.

TWN (2001), 'Re-thinking TRIPS in the WTO – NGOs demand review and reform of TRIPS at Doha Ministerial Conference', joint statement, accessed 6 December 2005 at www.twnside.org.sg/title/joint5.htm.

TWN (2002), 'Joint statement of NGOs and social movements: international civil society rejects WTO Doha outcome and the WTO's manipulative process', accessed 1 November 2008 at www.twnside.org.sg/title/ngo2a.htm.

TWN (2003a), 'WTO is the wrong venue for investment negotiations: report of the seminar on the nature and implications of a WTO investment agreement', TWN info service on WTO issues, 27 March, accessed 1 November 2008 at www.twnside.org.sg/title/twninfo10.htm.

TWN (2003b), 'Comment by TWN on the draft Cancún text of 13 Sept 2003', TWN briefing paper 19, October, accessed 6 December 2005 at www.twnside.org.sg/title2/briefing_papers/No19.pdf.

TWN (2008), 'Introduction', accessed 22 May at www.twnside.org.sg/twnintro.htm.

Tilly, C. (1984), *Big Structures, Large Processes, Huge Comparisons*, New York: Russell Sage Foundation.

Trade For People Campaign (2004), 'Urgent: invitation to joint NGO meeting on WTO, Geneva 24 May 2004', accessed 28 July 2008 at www.e-alliance.ch/media/media-5221.doc.

Trebilcock, M. and R. Howse (1999), *The Regulation of International Trade*, London and New York: Routledge.

Tsogas, G. (2000), 'Labour standards in the generalized systems of preferences of the European Union and the United States', *European Journal of International Relations*, 3(6): 349–70.

UN Global Compact (2007), 'What is the UN Global Compact?', accessed 6 February 2008 at www.unglobalcompact.org/AboutTheGC/index.html.

UNAIDS (2000), 'Report on the Global HIV/AIDS Epidemic', accessed 2 June 2007 at www.unaids.org/epidemic_update/report/Epi_report.pdf.

UNCTAD (United Nations Conference on Trade and Development) (1948), 'Final Act of the United Nations Conference on Trade and Employment: Havana Charter for an International Trade Organization', accessed 1 November 2008 at www.worldtradelaw.net/misc/havana.pdf.

UNCTAD (1999), *World Investment Report 1999: Foreign Direct Investment and the Challenge of Development – Overview*, New York and Geneva: UNCTAD.

UNCTAD (2000a), *A Positive Agenda for Developing Countries: Issues for Future Trade Negotiations*, New York and Geneva: UNCTAD.

UNCTAD (2000b), *Least Developed Countries Report 2000 – Aid, Private Capital Flows and External Debt: The Challenge of Financing Development in the LDCs*, New York and Geneva: UNCTAD.

UNCTAD (2005), *World Investment Report 2005 – Transnational Corporations and the Internationalization of R & D*, Geneva: UNCTAD.

UNDP (2003), 'Making global trade work for people', accessed 6 July 2007 at www.rbf.org/publications/globaltrade.html.

UNDP (2007), 'Globalization and the least developed countries', conference background paper, United Nations ministerial conference of the least developed countries: making globalization work for the LDCs, Istanbul, 9–11 July, accessed 1 November 2008 at www.undp.org/poverty/docs/istan/eng/12July07-Globalization_and_LDCs.pdf.

UNGASS (2001), 'Fact sheet. The secretary-general's global call to action against HIV/AIDS', accessed 1 November 2008 at www.un.org/ga/aids/ungassfactsheets/html/fssgcall_en.htm.

Union of International Associations (1999–2000), *Yearbook of International Organizations* (edn 36), Munich, Germany: K.G. Saur.

Union of International Associations (2004–2005), *Yearbook of International Organizations, Guide to Global and Civil Society Networks* (edn 41), Munich, Germany: K.G. Saur.

Union of International Associations (2008–2009), *Yearbook of International Organizations 2008–2009 – Vol 5: Statistics, Visualizations and Patterns* (edn 8), Munich, Germany: K.G. Saur Verlag.

Union of International Associations (2009), 'Statistics compiled by the UIA', accessed 3 November 2009 at www.uia.be/stats.

United Nations Sub-Commission on the Promotion and Protection of Human Rights (2000), 'Resolution 2000/7 intellectual property rights and human rights', UN Doc. No. E/CN.4/SUB.2/RES/2000/7 (2000), accessed 1 November 2008 at www.unhchr.ch/Huridocda/Huridoca.nsf/0/c462b62c f8a07b13c12569700046704e?Opendocument.

United Nations Sub-Commission on the Promotion and Protection of Human Rights (2001), 'Resolution 2001/33 access to medicines in the context of pandemics such as HIV/AIDS', UN Doc. No. E/CN/4/RES/2001/33, accessed 1 November 2008 at www.unhchr.ch/huridocda/huridoca.nsf/(Symbol)/E.CN.4.RES.2001.33.En?Opendocument.

United Nations Sub-Commission on the Promotion and Protection of Human Rights (2002), 'Resolution 2002/11 human rights, trade and investment', UN Doc. No. E/CN.4/Sub.2/RES/2001/11, accessed 1 November 2008 at www.unhchr.ch/Huridocda/Huridoca.nsf/(Symbol)/E.CN.4.SUB.2.RES.20 02.11.En?Opendocument.

USTR (Office of the United States Trade Representative) (2000), 'Generalized system of preferences (GSP); worker rights; deadline for submitting public comment on withdrawal of duty-free treatment of certain products imported from Swaziland', *Federal Register*, **65**(173): 54099–100.

Uvin, P. (2000), 'From local organizations to global governance: the role of NGOs in international relations', in K.W. Stiles (ed.), *Global Institutions and Local Empowerment: Competing Theoretical Perspectives*, New York: St Martins Press.

van de Ven, J. (2003), 'The breakdown of the WTO summit at Cancún: a blessing or a blow for developing countries?', occasional paper no. 13, October, Swiss Consulting Group, accessed 15 March 2006 at www.swissconsultinggroup.com/docs/13.pdf.

Vick, K. (1999), 'African AIDS victims losers of a drug war', *Washington Post*, 4 December, accessed 1 November 2008 at http://lists.essential.org/pharm-policy/msg00337.html.

Waer, P. (1996), 'Social clauses in international trade: the debate in the European Union', *Journal of World Trade*, **30**(4): 25–42.

Walker, R.B.J. (1994), 'Social movements/world politics', *Millennium: Journal of International Studies*, **23**(3): 669–700.

Wallach, L. and Sforza (1999), *Whose Trade Organization? Corporate Globalization and the Erosion of Democracy: An Assessment of the World Trade Organization*, Washington DC: Public Citizen.

Wallach, L., P. Woodall, and R. Nader (2004), *Whose Trade Organization? A Comprehensive Guide to the World Trade Organization* (2nd edn), New York: New Press.

Waltz, K.N. (1979), *Theory of International Politics*, Reading, MA: Addison-Wesley.

Wapner, P. (1995), 'Politics beyond the state: environmental activism and world civic politics', *World Politics*, **47**(3): 311–40.

Warkentin, C. and K. Mingst (2000), 'International institutions, the state, and global civil society in the age of the world wide web', *Global Governance*, **6**(2): 237–57.

WDM (World Development Movement) (2003), 'EU trade ministers told to drop WTO expansion plans: campaigners fear EU will demand WTO investment agreement as payment for CAP reform', press release, accessed 6 July 2007 at www.wdm.org.uk/news/archive/2003/palermo.htm.

Weiss, T.G. and L. Gordenker (1996), *NGOs, the UN, and Global Governance*, Boulder, CO: Lynne Rienner.

Wendt, A. (1987), 'The agent-structure problem in international relations theory', *International Organization*, **41**(3): 335–70.

WHO (World Health Organization) (1998), 'Resolution WHA52.19, revised drug strategy', accessed 1 June 2006 at www.who.int/gb/EB.WHA/PDF/WHA52/e19.pdf.

WHO (2001), 'Globalization, TRIPS and access to pharmaceuticals', WHO Policy Perspectives on Medicines 3, accessed 6 July 2007 at www.who.int/hiv/amds/regulations1.pdf.

Wilcox, C. (1949), *A Charter for World Trade 1948*, New York: Macmillan.

Wilkinson, R. (2002a), 'The contours of courtship: the WTO and civil society', in S. Hughes and R. Wilkinson (eds), *Global Governance: Critical Perspectives*, London and New York: Routledge.

Wilkinson, R. (2002b), 'The World Trade Organisation', *New Political Economy*, **7**(1): 129–41.

Wilkinson, R. (2005), 'Managing global civil society: the WTO's engagement with NGOs', in R.D. Germain and M. Kenny (eds), *The Idea of Global Civil Society: Politics and Ethics in a Globalizing Era*, London and New York: Routledge.

Wilkinson, R. and S. Hughes (2000), 'Labor standards and global governance: examining the dimensions of institutional engagement', *Global Governance*, **6**(2): 259–77.

Williams, F. (1999), 'Campaign over drug licensing to grow', *Financial Times*, 29 March.

Williams, M. (2005), 'Civil society and the world trading system', in D. Kelly and W. Grant (eds), *The Politics of International Trade in the Twenty-First Century: Actors, Issues and Regional Dynamics*, Basingstoke: Palgrave Macmillan.

Willetts, P. (1982), *Pressure Groups in the Global System: The Transnational Relations of Issue-Orientated Non-Governmental Organizations*, London: Pinter.

Willetts, P. (1996), *'The Conscience of the World': The Influence of Non-Governmental Organizations in the UN System*, Washington, DC: Brookings Institution.

Willetts, P. (2004), 'Remedying the World Trade Organization's deviance from global norms', in P. Griffith and J. Thurston (eds), *Free and Fair: Making the Progressive Case for Removing Trade Barriers*, London: Foreign Policy Centre.

Winters, L.A. (2003), 'Commentary 4.1: trade and labor standards: to link or not to link?', in K. Basu, H. Horn, L. Román and J. Shapiro (eds), *International Labor Standards: History, Theory, and Policy Options*, Oxford: Blackwell Publishing.

WIPO (World Intellectual Property Organization) (2008a), 'About WIPO', accessed 6 February at www.wipo.int/about-wipo/en/gib.htm#P23_2347.

WIPO (2008b), 'Paris Convention', accessed 6 February 2008 at www.wipo.int/treaties/en/ip/paris/trtdocs_wo020.html#P123_15283.

Wolf, M. (2001), 'What the world needs from the multilateral trading system', in G.P. Sampson (ed.), *The Role of the WTO in Global Governance*, Tokyo: United Nations University Press.

Wood, L.J. (2004), 'Breaking the bank and taking to the streets: how protesters target neoliberalism', *Journal of World-Systems Research*, **10**(1): 69–89.

World Bank (2003), *Global Economic Prospects and the Developing Countries 2003: Investing to Unlock Global Opportunities*, Washington DC: World Bank.

World Bank (2007a), 'Boards of directors – IBRD: votes and subscriptions', accessed 2 April at http://web.worldbank.org/WBSITE/EXTERNAL/ EXTABOUTUS/ORGANIZATION/BODEXT/0,,contentMDK:20124831 ~menuPK:64020035~pagePK:64020054~piPK:64020408~theSitePK:278 036,00.html.

World Bank (2007b), 'Outreach to Civil Society', accessed 2 April at http://web.worldbank.org/WBSITE/EXTERNAL/TOPICS/CSO/0,,content MDK:20094158~menuPK:220430~pagePK:220503~piPK:220476~theSit ePK:228717,00.html.

World Bank (2007c), 'Business center', accessed 2 April 2007 at http://web.worldbank.org/WBSITE/EXTERNAL/OPPORTUNITIES/0,,co ntentMDK:20061685~menuPK:51199931~pagePK:95647~piPK:95671~t heSitePK:95480,00.htm.

World Bank (2007d) 'About', accessed 25 June at www.worldbank.org/ icsid/about/about.htm.

WTO (World Trade Organization) (n.d. a), 'Countries, alliances and proposals', accessed 5 November 2007 at http://www.wto.org/english/tratop_e/ agric_e/negs_bkgrnd04_groups_e.htm.

WTO (n.d. b), 'Understanding the WTO: the organization, membership, alliances and bureaucracy', accessed 31 July 2008 at www.wto.org/ english/theWTO_e/whatis_e/tif_e/org3_e.htm.

WTO (n.d. c), 'Community e-forum', accessed 29 June 2007 at www.wto.org/ english/forums_e/chat_e/chat_e.htm.

WTO (n.d. d), 'Chat events', accessed 29 June 2007 at www.wto.org/english/ forums_e/chat_e/dg_chat2_e.htm.

WTO (n.d. e), 'Building Trade Capacity', accessed 1 November 2008 at www.wto.org/english/tratop_e/devel_e/build_tr_capa_e.htm.

WTO (n.d. f), 'NGO participation in ministerial conferences', accessed 4 December 2007 at www.wto.org/english/forums_e/ngo_e/ngo_e.htm.

WTO (n.d. g), 'TRIPS agreement', accessed 3 July 2007 at www.wto.org/english/docs_e/legal_e/27-trips_04c_e.htm#5.

WTO (n.d. h), 'TRIPS: a more detailed overview of the TRIPS agreement', accessed 3 July 2007 at www.wto.org/english/tratop_e/trips_e/intel2_ e.htm.

WTO (n.d. i), 'Frequently asked questions about TRIPS in the WTO', accessed 3 July 2007 at www.wto.org/english/tratop_e/trips_e/tripfq_ e.htm.

WTO (n.d. j), 'Intellectual property: protection and enforcement. Understanding the WTO: the agreements', accessed 3 July 2007 at www.wto.org/english/thewto_e/whatis_e/tif_e/agrm7_e.htm.

WTO (n.d. k), 'International intergovernmental organizations granted observer status to WTO bodies', accessed 1 November 2008 at www.wto.org/english/theWTO_e/igo_obs_e.htm.

WTO (n.d. l), 'Trade topics: investment', accessed 19 March 2006 at www.wto.org/english/tratop_e/invest_e/invest_e.htm.

WTO (n.d. m), 'Brazil – measures affecting patent protection', accessed 20 February 2008 at www.wto.org/english/tratop_e/dispu_e/cases_e/ds199_ e.htm.

WTO (1994), 'Marrakesh agreement establishing the World Trade Organization', accessed 1 November 2008 at www.wto.org/english/ docs_e/legal_e/04-wto_e.htm.

WTO (1996a), 'Guidelines for arrangements on relations with non-governmental organizations', WTO document number WT/L/162, accessed 2 March 2005 at www.wto.org/english/forums_e/ngo_e/guide_e.htm.

WTO (1996b), 'Trade and labour standards', WTO press brief, accessed 20 February 2008 at www.wto.org/english/thewto_e/minist_e/min96_e/ labstand.htm.

WTO (1996c), 'Indonesia: statement by H.E. Mr. Tungky Ariwibowo Minister of Industry and Trade', WTO document number: WT/MIN(96)/ST/22, accessed 6 February 2008 at www.wto.org/english/thewto_e/minist_e/ min96_e/st22.htm.

WTO (1996d) 'Pakistan: statement by Dr. Muhammad Zubair Khan Minister of Commerce and Head of Delegation Trade', WTO document number: WT/MIN(96)/ST/29, accessed 6 February 2008 at www.wto.org/english/ thewto_e/minist_e/min96_e/st29.htm.

WTO (1996e), 'Australia: statement by the Honourable Tim Fischer, M.P. Deputy Prime Minister and Minister for Trade', WTO document number: WT/MIN(96)/ST/26, accessed 6 February 2008 at www.wto.org/english/ thewto_e/minist_e/min96_e/st26.htm.

WTO (1996f), 'United States: statement by the Honourable Charlene Barshefsky, Acting United States Trade Representative', WTO document number: WT/MIN(96)/ST/5, accessed 6 February 2008 at www.wto.org/english/thewto_e/minist_e/min96_e/st5.htm.

WTO (1996g), 'Singapore Ministerial Declaration', WTO document number WT/MIN(96)/DEC, accessed 18 May 2007 at www.wto.org/english/ thewto_e/minist_e/min96_e/wtodec_e.htm.

WTO (1996h), "Trade and foreign direct investment" new report by the WTO, WTO Press Release, 9 October, accessed 1 November 2008 at www.wto.org/english/news_e/pres96_e/pr057_e.htm.

WTO (1997), 'Special report, concluding remarks by the chairman: "we have delivered" ', *WTO Focus*, **15**: 1–14, accessed 6 February 2008 at www.wto.org/english/res_e/focus_e/focus15_e.pdf.

WTO (1998a), 'United States: statement by H.E. Mr. William J. Clinton, President', accessed 6 February 2008 at www.wto.org/english/thewto_e/minist_e/min98_e/anniv_e/clinton_e.htm.

WTO (1998b), 'Norway: statement by H.E. Mr. Kjell Magne Bondevik, Prime Minister', accessed 6 February 2008 at www.wto.org/english/thewto_e/minist_e/min98_e/anniv_e/norway_e.htm.

WTO (1998c), 'South Africa: statement by H.E. Mr. Nelson Mandela, President', accessed 6 February 2008 at www.wto.org/english/thewto_e/minist_e/min98_e/anniv_e/mandela_e.htm.

WTO (1999a), 'Preparations for the 1999 Ministerial Conference WTO's forward work programme – proposed establishment of a working group on trade and labour'. Communication from the United States, 1 November, WTO document number: WT/GC/W/382, accessed 20 February 2008 at www.wto.org/english/thewto_e/minist_e/min99_e/english/about_e/prop_e.doc.

WTO (1999b), 'Preparations for the 1999 Ministerial Conference – proposal for a joint ILO/WTO standing working forum on trade, globalization and labour issues'. Communication from the European Communities, 5 November, WTO document number WT/GC/W/383, accessed 20 February 2008 at www.wto.org/english/thewto_e/minist_e/min99_e/english/about_e/prop_e.doc.

WTO (1999c) 'Statement circulated by H.E. Mr. M. Benaissa, Minister for Foreign Affairs and Cooperation of Morocco, President of the Ninth Ministerial Meeting of the Group of 77 and China', WTO document number WT/MIN(99)/ST/22, accessed 20 February 2008 at www.wto.org/english/thewto_e/minist_e/min99_e/english/state_e/d5220e.

WTO (1999d), 'Malaysia: minister's statement, by Asmat Kamaludin, Secretary-General, Ministry of International Trade and Industry', WTO document number WT/MIN(99)/ST/28, accessed 20 February 2008 at www.wto.org/english/thewto_e/minist_e/min99_e/english/state_e/state_e.htm.

WTO (1999e), 'Ministers consider new and revised texts. Chairperson: Vice-Minister Anabel González (Costa Rica)', WTO briefing note, 2 December, accessed 20 February 2008 at www.wto.org/english/thewto_e/minist_e/min99_e/english/about_e/resum02_e.htm.

WTO (1999f), 'Ministers start negotiating Seattle declaration', WTO briefing note, 2 December, accessed 1 November 2008 at www.wto.org/english/theWTO_e/minist_e/min99_e/english/about_e/resum01_e.htm.

WTO (2001a), 'Doha Ministerial Declaration', WTO document number WT/MIN(01)/DEC/1, accessed 20 February 2008 at www.wto.org/english/thewto_e/minist_e/min01_e/mindecl_e.htm.

WTO (2001b), 'TRIPS council's discussion on "intellectual property and access to medicines"', accessed 20 February 2008 at www.wto.org/english/tratop_e/TRIPs_e/counciljun01_e.htm.

WTO (2001c), 'Doha ministerial declaration on the TRIPS agreement and public health', WTO document number WT/MIN(01)/DEC/2, accessed 20 February 2008 at www.wto.org/english/thewto_e/minist_e/min01_e/mindecl_trips_e.htm.

WTO (2001d), 'European Communities: Mr Pascal Lamy, Commissioner for Trade, statement', WTO document number WT/MIN(01)/ST/4, accessed 1 November 2008 at www.wto.org/english/thewto_e/minist_e/min01_e/statements_e/st4.doc.

WTO (2001e), '"May I take it that this is agreeable?" Gavel, applause, Congratulations ....', accessed 6 July 2007 at www.wto.org/english/theWTO_e/minist_e/min01_e/min01_chair_speaking_e.htm.

WTO (2002), 'Procedures for the circulation and derestriction of WTO documents, decision of 14 May 2002', WTO document number WT/L/452, accessed 6 July 2007 at www.worldtradelaw.net/misc/derestriction1.pdf.

WTO (2003a), 'WTO symposium programme "Challenges ahead on the road to Cancún"', accessed 4 August 2008 at www.wto.org/english/tratop_e/dda_e/symp_devagenda_prog_03_e.htm#fntext.

WTO (2003b), 'Implementation of paragraph 6 of the Doha declaration on the TRIPS agreement and public health: fecision of the General Council of 30 August 2003', document number WT/L/540, accessed 1 November 2008 at www.wto.org/english/tratop_e/trips_e/implem_para6_e.htM.

WTO (2003c), 'Working group on the relationship between trade and investment, communication from Canada, Costa Rica and Korea – negotiating a multilateral framework on investment in the WTO', WTO document number WT/WGTI/W/162, accessed 6 July 2007 at www.wto.org/english/tratop_e/invest_e/invest_e.htm.

WTO (2003d), 'Cover letter of the draft Cancún ministerial text', accessed 1 November 2008 at www.wto.org/english/theWTO_e/minist_e/min03_e/draft_decl_covletter_e.htm.

WTO (2003e), 'Draft Cancún ministerial text (second revision)', accessed 28 July 2008 at www.wto.org/english/thewto_e/minist_e/min03_e/draft_decl_rev2_e.htm.

WTO (2003f), 'Day 4: as ministers comment on new draft, chairperson warns of dangers of failure', accessed 28 July 2008 at www.wto.org/english/thewto_e/minist_e/min03_e/min03_13sept_e.htm.

WTO (2003g), 'Day 5: conference ends without consensus', accessed 28 July 2008 at www.wto.org/english/thewto_e/minist_e/min03_e/min03_14sept_ e.htm.

WTO (2004), 'Text of the "July Package" – the General Council's post-Cancún decision', accessed 3 December 2007 at www.wto.org/english/ tratop_e/dda_e/draft_text_gc_dg_31july04_e.htm.

WTO (2005a), 'My day at the ministerial conference: director-general Pascal Lamy's ministerial conference diary', accessed 29 June 2007 at www.wto.org/english/thewto_e/dg_e/pl_visitors_e/min05_blog_e.htm.

WTO (2005b), 'Hong Kong ministerial declaration', WTO document number WT/MIN(05)/DEC, accessed 20 February 2008 at www.wto.org/ english/thewto_e/minist_e/min05_e/final_text_e.htm.

WTO (2005c), 'Members OK amendment to make health flexibility permanent', WTO press release (Press/426), 6 December, accessed 17 November 2006 at www.wto.org/english/news_e/pres05_e/pr426_e.htm.

WTO (2007a), 'The WTO: secretariat and budget: WTO secretariat budget for 2007', accessed 5 August 2008 at www.wto.org/english/thewto_e/secre_e/ budget07_e.htm.

WTO (2007b), 'Background information WTO public forum 2007: "How can the WTO help harness globalization?"', accessed 24 May 2008 at www.wto.org/english/forums_e/public_forum2007_e/forum07_e.htm.

Yandle, B. (1983), 'Bootleggers and baptists: the education of a regulatory economist', *Regulation*, **7**(3): 12–16.

Young, O. (1982) *Resource Regimes: Natural Resources and Social Institutions*, Berkeley, CA: University of California Press.

Appendix

INTERVIEW SOURCES

Global Trade Watch Australia representative, 5 December 2005, Melbourne, Australia.

International Confederation of Free Trade Unions representative, 29 September 2006, Geneva, Switzerland.

Médecins Sans Frontières representative, 19 September 2006, Paris, France.

Oxfam Community Aid Abroad Australia representative, 6 December 2005, Melbourne, Australia.

Oxfam International, Geneva advocacy office representative, 27 September 2006, Geneva, Switzerland.

World Trade Organization, external relations division representative, 28 September 2006, Geneva, Switzerland.

Index